Historic Replica Construction

14th Century: Volume 1

Edited by Stephen 'Sven' Wyley

MELBOURNE

Front cover picture (Photo 1): One of the two 14th century hutch chests made by Stephen *'Sven'* Wyley, made from recycled shelving, photographed by Morgan Wyley.

Copyright © 2023 by Wyley, Fraser, Robinson.

All rights reserved. No part of this publication may be reproduced, distributed or transmitted in any form or by any means, including photocopying, recording, or other electronic or mechanical methods, without the prior written permission of the publisher, except in the case of brief quotations embodied in critical reviews and certain other non-commercial uses permitted by copyright law. For permission requests, write to the publisher, addressed "Attention: Permissions Coordinator," at the address below.

Wyley, Fraser, Robinson. C/- Intertype
Unit 45, 125 Highbury Road,
BURWOOD VIC 3125.
www.intertype.com.au

Ordering Information:
Quantity sales. Special discounts are available on quantity purchases by corporations, associations, and others. For details, contact the "Special Sales Department" at the address above.

Historical replica construction in wood, metal and leather – 14th Century – Volume 1/ Wyley, Fraser, Robinson. —1st ed.
ISBN 978-0-6486131-1-4

Acknowledgements.

Special thanks to the following people for taking their red pen to this manuscript including: Wayne Robinson, Rey Croucher, Katrina 'Kat' Lambert, Hugh McDonald and others.

Thanks to following for their assistance:
- Alison Archibald, Collection Care Department, British National Archives;
- Nikki Braunto, Senior Picture Researcher, Museum of London;
- Cristina D'Alessandro, Scala Archives;
- Richard Dabb, Picture Researcher and Editor, Museum of London;
- Susanne Edelmann, photographer, City of Nuremberg - City Library in the Nuremberg Education Campus. Historical and Scientific City Library, Nürnberg;
- Peter Hewitt, Museums Officer, Collections West, The Stewartry Museum, Kirkcudbright, Scotland;
- Paul Johnson, Image Library Manager, The National Archives, United Kingdom;
- Dr Emil Krén, Editor, Web Gallery of Art;
- Daniel Korachi-Alaoui, Archives and Library Assistant, Canterbury Cathedral Archives and Library;
- Sandra Powlette, Image and Brand Licensing Manager, British Library;
- Nathan Smith, Company of the Phoenix;
- Jonathon Vines, British Library, Image Licencing;
- Morgan Wyley, Photography and photoshopping;

- B. Wyley, Painting of the Treaty of Calais chest;
- Madame Zerkane, Royalties, Department Images and digital services department, Bibliothèque nationale de France.

The following people have contributed over a long period to the development of the knowledge that has culminated in this book:
Jenny and Gary Baker, Dr Peter Beatson, Dr Tim Dawson, Stephen Lowe, Hugh McDonald, Christopher Morgan, Steven Nicol, Wayne Robinson, Keith *'Chips'* Whitehead, Frank Wyley (my Dad), and Andrew Young.

And thanks to all the customers and stakeholders associated with *'Sven the Merchant'*, without your support and purchases this would never have happened.

We are grateful to all the institutions and individuals listed for permission to reproduce the material in wish they hold copyright. Every effort has been made to determine and contact the copyright holders, we apologise for any omission and we will try to add any necessary acknowledgement in the subsequent editions.

Dedication:

To my Mum, who taught me by example that you are never too old to learn something new.

S.Wyley.

Table of Contents.

Introduction	9
Holding your work	12
Cleating nails.	16
Interpretation of the remains. Is it a table or a bench? It is not a chest.	18
Making a proportional representation of a depicted item.	20
Plans.	25
Resizing plans to fit the length or width of the plank available.	25
Take the dimensions with a pinch of salt.	29
Painting furniture.	31
Safety.	36
Chest lock survey – Turnkey locks.	40
Leatherwork.	42
Tool protection.	43
Warp protection and grain direction.	45
Bede's chair.	46
The Pillager's Hutch Chest.	60
Lock plate.	81
The Santa Croce Sitting Bed.	101
The Taciunum Sanitatis table - Making Spaghetti.	114
The Luttrell Psalter Trestle Table.	128
Hanging Salt Box of Buda, Hungary.	149
The Bellows from the Smithfield Decretals.	162
The Frame Saw (Santa Croce).	174
The Costrel from Baynard Castle Dock, City of London.	186
The Heater (Shield).	266

Appendix 1 – Nail making.	291
Appendix 2 -Wider boards and how to make them.	294
Appendix 3 – Hutch chest – Large.	299
Appendix 4 – Hutch chest – Small.	301
Appendix 5 – Treaty of Calais chest.	305
Appendix 6 – Bede's Chair – Flat pack.	306
Appendix 7 – Bed, longer version based on the bed I made for myself.	309
Appendix 8 – Useful conversions.	310
Appendix 9 – Chest lock Survey – Chests with turnkey locks from 10th to 16th century.	313
Appendix 10 – Typologies of locks.	321
Appendix 11 - Trenails (Wooden pegged Construction).	325
Appendix 12 – Making square washers.	341
About the authors.	344
Stephen Francis (Sven) Wyley.	344
Andrew Fraser.	346
Wayne Robinson.	347
Bibliography.	349
Further Reading.	355
Links.	356
Photographs.	366
Drawings.	382
Illuminated Manuscripts and Frescos.	387
Forthcoming works.	389
Previous Publications.	389

"I believe in the sharing of knowledge, not the hoarding of it."

S.Wyley

Introduction

The 14th century was a time of war and wonders and was the beginning of the Renaissance, where the arts and architecture reached new heights and degrees of sophistication. The rise of international trade in the period,
 - which brought about the rise of the merchant class, and saw the rise of city states like Florence and Pisa,
 - and the flow of knowledge was assisted by the establishment of more universities.

Then there was plague, known as the *'Black Death'*, which killed over 25 million people, and the *'Hundred Years War'* between England and France (which lasted for 116 years, but who's counting?), making it all an interesting time to live and for us to reflect on.

The first part of the book covers a range of information which will aid you in your future projects including: holding your work, cleating nails, proportional replicas from manuscripts, interpretation of the extant remains (was it a table or a bench, leatherwork, a study of chest turnkey locks, making a proportional representation of a depicted item, painting furniture, resizing plans to fit the available timber, safety, take the dimensions with a pinch of salt, tool protection, triple checking the dimensions provided, warp protection, The main body of the book is comprised of various 14th century projects that include:

- Bede's Chair (*St.Paul's Church, Jarrow, County Durham, United Kingdom*) by Stephen Wyley;
- The Pillager's chest (*MS Royal manuscript, British Library, UK*) by Stephen Wyley;

- The Sitting bed (*The Preparation of the Cross, Santa Croce Fresco, Florence, Italy*) by Stephen Wyley;
- Table - Making Pasta (*Taciunum Sanitatis of Vienna manuscript, BNF, France*) by Stephen Wyley;
- The Luttrell Psalter Table by Stephen Wyley;
- The Hanging Salt Box (*Budapest Historical Museum, Hungary*) by Stephen Wyley;
- The Bellows (*Smithfield Decretals manuscript, British Library, UK*) by Stephen Wyley;
- The Frame Saw (*The Santa Croce Fresco, Florence, Italy*) by Stephen Wyley;
- The Costrel (*Museum of London, UK*) by Wayne Robinson;
- The Heater Shield by Andrew Fraser and Stephen Wyley.

This book assumes a basic level of competence with working in wood, metal and leather. As you complete the projects your skill will naturally increase, however, safety is paramount. Do not use tools or equipment with which you have no experience in using them, or without the appropriate personal protective equipment. If you are lacking experience or skill, it is recommended that you obtain training from your local training institution or a more experienced worker of wood, metal and leather, or when all else fails there is '*YouTube*'. The subject of metal work will be touched upon in more detail regarding the manufacture, purchase and fitting of metalwork such as chest hinges, hasps and handles. The project dimensions are in the metric system with Imperial/US customary measures parenthesised. Timber and metal lengths are rounded to the nearest $\frac{1}{16}$ inch and drill sizes to the nearest $\frac{1}{64}$". A conversion chart is also provided in Appendix 8. Each system of units is consistent within each project, so pick one and stick with it. Cutting some pieces to metric sizes and other pieces to imperial measurements will create various problems. Minor adjustments may still be necessary due to the rounding errors or local variations in standard timber sizes. Always test fit everything prior to permanent assembly.

Common Era (CE) and Before the Common Era (BCE) dating conventions are used throughout this book. The two notation systems are numerically equivalent, 1450 CE and AD 1450 refer to the same year. CE notation has been widely adopted for archaeological and historical academic use and nothing other than consistency with the academic sources is implied by its use here.

In this volume we have added leather work in the form of parts of the bellows and the costrel. Leather work is a worthy skill for making clothing, accessories and accoutrements. Leather is a wonderful material which can be treated like a fabric when soft and pliable and like wood when stiff and hard.

We don't plan to repeat the general information found the *"Vikings - Volume 1"* (2021), and we recommend that you obtain a copy if you want to know about historical sources and how to use them, the form and function of furniture, about the time and materials needed to make items, plans and patterns, making the most of every plank, and chest fittings and locks.

Good luck, and may the force be with you.

Holding your work

Holding a workpiece (*be it wood, metal or bone etc.*) in your hand or against your body can result in a slip or loss of control which can result in an injury (*needing sutures or in some cases surgery*). It is easier and safer to hold your workpiece with a range of devices to hold or stop the workpiece moving, which vary in material and complexity - see Table 1. An example of a bench stop on a Roman workbench, Photo 2, shows Perdix cutting mortises with a chisel and hammer, from a wall painting from the north triclinium, the House of Vettii, Pompeii, mid-1st century.

Photo 2. Fresco showing Perdix cutting mortises with a chisel and hammer while the timber is held in place by pegs in the top of a workbench.

An 11th century illuminated manuscript Cynegetica (Cod Z 479), folio 36r, held in the Bibliotheca Marciana Venice Italy, shows an ivory worker with an adze working on a bench with a holdfast or endstop.

Figure 1. Amb. 317.2 Folio 21 recto (Mendel I), Karl Schreyner (carpenter) – 1425 CE. A carpenter planes a piece of timber on a workbench with three end stops for the top of the plank and a fourth stop on the right hand side of the plank to stop sideways movement.[1]

---

[1] Stadtbibliothek im Bildungscampus Nürnber, Die Mendelschen und Landauerschen Hausbücher Amb. 317.2° (Mendel I), fol 21r. https://hausbuecher.nuernberg.de/75-Amb-2-317-21-r

I have not yet found any similar workbenches until the 15th century in the illuminations showing the various trades in *"The Mendelian and Landauer house books"* - see Figure 1, which show two different stop configurations.

Name	Description
Table 1. Various holding devices.	
Bench stop - peg	Removable wooden pegs that fit into holes in the workbench.
Bench stop – 'Z'	A wooden board with a board across each end. One end rests against the edge of the workbench while the workpiece is held against the other block. Handy for cutting smaller pieces of timber.
Clamp	Can come in a range of types, shapes, sizes and materials with two sides that can be tightened to secure the work. Clamps can be used to hold a workpiece together or hold the workpiece on to the workbench.
Dog	A metal staple with sharpened ends used to hold a log or beam of wood in place on a bench or trestle. One end of the dog is driven into the bench and the other into the log or beam.
Hand clamp	A hand held clamp for small work used by jewellers and horn workers. The two sides are drawn together by a screw and nut or a wedge arrangement.
Hold Fast	A metal rod in the shape of an inverted "L" for Medieval or "J" for Roman hold down, where the long end goes through a hole in the workbench, and the shorter end sits on top of the work. The top of the hold down is struck downwards, causing the hold down to change shape and put pressure on the workpiece. To remove the hold down the long end is struck upwards relieving the pressure on the

Name	Description
	workpiece.[2]
Shaving horse	A bench that is sat bestride like riding a horse by the operator. Leg power is used to provide pressure on an adjustable clamp to secure a workpiece. A drawknife is often used to work on the workpiece in the clamp.
Vice	A bench mounted clamp that comes in various sizes with dual jaws that are closed by turning a threaded shaft which brings the two jaws together.
Vertical log holder	The Egyptians cut logs longitudinally by lashing the log upright to a wooden post fixed in the ground.[3]

Table 1. Various holding devices.

---

[2] There was a fresco in Roman Herculaneum that showed a hold down on a workbench. Sadly, it has deteriorated. We can see this on an etching from 1773.

[3] Eighteenth dynasty, the tomb of Rekh-mi-re at Thebes.

Cleating nails.

Cleated nails are used to hold fittings in place (think of a staple for paper). The nail goes through a nail hole in a fitting, through the wood (always pre-drill the timber with a drill bit just a bit smaller that the nail) and then the protruding end is bent over (either with a pair of pliers or a hammer) and curved downwards. The bent nail is then hit into the wood with a hammer[4] downwards into the wood, with a block of steel supporting the nail head.

Photo 3. These cut nails hold the lock on the front of the chest and need to be cleated (bent over) or else the lock can be pulled off.

---

[4] I use a '*cobblers*' hammer with the back wedge cut off, it gives more room to swing a hammer inside the chest.

Photo 4. A block of steel is placed under the head of the nail to act as an anvil.

Photo 5. A hammer is used to bend the nail shaft down to the timber of the chest. The tip can be bent into a curve to act as a staple.

Photo 6. The cleated nails are bent in opposite directions so the fittings cannot be easily removed.

Interpretation of the remains. Is it a table or a bench? It is not a chest.

Archaeologists, curators and writers are not always correct in their interpretation of objects. They are not always skilled in the procedures and processes of wood or metal working, so a few of their interpretations could be wrong.

An example can be found in the woodwork finds from mid-14th century York (*no. 8941 from 16-22 Coppergate - Ottaway (1992)*) which is listed as the lid or side of an oak chest, measuring 539 mm L x 268 mm W x 23 mm thick (21 $^{7}/_{32}$" x 10 $^{35}/_{64}$" x $^{29}/_{32}$"). The board is radially split, with two 27-28 mm (1 $^{1}/_{16}$" - 1 $^{7}/_{64}$") diameter holes along an intact edge. There appears to be part of a hole in the upper left corner and the top right corner is missing. I believe this is not a *'lid or side of oak chest'* but either a table or a bench similar to the Oseberg table or the many workbenches depicted in the "*Hausbücher of the Mendelschen and Landauer Nürnberger Zwölfbrüderstiftungen*" (dating from 1425 CE) - see Figure 1. I am not aware of any chest which has holes like those shown in No. 8941.

If nothing but metal fittings remain, looking at the fittings themselves can imply the size of the chest when compared to similar extant remains. If there are good archaeological find reports that show the relative positioning of the pieces to each other, this will indicate the size of the chest (e.g. the Birka grave finds, like grave 639, *Arbman (1940)*).

No one is perfect, so question the research and come up with your own conclusions. Be prepared to be questioned on it, and as information becomes available you should be willing to change your mind.

Making a proportional representation of a depicted item.

When taking information for a replica from a fresco, painting, sketch or an illuminated manuscript you must take the following into consideration:
- The fresco, painting, sketch or an illuminated manuscript is a secondary source of information and is an interpretation by the artist of the item in question;
- A subject in the foreground is normally shown in more detail;
- The scale of an item in a picture can denote its significance in the work. The larger items are important and smaller items in the background may appear small because they are just *'window dressing'*;
- A picture is just a two-dimensional rendering of an item and most of the time you are not shown the back etc., so some aspects of an item have to be speculated on.

Six of the projects in this volume are based on depictions, from the Pillager's chest to the frame saw, all of those projects have been made, used and found to be good. Feel free to modify the dimensions to suit your situation.

Figure 2. The "*Pillagers*" from the Chroniques de France ou de St Denis (Chronicles of France and St. Denis), British Library.

Let's look at the *"Pillagers"* in the Chroniques de France ou de St Denis (Chronicles of France and St. Denis), held in the British Library (*MS Royal 20 C VII 41v*), dating from 1381-1399, see Figure 2 (yes, I will go into detail of how to make a replica of the chest later in the book, be patient). Folio 41v shows various infantrymen standing around enjoying a drink of what appears to be red wine while their companions pillage the house. The house appears to be out of scale with the infantryman on the back end of the chest and those hanging out the windows.

Figure 3. MS Royal 20 CVII, f. 41v. British Library, detailed view of the chest.

The chest is the item of interest in this manuscript illumination. The chest is currently locked, but a few blows with the war hammer that is being used to broach the wine cask would remove the hasp of the lock quickly. The chest is shown with 'fleur di lis' ended hinges, a scalloped edge hasp plate with a single hasp lock. There is no definition of separate planks for the legs and the end piece is twice as thick as the front or the lid.

If we assume that the infantryman's palm on the left is about 120 mm (4 $^{23}/_{32}$") wide and then measure a printed copy of the illumination where the gap at the end is 4 mm ($^5/_{32}$"), then we can assume that 1 mm on the picture = 30 mm (1 $^3/_{16}$") in life size, thus this can be used to create a plan of the chest at 1:30 scale. See Drawing 1 for the details of the calculations.

Drawing 1. Plan of chest with conversions of chest measurements to a full size chest.

Plans.

The plans in Drawing 1 are a guide on how to reproduce a replica based on the original item. In some cases the example is from a manuscript and certain assumptions have to be made about shape, form, joints and detail. In other cases there are complete objects, or the remains of extant item, which may not have been square when it was made, or it was damaged during its use, and found centuries after being tossed into the ditch, well or harbour or the item was damaged in the intervening years (*e.g. Bede's Chair*).

The plans in this volume are provided to make a replica using square and true timber thus producing a replica based on the original item. It is up to you if you want to produce a replica with every chip and warp (*e.g. the Hanging salt box*).

Resizing plans to fit the length or width of the plank available.

If the widest plank you can get to make a chest is only a certain size (say 24 cm rather than 29 cm (say 10" rather than 12")), you can make a proportionally sized version by calculating a ratio of the length versus height of the chest:
= 29 * 1.7 = 49.3 cm. (So if the chest is 29" long and 16½" wide the ratio is 29/16.5 = 1.77. Therefore the length of a replica using a 12" wide plank = 12 * 1.77 = 21".) For design purposes you also have to take the thickness of the planks into consideration. You will end up with something like the chest in Photo 7, compared to Photo 8.

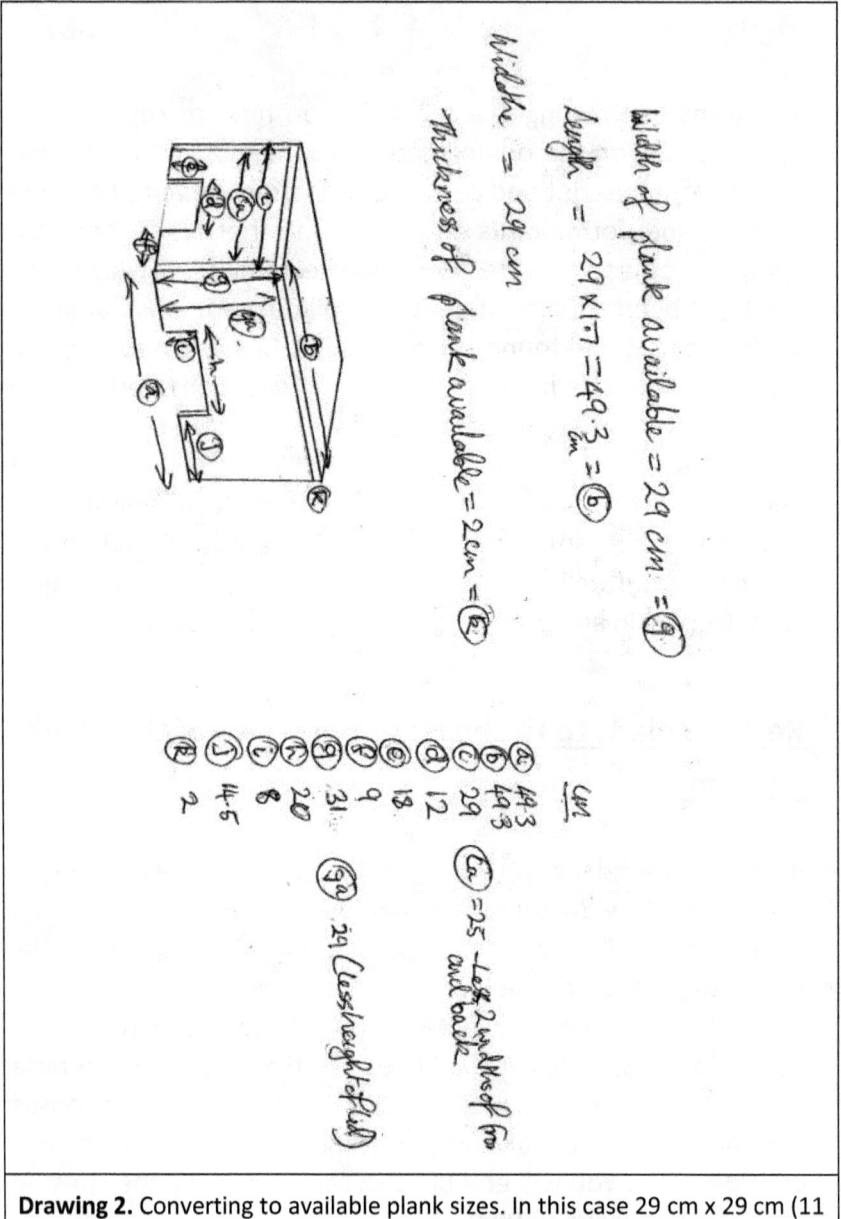

Drawing 2. Converting to available plank sizes. In this case 29 cm x 29 cm (11 $^{27}/_{64}$ ").

If the chest is 72 cm (28 $^{11}/_{32}$ ") long and 42 cm (16 $^{17}/_{32}$ ") wide the ratio is 72/42 = 1.7. Therefore the length of a replica using a 29 cm (11 $^{27}/_{64}$ ") wide planks

Photo 7. Hutch chest in pine with hasp closure.

Photo 8. A bigger version of the hutch chest with separate legs for the front and back.

The transition to three separate pieces for the front and the back of a chest is worthy of a research project. One of the earliest chests with this design is the Crusader chest of Bunratty Castle (*Ireland*).[5] The change in design allowed for much bigger chests without having to fell and process even bigger trees. The design raised the chest further off the ground, giving less opportunity for water damage to the valuable items inside. The change also made it harder on the people that had to lug them around from residence to residence as a lord toured their fiefs. For drawings and information on the larger version see Appendix 3, and for a smaller version see Appendix 4.

Take the dimensions with a pinch of salt.

When researching an item check that you have the dimensions correct, then ask yourself the question, is this right? This has happened to me twice, the first time involving the Vox Torp Chest (*from the Vox Torp Church, Smaland, Sweden, Statens Historiska Museum, Stockholm, No. 4094*). I even made a scaled down version in cardboard, then a full size version in timber, only then did I twig that something was wrong, I made further enquiries, I had the dimension the wrong way round. I now use that chest to store some of my re-enactment kit because I can't use it at displays.

The second time involved a chest from Bunratty Castle in Ireland (*Co. Clare*) houses the Gort Furniture Collection. Amid the collection is an iron-bound 12th century chest (*Acc. no. 292, item number 33*), rectangular in shape, standing on short

---

[5] Gort Furniture Collection, Bunratty Castle, County Clare, Ireland.

legs made by extending the ends past the bottom. On the original web page (*now no longer available*), the dimensions were given as "110cm L x 170cm H x 41cm W" (43½" L x 67" H x 16" W to the nearest half inch). This did not match the photo and the provided dimensions would produce a very stout chest. I presume that the writer or person doing the measurements got the length and height around the wrong way, either due to confusion or simple transposition of the numbers.

If the measurements don't seem right, I suggest that you seek out other sources, or ask the collection curator to confirm the measurements.

Painting furniture.

Photo 9. Treaty of Calais Chest (*British National Archive - E 30/153 case. (National Archives 2022)*).[6]

Furniture in the 14th century was sometimes painted and this was true for some chests. The colours were supplied by a range of chemical compounds mixed with water and a binding medium such as egg yolks, called tempera or '*egg tempera*'. Some examples of the compounds can be found in Table 2.

---

[6] Thanks to Paul Johnson, Image Library Manager, The National Archives, United Kingdom

Table 2. Examples of compounds used in some medieval paints.[7]

Colour used	Likely ingredient
Red	Red ochre (iron oxide)
Umber (brownish red)	Mixture of iron and manganese oxides and hydroxides
Yellow	Yellow ochre (iron oxyhydroxide)
Green	Copper (II) carbonate or copper acetate
Blue	Deep blue made from ground lapis lazuli
Black	Carbon black
White	Lime White (calcium carbonate)

An example of painted furniture is the Treaty of Calais (TOC) chest (*currently held in the British National Archive, - E 30/153 case*)[8]. See Photo 9. Tree ring analysis of the timber shows the wood was felled around 1360 CE. The TOC chest is a 6 boarded rectangular box which was purported to have held the Treaty of Calais[9], a peace treaty between England and France, signed in 1381.

The exterior of the chest is painted with various heraldic devices of the countries and nobles involved, with four large shields on the front, 6 smaller shields on the lid, and an

---

[7] Some paints had toxic ingredients like copper and lead and should be avoided.

[8] There is another chest very similar to the TOC chest, which could have been made by the same workshop to the same dimensions, fitting and artwork. It is the David Bruce's Ransom chest (no. 39/36 case), and the red rampant lion on the front even has the same blue leg. National Archives (n.d.) E27

[9] The treaty itself is not extant nor are the details of the treaty recorded. Such is the transient nature of peace, and the Hundred Years War continued until 1453 CE, lasting 116 years...

inscription on the rear section of the lid which reads: *'Pax facta Cales inter reges et regna Anglie et Francie die xxiv'* (Peace made at Calais between the kings and kingdoms of England and France on the 24th day [October 1381]).

The front, back and side have a red background and the lid has a yellow/green background. The metal work consists of two plain strap hinges, a central handle in round bar, a plain hasp strap on the centre of the lid which belonged to a now missing lock that left a shadow in the centre of the front. The shadow of the lock plate shows a scalloped base and sides, and a straight top. There is a circular hole in the front of the chest where the lock mechanism would have sat. See Appendix 5 for the plans to make your own Treaty of Calais chest, including the fittings.

The identification of the various heraldic devices is incomplete due to their damaged condition (the right hand end of the lid), or the owner of some of the heraldic devices has not yet been identified, see Photo 10. On the lid from left to right there is; Richard Fitz Alan, The Dauphin, England, France, The Black Prince, and Unknown. On the front from left to right there are; John Buckingham, Guy De Bryan, Nicholas De Loveyne (possibly) and someone unknown

Photo 10. The heraldry on the Treaty of Calais chest. (*British National Archive*).

A replica of the Treaty of Calais chest has been made, see Appendix 5 for the plans, however the painting of the replica chest was not completed at the time of publishing but will hopefully appear in a second issue, or a complete article. It is highly recommends that the painting of such a work take place before the fittings are attached to the chest as it makes the painting more laborious, especially with scaling and accessibility. See Photo 11.

Photo 11. Replica of Treaty of Calais chest with painting in progress. I have *'cheekily'* included the heraldic device for Sir John Hawkwood of the White Company on the far right in place of the obliterated device.

Safety.

Personal safety, and the safety of those around you, is of paramount importance. The activities undertaken in the process of historical replica construction must not put yourself or others at risk of an incident causing harm or even a fatality.

Some basic rules should include:
- Read, understand, and follow the equipment maker's instructions;
- Use the tools the way in which they were intended (i.e. a chisel is not a screwdriver);
- Wear the appropriate personal protective equipment (PPE) (i.e. eye, ear and respiratory protection, safety boots, gloves as appropriate and a leather apron for the torso, no bare skin on torso and limbs), long hair, be it head or beard hair, must be tied back, no loose clothing or jewellery (have your heard of degloving?, look it up);
- Keep tools and equipment clean, in good condition and sharp;
- Provide adequate ventilation in the work space;
- Keep the work area clean, tidy and free of slip, trip and fall hazards;
- Ensure that equipment is firmly affixed to the floor or a bench (i.e. grinders and pedestal drills);
- If standing in one place for long periods, use rubber fatigue mats;
- If you are using power tools ensure that the power cords are not damaged, and the guards are in place and operational.

Table 3. Hazard identification and control.[10]

Hazard	Controls
Chemicals	Read and follow the Safety Data Sheet (SDS), provided adequate ventilation, PPE (Gloves, safety glasses, respirator). Long pants, long sleeve shirts.
Drugs, medications and alcohol	Don't work under the influence of drugs, medications that impair your decision making skills or alcohol.
Dust	Mechanical extraction, ventilation, PPE (respirator). Choose operations that produce coarse chips rather than dust when practical. Clean up dust with a vacuum cleaner.
Electrical	Maintain electrical leads and cords. Residual current device (RCD) on electrical switchboard.
Entanglement	Tie back long hair. Do not wear loose clothing. Remove jewellery (or wear gloves). Note: Some people believe that gloves themselves are an entanglement hazard.
Equipment	Good maintenance on

---

[10] A hazard is a thing that can cause an incident causing harm or damage. The risk is the subjective assessment of the level of harm or damage a hazard may cause. A control is a mitigating thing or practice to reduce or remove the effect of the hazard.

Table 3. Hazard identification and control.[10]

Hazard	Controls
	equipment. Guards in place. Safety switches are operational.
Ergonomics	Set up of workshop (heights of benches and equipment, storage of most often used tools in reach zone, avoid awkward positions).
Fatigue	Take regular breaks (10 minutes every hour). Install rubber fatigue mats on the floor. While craft work is a great way to destress after a rough day at work, maybe it's not the best thing to do when you're exhausted.
Flying debris (from cutting, grinding etc.) and sharp objects.	PPE (Gloves, safety glasses or face shield). Long pants, long sleeve shirts.
Heat	Schedule work in the early morning or evening avoiding the hottest part of the day, take regular breaks (10 minutes every hour), and keep hydrated. Situations (i.e. forge). Use heat shields, PPE (Gloves, safety glasses or face shield). Long pants, long sleeve shirts.
Manual handling	Good manual handling can be

Table 3. Hazard identification and control.[10]

Hazard	Controls
	helped by the set out of your workshop. Store regularly used tools in easy reach. Store heavy items between shoulder or knee height. Use correct lifting techniques, 2 person lift, or mechanical lifting equipment.
Noise	Distance from source, noise dampening materials, baffles or barriers between source and ears. PPE (plugs (correctly installed) or ear muffs).
Sharp tools	Provide covers, store in a way to avoid unnecessary contact, always cut away from your body.
Slips, trips and falls	Remove slip, trip and fall hazards, clean-up workshop after each job, practice good housekeeping.

"*Good housekeeping is about having 'a place for everything and everything in its place'.*"

S.Wyley.

Chest lock survey – Turnkey locks.

This is a short survey of 23 chest's 'turnkey' locks from the 10th to the 16th centuries, based on external set up, that gives a glimpse into how locks were made in the Medieval world and a typology (*similar to Petersen's sword typology*[11]) has been developed *See Appendix 9*. Goodall provided a limited typology and Linlaud's is quite comprehensive, both are based on internal lock mechanism (which is invisible for those locks fixed on the inside of the chest).[12]

This is not an exhaustive study and there will need to be a lot more work done, but some preliminary statements can be made about the results so far that the majority of the locks had:
1) the hasp on the left hand side as you look at the chest;
2) the key hole in the centre of the lock;
3) rectangular lock plates, and some had rectangular lock plates with scalloped edges or decorated corners.

The most unique lock plate belongs to the Casket[13] of the Blessed Juliana of Collalto (*Byzantine*), which had a circular lock shaped like a *'starburst'* from the circular surface, and a later period rectangular lock.

---

[11] Jan Petersen, De Norske Vikingsverd ("The Norwegian Viking Swords") published in 1919. Followed by Oakeshott's typology in "The Archaeology of Weapons: Arms and Armour from Prehistory to the Age of Chivalry" (1960), which was based on Petersen's work.

[12] When I get time I will expand the survey.

[13] They call it a 'casket' but its dimensions are 175 x 69 x 84 cm (68 $^{57}/_{64}$ x 27 $^{11}/_{64}$ x 33 $^{5}/_{64}$ "). I believe this is a *'chest'*, and would call any storage box less than 30 cm in height or length a casket. A casket is for storing small valuables, jewellery or relics, whereas a chest is for storing larger items like arms, armour, silverware, vestments etc.

The chest lock typology for turnkey locks[14] is based on the position of the hasp (*left, centre, right*) in combination with the position of the key hole (*left, centre, right*). The chest lock on the '*Pillages*' chest appears to be a type 5CB, with its hasp on the right hand side of the lock plate, as you are looking at the chest, with a central keyhole. Knowing the setup of where the hasp and key hole are located indicates the internal working of the lock, and makes it easier to make a replica (*or pick*).

See Drawing 12 for parts of the Pillager's chest turnkey lock.

See Appendix 9 for the complete study.

---

[14] The chest lock typology for slide locks can be found in a forthcoming publication 'Vikings – Volume 2'.

Leatherwork.

Humans have used animal hides since prehistoric times. The Neolithic man, *'Ötzi'*, from Northern Italy is a good example. Leather was used for securing all manner of 'bits and bobs' that need to be carried from place to place in form of bags, pouches, quivers, sheaths and bottles. Other leather was used for garments, gloves and shoes. The types of animals used to provide that leather ranged from goat, sheep, cattle (calf skin was very popular) and maybe some deer and swine. The improvement in tanning technology increased the material's durability and wearability.

In the medieval period pouches, purses and cases were used to secure and transport all manner of personal items such as combs, ear spoons, or keys, dice and coins, as well as writing tablets and styluses.

Wayne Robinson's piece on the costrel from Baynard Castle Dock, City of London, will cover the techniques for making the jigs needed to make a costrel. These were used to carry water (and other liquids) on one's person.

Tool protection.

Tools take a fair bit of effort to make or potentially cost a lot of money to buy. No-one wants to have to replace them if they're damaged. It's important to carry out regular care and maintenance. See Table 4 for some suggestions.

Table 4. Tips for protecting and using tools.	
Issue	*Solution*
Sticking saw	Apply wax, soap, or fat to blade
Dry / cracking wooden handles	Apply boiled linseed oil
Rust on iron/steel	Use steel wool and/or a solution containing vinegar.
Protecting blades	Store in slotted wooden racks.
	Store with a leather or wooden cover or in leather storage rolls. See photo 12 for a wooden axe sheath.
Blunt blades	Sharpen at the correct angle for the tool.
	Remove burr using a strop.
Housekeeping	Clean up after a job, put everything back where it belongs.

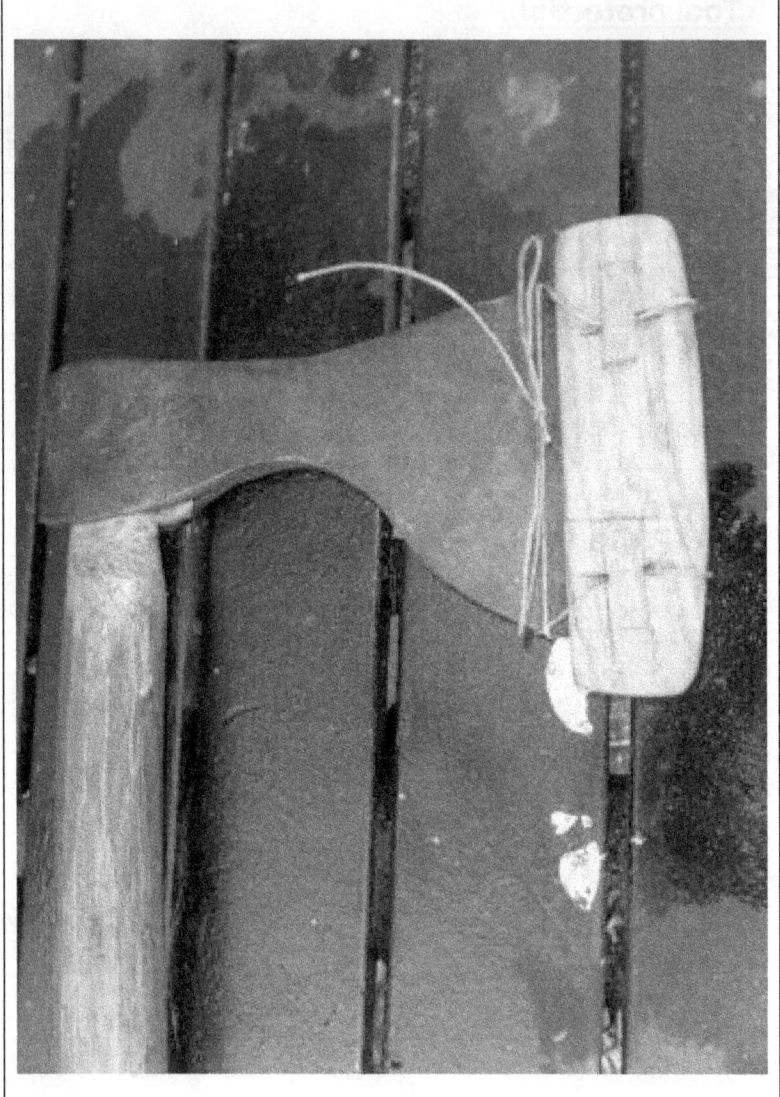

Photo 12. Wooden axe sheath from Haithabu No. 4, HbH.432.003 on an axe based on the axe found near the Mastermyr chest find.

Warp protection and grain direction.

Heelas (*1944*)[15] supplies great advice regarding timber and dealing with warping. Wood is wet when cut and needs to be properly seasoned before use. The drying process removes the sap from the wood, which stops rotting, warping and splitting. Timber needs to be stored in a dry place, and kept flat and well spaced to allow air flow between timbers. The timber that is used in the construction of a piece of furniture needs to be used as soon as possible after cutting to size and shape to avoid warping, splitting and shrinkage.

When joining wide boards together you can overcome warpage by arranging the wood with the heart sides towards the same face and not alternating directions. If it does warp, it will warp in the same direction.

When making a butt joint, it's easiest to mark the direction of the grain on the timber with arrows in pencil. Then align the grain using the pencil lines when you glue them together. If the timber is figured (patterned) try to match the figuring.

---

[15] Craftwork in Wood by Edgar H. Heelas, pages 81-82.

Bede's chair.

By Stephen Wyley.

Bede's chair – High backed chair.	**When**: 14th century CE
Stored: St.Paul's Church, Jarrow, County Durham, United Kingdom	**Material**: Oak
Size: Depth 48 cm, Width 60 cm, Height 147 cm[16] (Depth 19", Width 23½", Height 58")	

Photo 13. Bede's Chair from front left.

---

[16] From the provided height of 147 cm (57 $^7/_8$ ") the other dimensions can be ascertained - see page 9, 'Making proportional representation, and supported by information supplied by Wayne Robinson (photography and personal observations).

Photo 14. A replica made from old student desks (*timber unknown*). Oak for some backboards and the front of the seat, and pine for the top rail and bracing across the bottom of the sides.

Introduction.

Throughout history the type of chairs you owned and used represented your wealth and status in society. Compare the Viking three legged stool of Lund (*see Viking Volume 1*) to the bronze throne of Dagobert I (dated to probably the middle of the 7th century). No more so with box chairs, because of the amount of oak used and the time and skill it took to manufacture. See Table 5 for more examples.

Bede's chair is a multi-piece high backed box chair, covering the user on three sides, and good for keeping the draughts at bay. The chair is housed in St. Paul's Church in Jarrow, County Durham, United Kingdom. The site was an Anglo-Saxon monastery in the 7th century and is associated with the '*Venerable Bede*'.[17] According to some sources the date is attributed to the 11th century by Carbon 14 dating with the associated errors; unfortunately I have not been able to sight a Carbon 14 dating report.[18] Other sources assign a date of the 14th century, including the British Library, which may be simply quoting Cox and Harvey.[19] The type of timber is oak and the

---

[17] English Heritage (n.d.) St Paul's Monastery.

[18] Bede was a saint of the Roman Catholic Church and has been considered a noted historian and scholar, writing the earliest history of England. Regarding Perry (2019). I have written to the author asking for the Carbon 14 dating report details. I have received no reply as yet. An 11th century date would coincide with a fire at the church in 1069 CE – Cox and Harvey (1908).

[19] English Church Furniture by Cox and Harvey (1908), who quotes Savage (1900). Savage in Arch. Ael. Vol. xxii, p48 in turn cites Hitchinson (1782) Arch. Ael. Vol. ii. p. 477, but also notes that in 1745-6, it was known as Cuthbert's Chair. Newcastle Courant, Jan. 18-25, 1745-6.

height is four feet ten inches (147 cm) according to Popular Science Monthly of 1898.[20]

Photo 15. The side of the top of the chair showing the end of the top rail, the end of the boards attached to the back, and the damage to the top of the side board.

---

[20] Attempts have been made, without success, to verify the carbon dating of the chair and the dimensions.

Photo 16. Side of the chair, showing the mortise and tenon for the back of seat, and how side of the seat sits on the ledge of the sides, how the front of seat is supported by a square railing running between both sides of the seat.

Photo 17. Detail of side of chair, showing what appears to be a wedge on the right side of the tenon, and two nails, one through the side of the chair which could go into the seat between the tenon and the front of the seat, the other through the side of the chair under the level of the front of the seat.

Table 5. Example of similar chairs.

Source	Description	Size	Dated
The choir chair in Hol Church, Hallingdal, KHM, C17902,	A high sided and backed box chair in pine. Sides decorated in carved leaf and vine decoration, a Romanesque – Gothic style and circular plates at the apex of both sides, made in pine.	H 161cm W 71cm D 38cm H $63\frac{3}{8}$" W 28" D 15"	13th century, possibly late 13th century CE.
Ab Urbe Condit, ms. BNF Francais 268, Folio 152V.	Panelled vertical sides supported on a cross beam with arched supports at either end, sloped arm down from back, back height mid upper arm of the user, indicating that the chair is supported by four legs.	Illuminated manuscript	3rd quarter 14th C - 1390-1400 CE.
8594 St.	'L' shaped	Unknown	14th Century CE

Table 5. Example of similar chairs.

Source	Description	Size	Dated
Augustine's Chair, from St James Church of Stanford Bishop, in Herefordshire. This chair is believed to be the one in which St. Augustine was seated when he received the British Bishops at Augustine's Oak. Owned by the Royal Museums in Canterbury, on permanent loan to St James Church, Stanford Bishop.	sides supporting single back board, seat and front of seat are two boards at right angles to each other, suspected mortise and tenon joints between horizontal timbers and sides.		(a 1943 examination concluded most was from the 18th century, see Upton, 2014)
A box seated table chair,	Planked table top on two	H 114.3cm W 63.5cm	1490 CE

Table 5. Example of similar chairs.

Source	Description	Size	Dated
English, Stock No. 1349.[21]	runners folds up to form a back chair on a panelled and framed box.	D 45.7cm H 45" W 25" D 18"	
A choir bench (cathedra) from Verne's Church in Stjørdalen, Norway.[22] Museum No. T3193. 'The 'Værnes Chair', made in 1685 as the private pew for the squire of Værnes (General Schultz and his wife)" is mentioned on a web page for the Church. [23]	Back of the bench consists of 3 planks dowelled into sides, both sides are carved, the left side (as you look at it) is a dragon with a human master and the right side is topped by a circle with a spiral carved from the outside.	Unknown	1685 CE

The following are basic instructions on how to make a replica of the Bede's chair. I will also provide instructions for a flat packable version in Appendix 6.

---

[21] Simmoni, J. and J. (n.d.)
[22] Master Marinus. (2015)
[23] SpottingHistory (n.d.).

Materials.

Timber (oak preferably but pinus radiata will do). See Table 6 for the cutting list. See Appendix 2 for wider boards and how to make them, if they are not available.

Table 6. Timber cutting list.
Imperial/customary measures in parenthesis.

Part	Length	Width	Height / Depth
2 x Sides	150cm (60")	44cm (17 $^{21}/_{64}$")	4cm (1¼")
1 x Seat	60cm (23½")	48cm (19")	4cm (1¾")
4 x Planks for back of seat	60cm (23½")	25cm (10")	1cm ($\frac{3}{8}$")
2 x Cross beams (top and under front of seat)	60cm (23½")	4cm (1¾")	4cm (1¾")
2 x Back beams	150cm (60")	4cm (1¾")	4cm (1¾")

<u>Tools.</u>

Rulers (30cm, 60cm, and 100cm (12", 24" and 36")), set square, chisels (25mm (1") and 7mm (¼"), plain edge), files (coarse - flat bastard, fine - square bastard), tenon saw, hand saw, plane, G clamps, scrap wood (*for holding work without damaging it*), claw hammer, wooden mallet, bench vice, pencil, hand drill with 4mm ($\frac{5}{32}$") bit.

Construction Process. See Drawing 3, 4 & 5.

Back beams.
1. Mark out and cut out timbers to size.

Sides.
1. Mark out and cut out timbers to size.
2. Cut the '*cut out*' for the rail under the seat.
3. Mark out and drill out mortise for seat, trim to shape with mallet and chisel.

Seat.
1. Mark out and cut out timbers to size.
2. Cut tenons on either side.
3. Cut and round off the leading edge of the seat.

Seat and top rails.
1. Mark out and cut out timbers to size.
2. Round top edges of top rail.

Back boards.
1. Mark out and cut to length. Note: Earlier photos show a range of different widths were used.

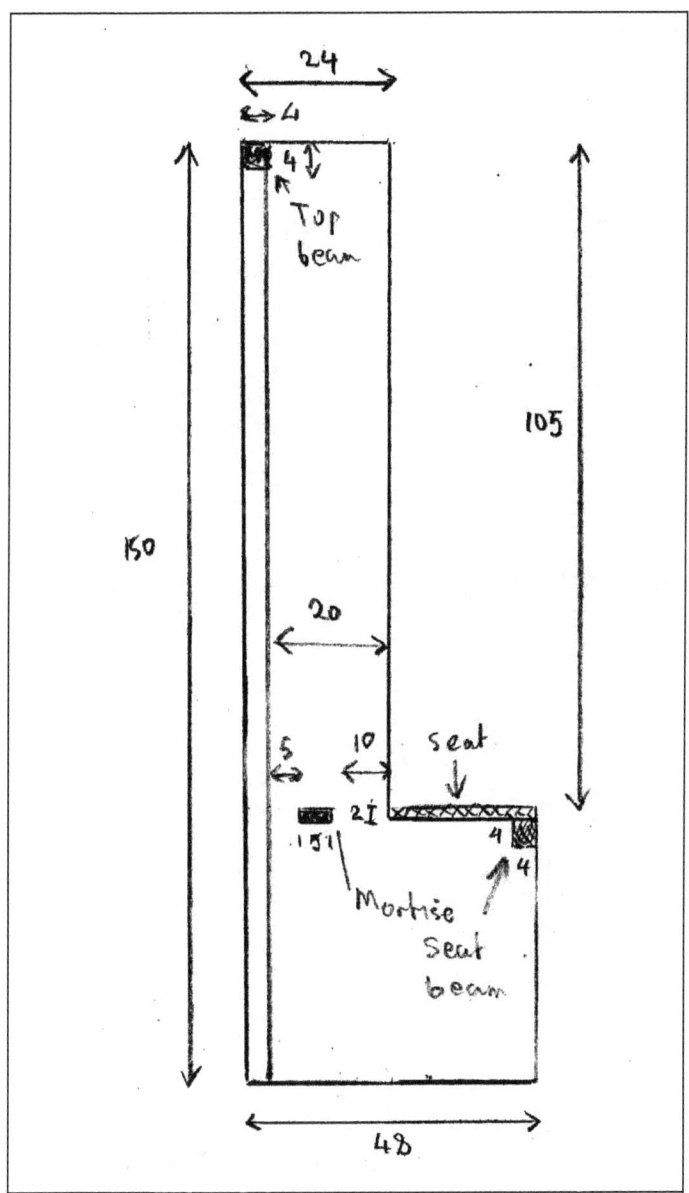

Drawing 3. Side on plan of the chair in large planks. Dimensions in cm.

Assembly.

1. Attached back beams to the rear end of the side boards with glue, nails or dowels.
2. Join sides and seat, hold in place with sash clamps.
3. Glue and nail or dowel sides to seat, between mortise and tenon and seat that sits on top of the side pieces.
4. Wedge the mortises and tenons in place.
5. Fit the bottom rail under the seat, glue and nail or dowel in place.
6. Glue and nail or dowel the top rail to the top of the sides.
7. Nail the back boards in place on back beams.
8. Apply a coat of linseed oil to treat the timber.

Note: a flat pack version can be found in Appendix 6.

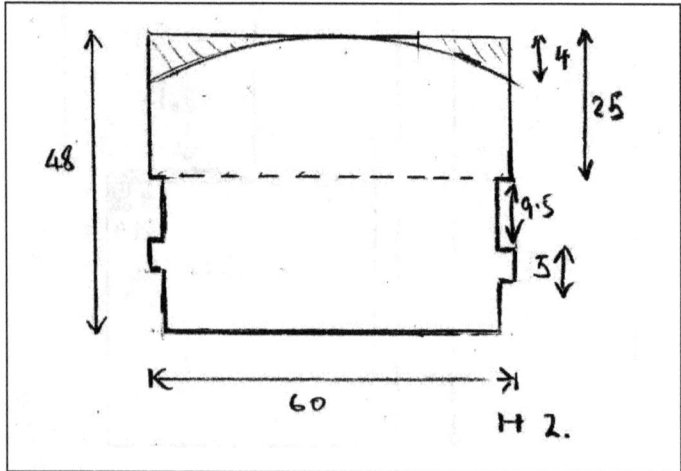

Drawing 4. Plan of the seat in large plank. Dotted line represents join in smaller planks. Dimensions in cm.

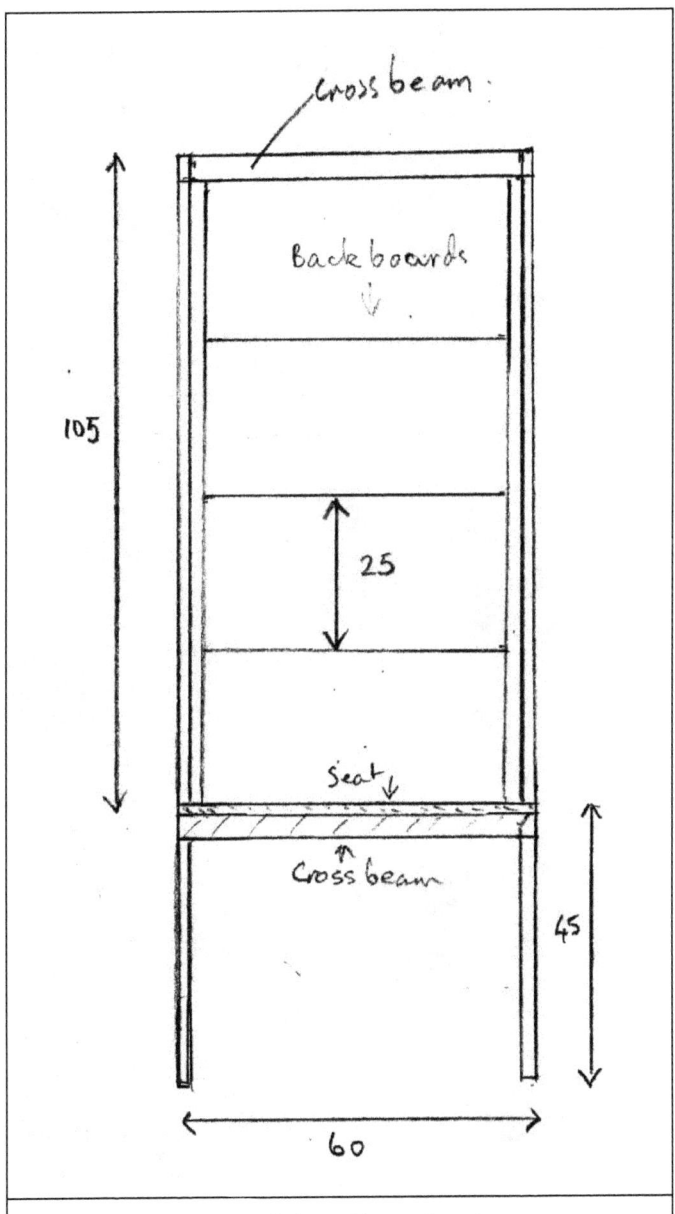

Drawing 5. Front view of chair. Dimensions in cm.

The Pillager's Hutch Chest.

By Stephen Wyley.

The Pillager's Hutch chest – illuminated manuscript.	**When:** Late 14th century – 1380 CE.
Stored: British Library	Chroniques de France ou de St Denis (from 1270 to 1380) - Rioters pillaging a house in Paris. Collection: BL MS Royal 20 CVII, f. 41v.

Figure 3. MS Royal 20 CVII, f. 41v, details of the Pillager's with the chest, British Library.

Photo 18. A hutch chest that I made, with CNC laser cut hinges. Note: I have reinforced the corners of this chest with steel brackets nailed in place. The timber used was recycled and needed some reinforcing.

Introduction.

According to Eames (*1977*)[24] chests were probably the most widely used piece of furniture in the medieval period. Hutch chests were used for storage and as luggage in the wealthy homes of merchants, nobles, or churches. They were used for storing clothes, linen, money, ecclesiastical vestments,

---

[24] Eames P, (1977) *Medieval Furniture in England and France and the Netherlands from the 12th to 15th centuries* (Furniture Hist. Soc. Journal 13).

silverware or documents. *See Table 7 for some examples from a range of sources.*

Clamp fronted or 'Hutch' chests were made and used from the 12th to the 17th century. The front consisted of a horizontal panel (which could be single or multiple boards), joined to legs or 'stiles' at either end. This permitted bigger chests than could be made with the 'six boarded' chest which was constrained by the width of the boards and allowed cross grain movement as the timber's moisture content changed.

The hutch chest from Figure 3 shows soldiers pillaging a house during the Hundred Years War. The manuscript shows two soldiers carrying a relatively small chest, so I am assuming that it is heavy and that it may contain something valuable, perhaps coins. As the illumination does not show a differentiation of separate legs I have assumed that the front and the back are made from single pieces of timber.

The hinge terminals on the chest are *'fleur di lis'* in shape and the lock plate is concave on both sides and bottom, which shows considerable skill of the maker and would have cost a lot even in the 14th century.

Table 7. Example of similar chests.

Source	Description	Size	Dated
Crusader Chest - Gort Furniture Collection, Bunratty Castle, County Clare, Ireland. (ACC No. 338, Item No. 8., Oak.	Chest is raised up on legs, front inserts to the legs. Legs are pierced by a "D" shaped cut out near the base, reversed "D" on the left leg. Three square shaped lock plates for turnkey locks. Three iron straps reinforce the front to the left of each lock plate. Each front corner (only the front is shown) has two reinforcing straps, joining the legs and the ends. Strap hinges but no detail shown.	L 190cm W 43cm H 72cm L 75" W 17" H 23½"	12th century CE
Hutch chest with chip carving on front, Victoria and Albert Museum, Museum Number W. 30-1926, possibly from a church in Hampshire. Wood; Oak. (*VAM 2004*)	Clamp fronted chest, the base of each leg curves up to join the front of the chest. Three different circular geometric chip carvings adorn the centre of the front legs and the centre of the front panel. Current lock is later in design, consisting of an internal latch turnkey lock. Ends consist of crossed stiles over a plank. Hinges appear to be internal, with no indication that they were ever external.	L 111cm W 49.5cm H 53cm L 43¼" W 19½" H 21"	1200-1300 CE
Little	Based on line drawing, clamp	L 107.9cm	13th

Table 7. Example of similar chests.

Source	Description	Size	Dated
Canfield Coffer found in Canfield, Essex, England. (Roe 1929)	fronted chest, "D" shaped cut away in base of front legs, "D" reversed on left leg. Circular lobes at the top of the bottom of the straight section of each "D". Rounded lobe on curved section of left leg's "D". 3 hasps for padlocks, a hasp for each leg and one hasp in the centre of centre panel of front. Top of the hasps appear to be on the underside of the lid. Hinges for lid not shown, assuming they are attached to the underside of lid.	W 52.1cm H 64.1cm L 42½" W 20½" H 25¼"	century CE
Chest from Kloster Isenhagen Chapter house, (Lower Saxony, Germany) No. TR-NR-409/ISN Ba 83.[25]	Stout clamp fronted chest, thin central panel between legs, and central timber with scalloped shaped cut out of base. Reinforcing metal strips on end edges of lid and above lock, turn key lock, lock plate with scallops on all four sides. End in-stepped from legs.	H 69cm W 85cm D 53.9cm H 27" W 33½" D 21¼"	1375 CE

---

[25] Master Marinus (2012)

Table 7. Example of similar chests.			
Source	*Description*	*Size*	*Dated*
Oak clamp front chest – Fitsimmons (*2021*) (Note: Lock plate scalloped on 4 sides.)	Clamp fronted chest, centre panel consist of two horizontal planks, dowel joined to thin legs, with one lock plate with deep scalloped edges, turn key lock, hasp hole but no evidence of hasp on lid. "U" staple in front of the chest to the left of the lock plate with no evidence for hasp. External strap hinges with round lobed terminals, and are hinged through a flattened loop which is then stapled to the rear legs. Lid consists of two parallel planks supported at either end by curved bottom styles that fit over the outside of the ends and slot into the front legs. The bottoms of the styles are curved and the back ends for a dowelled hinge through the rear centre panel. A storage till is located against the left end of the chest. The ends are made up of three planks which are mortises into the legs, and dowelled through the side of the legs.	L 140.3cm W 68.6 cm H 73.3cm L 52¼" W 27" H 29"	1390-1400 CE[26]

---

[26] von Stülpnagel (2000)

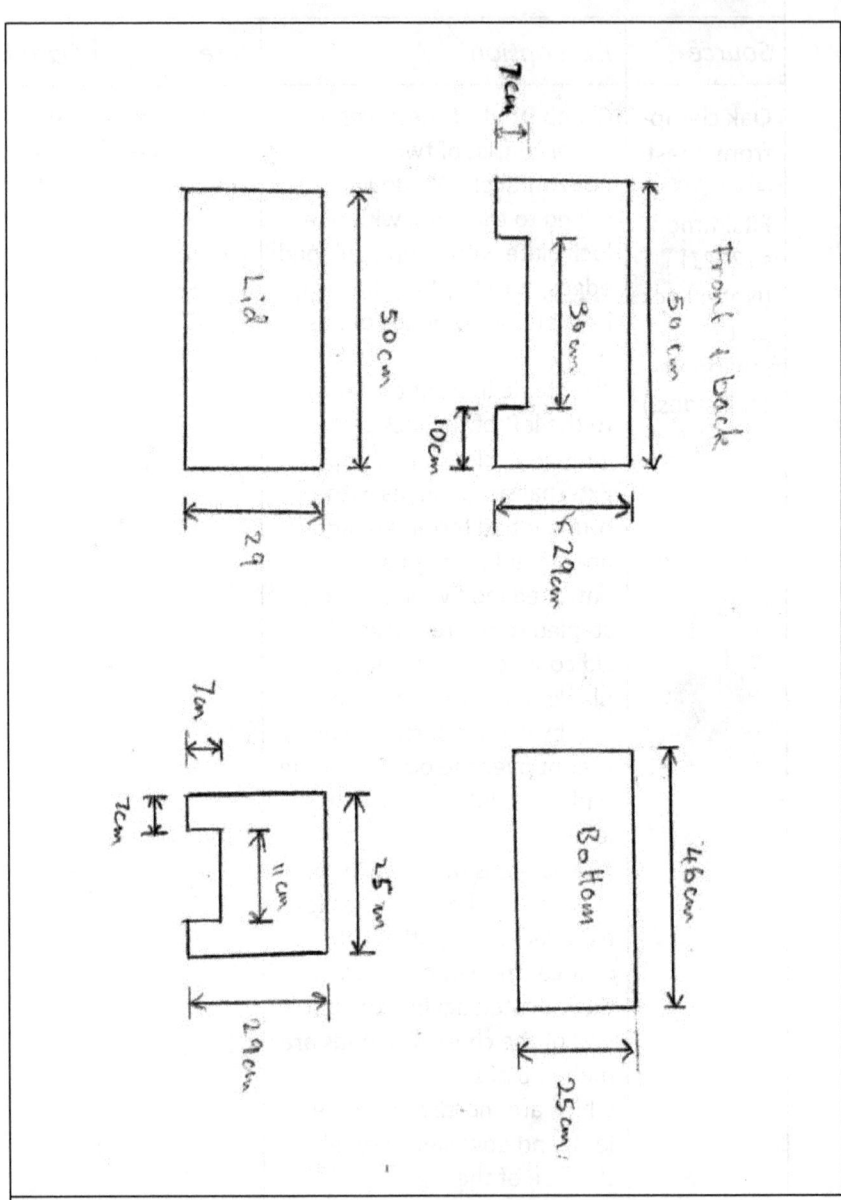

Drawing 6. Hutch chest plans. Larger and smaller versions can be found in Appendix 3 and 4. Dimensions in cm.

Materials.

Timber (oak preferably but pinus radiata will do). How much timber do you need? Answer = exactly 246 cm (97") but I recommend getting at least 300 cm (120"), just in case there is a warp, fiddle, knot or crack to be avoided. See Table 8.

Table 8. Timber cutting list in centimetres (inches).			
Part	Length	Width	Height/Depth
Front and Back	50 (19¾")	29 (11½")	2 (¾")
Ends (make 2)	25 ($9\frac{3}{8}$")	29 (11½")	2 (¾")
Lid	50 (19¾")	29 (11½")	2 (¾")
Bottom	46 ($11\frac{1}{8}$")	25 ($9\frac{3}{8}$")	2 (¾")

These measurements are based on the original chest.
Plans for a larger version are in Appendix 3.

Metal.

Nails, steel for fittings (hinges, hasp, hasp plate). See Tables 9 and 10.

Table 9. Metal cutting list in millimetres (inches/metal gauge).			
Part	Length	Width	Thickness
2 Hinges – Fleur di lis	270 (10¾")	30 (1¼")	2 (14ga)
2 Hinges – Strap for back	215 (8½")	24 (1")	2 (14ga)
Hasp	310 (12¼")	24 (1")	2 (14ga)
Lock plate	100 (4")	10 (4")	2 (14ga)
Slide	85 ($3\frac{3}{8}$")	18 ($\frac{23}{32}$" [27])	2 (14ga)
2 Slide guides (lugs)	25 (1")	20 (¾")	2 (14ga)
2 Keys	140 (5½")	20 (¾")	2 (14ga)
Ward plate	35 ($1\frac{3}{8}$")	47	1 (18ga)
Ward (attached to lock plate)	25 (1")	10 ($\frac{3}{8}$")	1 (18ga)
Spring	60 ($2\frac{3}{8}$")	10 ($\frac{3}{8}$")	1 (18ga)

[27] Cut to ¾" and file to fit if you can't measure to this precision

Table 10. Number of nails required.

Body of chest	24
Hinges	12
Hasp and hasp plate	6
Total	**42**

Tools.

Rulers (30cm, 60cm, and 100cm (12", 24", 36")), set square, chisels (25mm (1") and 7mm (¼"), plain edge), files (Coarse - flat bastard, fine - square bastard), tenon saw, hand saw, plane, G clamps, scrap wood (for holding work without damaging it), claw hammer, wooden mallet, bench vice, pencil, hand drill with 3mm ($\frac{1}{8}$") and 4mm ($\frac{5}{32}$") drill bits.

Construction method.
See drawing 6.

The Box.

1. Mark out the bottom and ends and cut them out.
2. Cut out the pieces in the end boards.

Photo 19. Cut outs in the end boards.

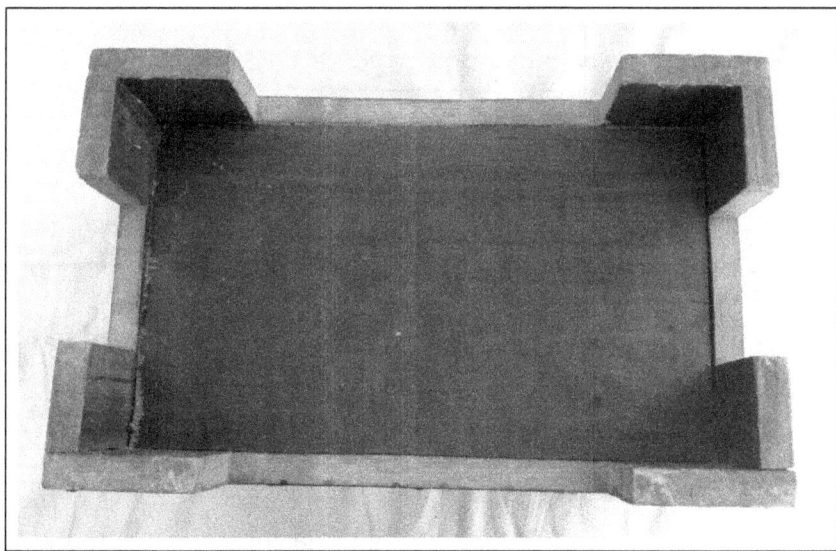
Photo 20. Bottom in place.

3. Glue and nail ends to bottom (forms an 'H').
4. Check that it is square.
5. Cut Front and Back to fit bottom and ends.
6. Cut out cut outs in Front and Bottom.

Photo 21. Cut out sections in front and back.

7. Glue, nail and allow glue to dry.
8. Turn the box over on the timber for the lid and use as a template, mark with pencil, and mark which part of the lid is the front and back of the chest (your chest may not be square or to the exact size as the plans).
9. Cut out the lid, clean up the edges.

<u>Making the hinges.</u>
See Drawing 7.

Hinges can be forged, cut and ground or Computerized Numerical Control (CNC) laser cut. Forging takes access to a forge and lots of skill, cutting and grinding takes a lot of work or money, whereas a CNC laser cut looks good and takes less time. Consult the internet for your local metal cutter, they may charge for loading the job to their machine but they will have it on file if you need more.

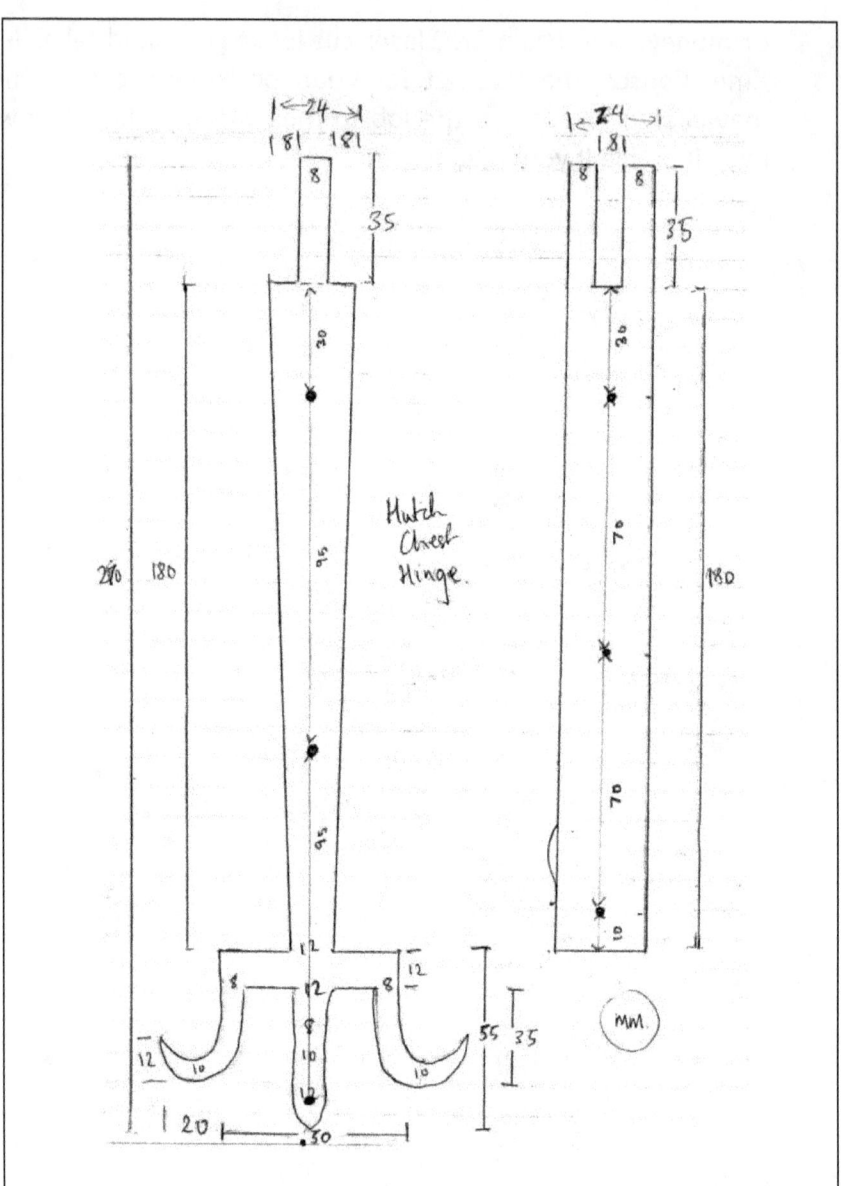

Drawing 7. S trap hinge, with a *'fleur de lis'* terminal, made from mild steel from flat bar. Dots are nail holes. Dimensions in mm.

Making hinges by cutting and grinding.

1. Mark out and cut to length.
2. Use an angle grinder with a cutting disc to cut out the basic shape.
3. Clean up with hand files.
4. Assemble the hinge parts cold since it is only mild steel, or hot if you have a forge or a gas torch. Bend over parts of the hinge over a round bar to form a round barrel, insert rivet and peen over end, without squashing the hinge, to secure the hinge.
5. Blacken with gas torch (i.e. Liquid Petroleum Gas (LPG) etc.) and oil to provide a rust proof surface.
6. Mark out, punch and drill nail attachment holes. If using 20 mm (¾") thick timber the hole closest to the hinge should be 30 mm (1¼") in from the hinge. The next hole is in the middle of the hinge, and the third hole should be in the apex of the fleur di lis.

Attaching the hinges.

1.   Ensure that the lid is sitting properly and square on the chest. Attach hinges to the back and then the lid of the chest.
2. Ensure that the hinges are sitting square to the back and the lid with a set square.
3. Pre-drill the holes through nail holes in hinges using drill bits smaller than the shank width of the nail used to attach the hinges.
4. Cleat nails on the inside of the chest. See *'Cleating nails'* on page 20 - 22.

Photo 22. Hinges attached to the top of the chest.

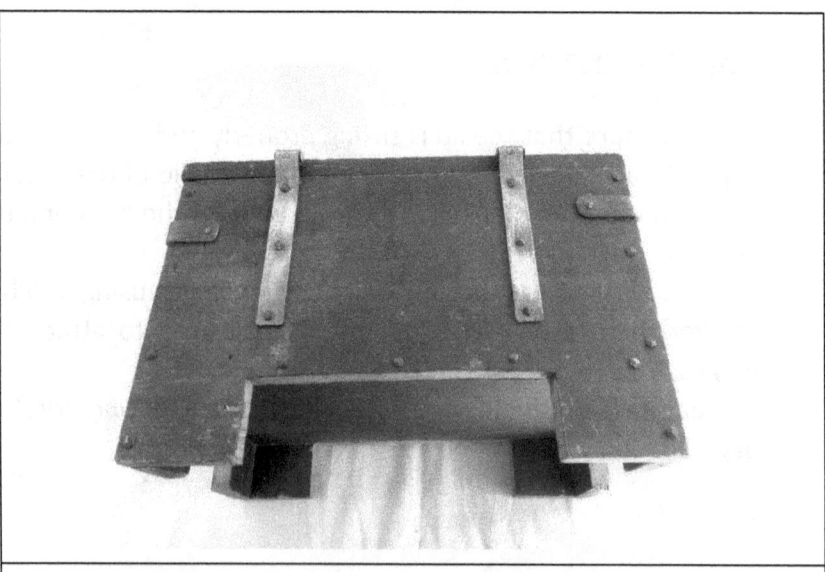

Photo 23. Hinges attached to the back of the chest.

Photo 24. Back of the hinges are bent to take the position of the hinge pin. Note: the corner brackets are not on the original illumination.

The Lock.

Lock smithing is no longer a prevalent skill and it is a sad thing that such skills have been lost. The lock in this case is a complicated mechanism with eleven parts and requires finer skills than a common blacksmith. [28]

The lock is made up of multiple parts which need care and accuracy in both their making and attachment to the lock, and once attached they need to work together to make a

---

[28] Here is a link showing what a lock looks like inside and how it works. https://www.youtube.com/watch?v=cC90-fqXthk (Sven Skildbiter, 2021)

functional mechanism for securing the chest from unwanted egress.

How the lock works.

The key is inserted in the key hole and the swivel point slides into the hole in the ward plate. To unlock the lock, the key is rotated anticlockwise (to the left as you look at the chest). The notch in the key passes the ward attached to the lock plate. As the key rotates further, it engages the notches in the slide. This in turn overcomes the downward pressing of the spring on the slide, which moves the slide to left, unlocking the lock. The locking process is just the reverse of the above process. See Drawing 8 & 9.

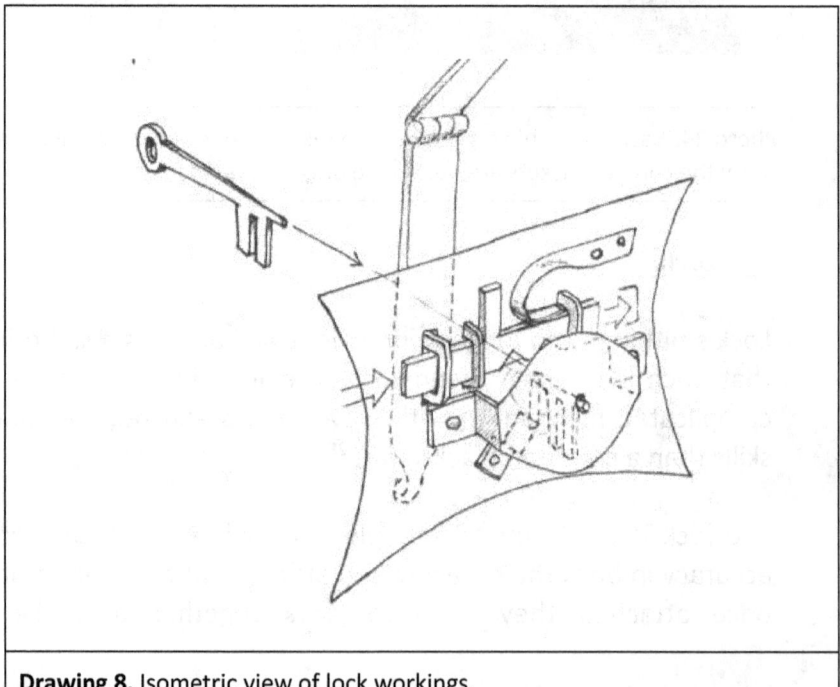

Drawing 8. Isometric view of lock workings.

If you have not made a lock before, the following instructions should be of assistance. I recommend concentrating on each piece at a time, it's just like *'Eating a Mammoth'*.[29]

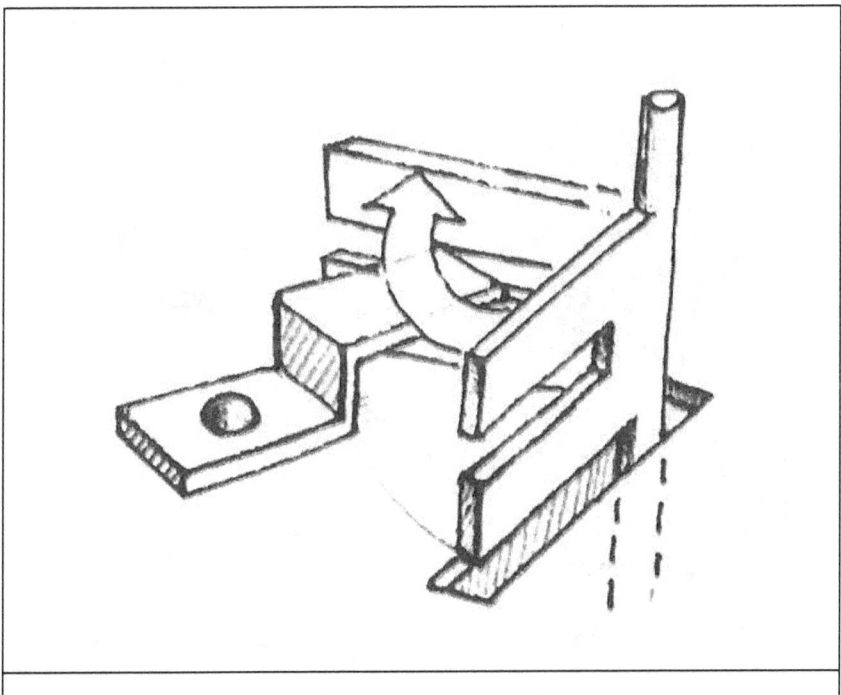

Drawing 9. Isometric view of how the key passes the ward.

Keys.

1. Mark out, cut out and file to shape.
2. Mark out, pouch and drill hole in grip.
3. File a round shaped swivel point that sits in the hole in the ward plate so it rotates.
4. Round throat behind key head so it rotates in keyhole.

---

[29] *"Question: How do you eat a mammoth? Answer: Well first you have to go to Siberia and dig one up…"* S.Wyley.

5. Place the key in the lock and rotate until the key comes into contact with the ward. Mark where slot(s) need to be cut.
6. Cut slots for wards once the wards are attached. See wards and lock assembly.

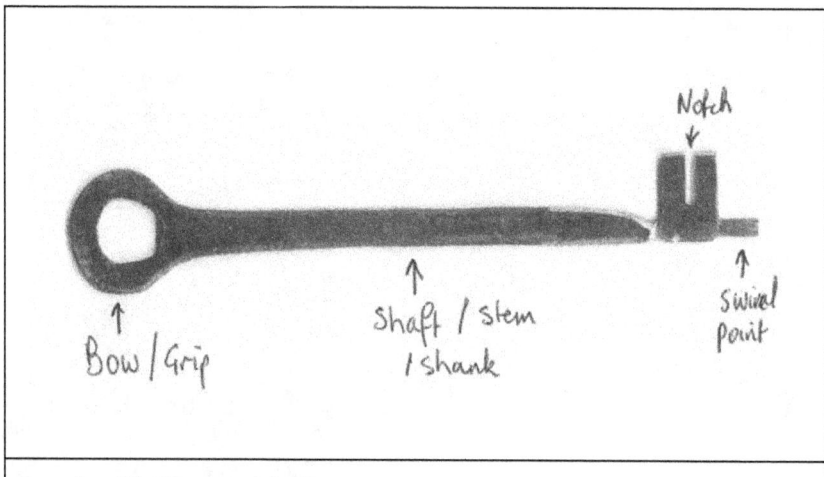

Drawing 10. The parts of a key.

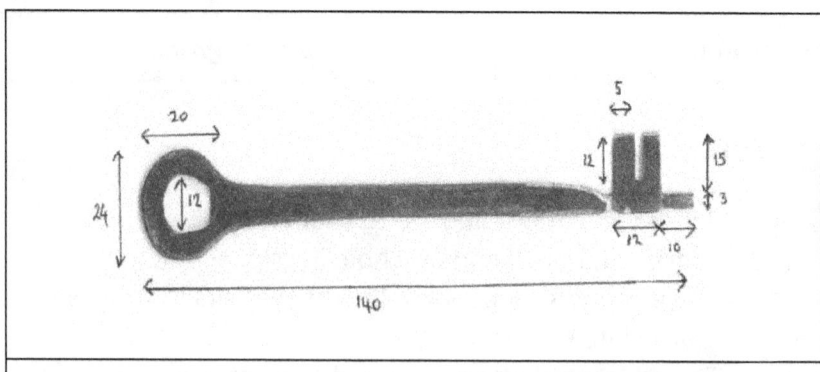

Drawing 11. The measurements of the key. Dimensions in mm.

Lock plate.

See Drawings 12 & 13.

1. Mark out and cut the lock plate (either with cold chisel, hammer and anvil (protect anvil from damage (I use a block of steel, not a real anvil).
2. Mark out and drill corner nail attachment holes, size of holes depends on size of nails to be used. The larger the nail the further from the edge of the plate.
3. Counter sink nail holes if the nail has a shoulder.

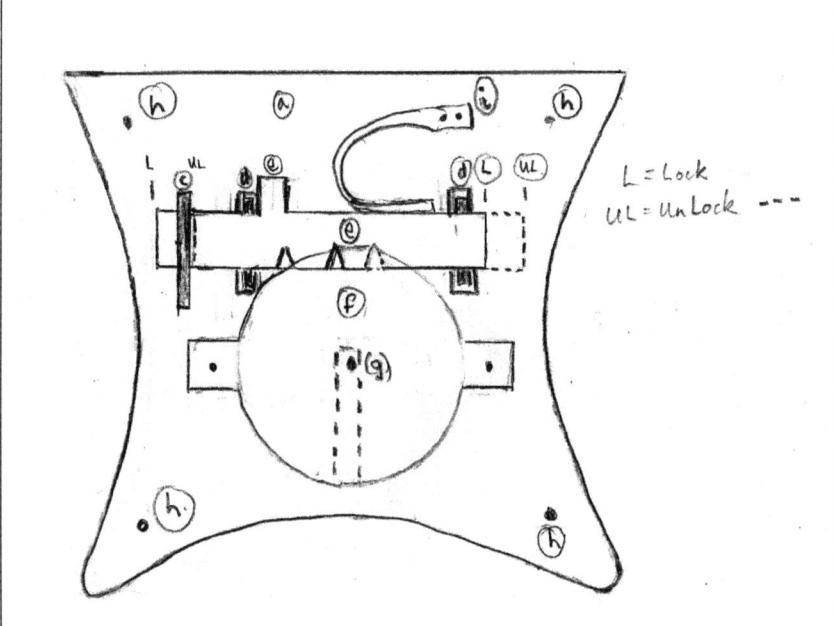

Drawing 12. Lock parts, slide and ward plate.
(a) lock plate, (b) slide stop, (c) hasp lug, (d) slide lugs, (e) slide with notches, (f) ward plate, (g) swivel hole in ward plate, (h) nail hole, (i) spring. Slide travel: L= Lock, UL = Unlock.

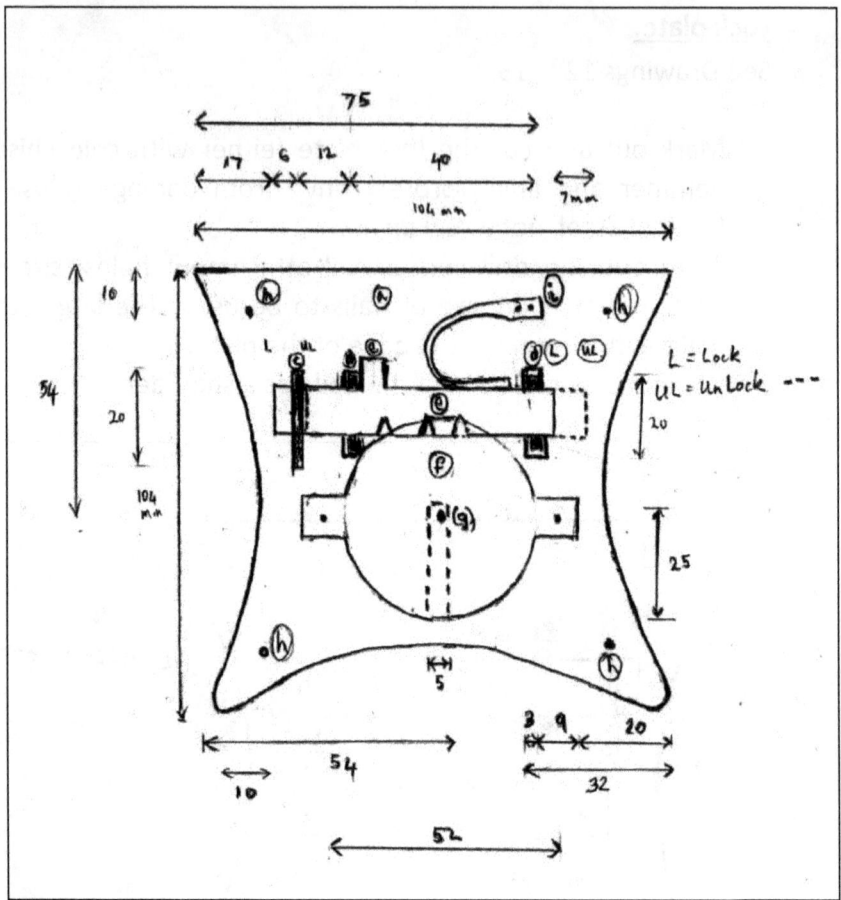

Drawing 13. Lock. Dimensions in mm.

Photo 25. The lock plate can be cut out with a cold chisel, hammer and anvil. Note: Protect the anvil from damage.

Slot for the hasp lug.

1. Line up slot with position of the slide, where the hasp fits between the lug rivets and the nail in the corner of the lock plate, so the hasp sits flat against the lock plate.
2. Mark line of hasp on lock plate, punch the line with punch, hammer and anvil.
3. Drill out holes with 3 mm ($\frac{1}{8}''$) drill bit and drill.
4. Cut with cold chisel, turning it over and cutting with cold chisel until a big enough hole to fit a file into.

5. File and out slot to fit hasp lug.

NB: you may need to file down the end of the slide to make a wedge shape, tapering back from the leading edge to aid the entry of the end of the slide. Ensure that the slide will slide into the lug on the hasp in the *'locked'* position.

Hasp.

1. Mark out and cut to length.
2. Cut out the slot at the end of hasp.
3. Cut out tongue at end of hasp.
4. Cut out taper on the other end of hasp, roll taper for form loop.[30]
5. Ensure there is play of least 1 mm ($\frac{1}{16}$") between the slot and tongue.
6. Roll slot and tongue to form loops (this can be down hot (forging) or cold since you are using mild steel).
7. Slide tongue into slot, insert rivet, ensure hinge of hasp rotates freely, peen over rivet in place.
8. Drill and attach lug, rivet lug in place on lug.
9. Ensure the hole in the lug matches the slide bar of the lock.

---

[30] Since the metal I recommend you use is just mild steel you don't need to heat it up to bend it over the horn of an anvil. Just hit it over the horn to make a crescent shape, place the opposite end of the hasp on the anvil and hit it downwards to bend the tip further round. Lie the hasp flat on the anvil and hit the tip of the loop until it forms a loop and touches the body of the hasp.

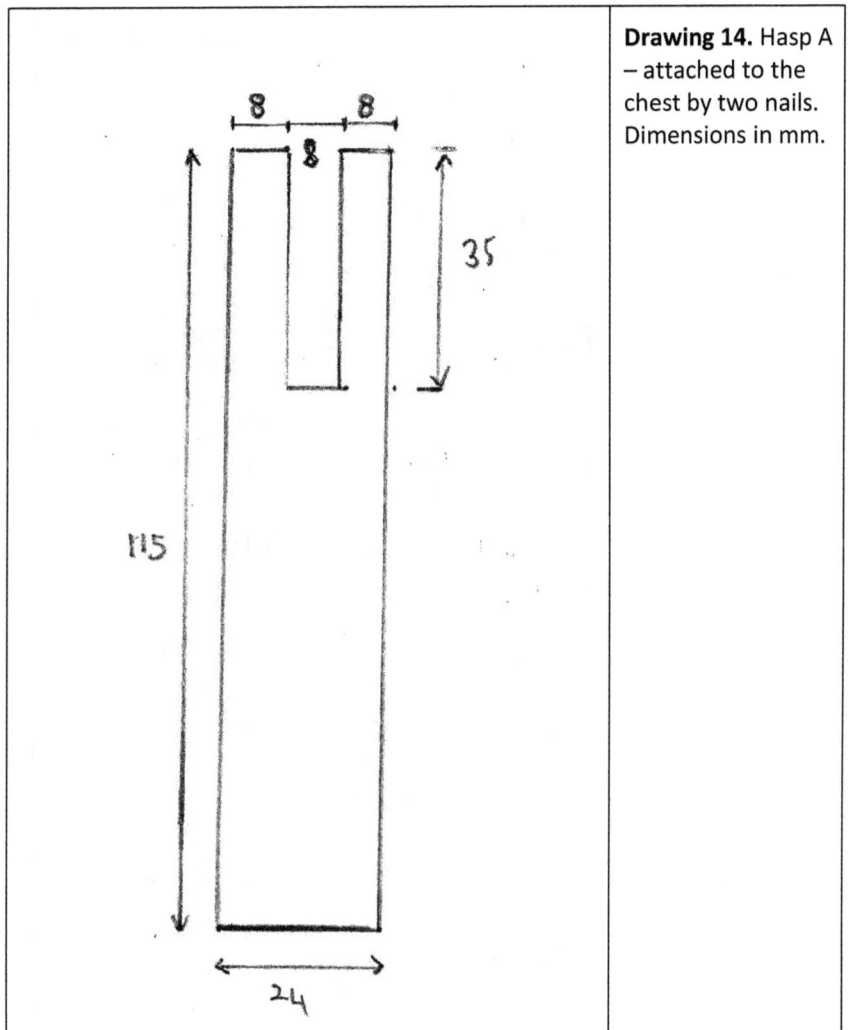

Drawing 14. Hasp A – attached to the chest by two nails. Dimensions in mm.

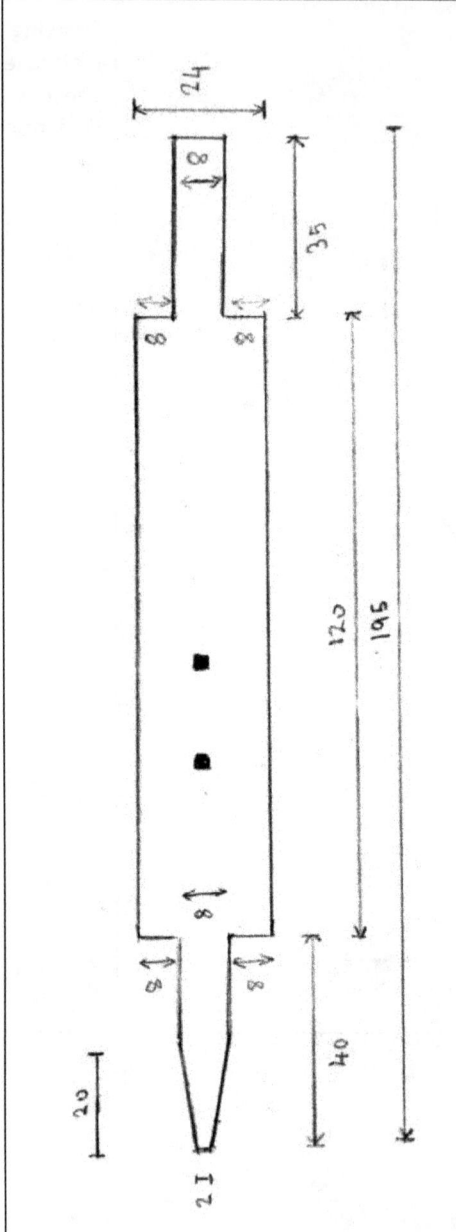

Drawing 15. Hasp B – Hinged to part A, Point rolled into a ring and the black dots on the body of the hasp represent where the lug is placed, through which the lock slide slides through to lock the chest. Dimensions in mm.

Photo 26. The turned up tip of the hasp.

Lugs.
See Drawing 16.

1. Mark out, cut out and file to shape. Note: The lugs have 10 mm ($\frac{3}{8}$") long legs to help hold them in place when you are fiddling around but when you rivet them you cut them down to 5 mm ($\frac{3}{16}$").

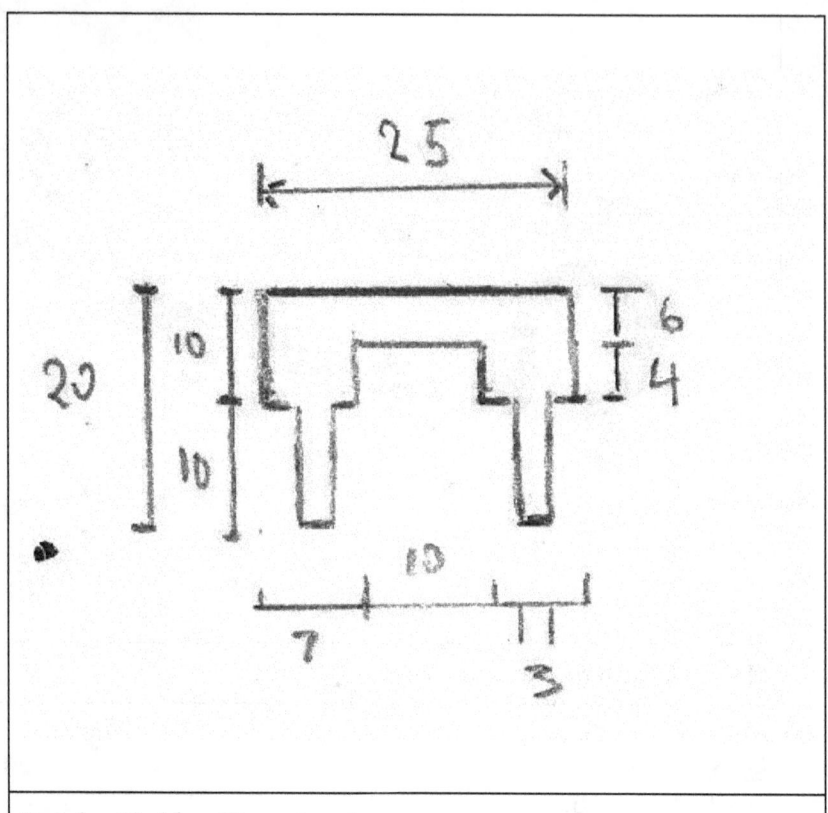

Drawing 16. A lug. Dimensions in mm.

Ward plate.
See Drawing 17.

1) Mark out, cut out and file to shape.
2) Mark out, pouch drill holes, drill holes in ends and centre of plate for attachment to lock plate.
3) Mark 'L' and 'R' (with permanent pen) to make sure you can keep the pieces to the correct side. Attach temporarily with 3 mm ($\frac{1}{8}$") bolts and nuts.

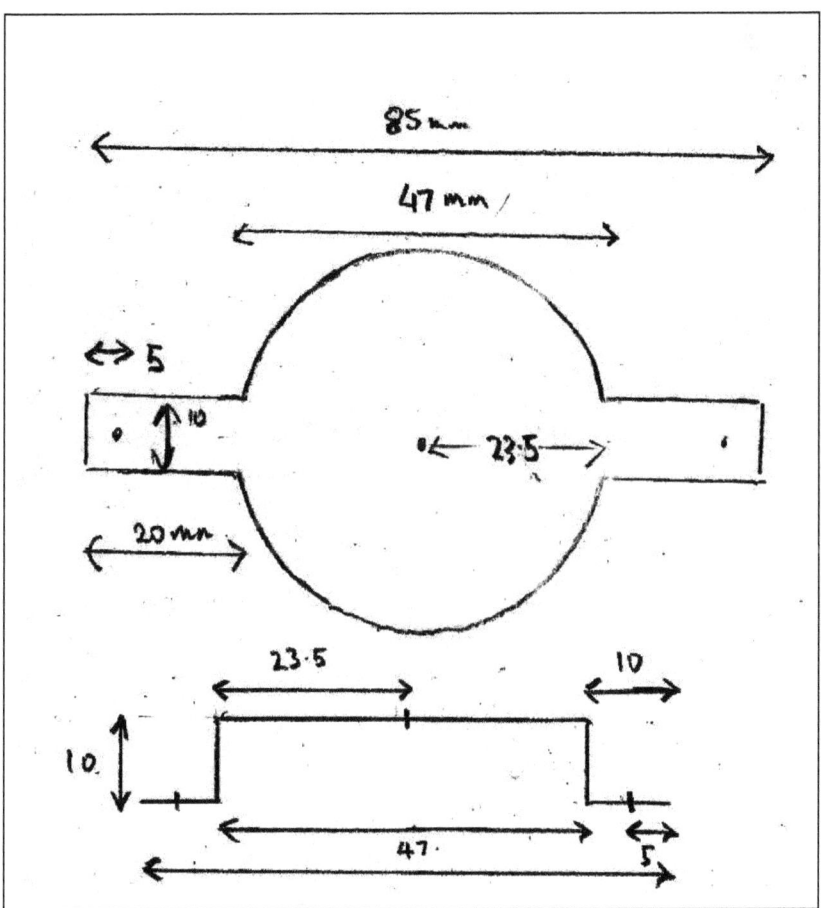

Drawing 17. (a) Top view of the ward plate, (b) Side view of ward plate. Dimensions in mm.

Wards.

There are two types of wards: 1) the wards that are attached to the ward plate or lock plate that are at 90 degrees to the lock plate; and 2) the wards that are parallel to the lock plate. You can keep it simple by having one ward. If you use more wards it is more complicated, meaning more work, and more to go wrong.

1. Mark out, cut out and file to shape.
2. Mark out, pouch hole, and drill 3 mm ($\frac{1}{8}$") drill bit.
3. Bend to shape, ('90 degrees' wards are just a right angle, '*Parallel*' ones are a flat 'Z' with right angles).
4. Wards are often riveted with a single round shaft rivet. This can rotate, so I recommend filing the rivets and holes square before riveting.
5. Rivet wards to the ward plate before the ward plate is riveted to the lock plate.

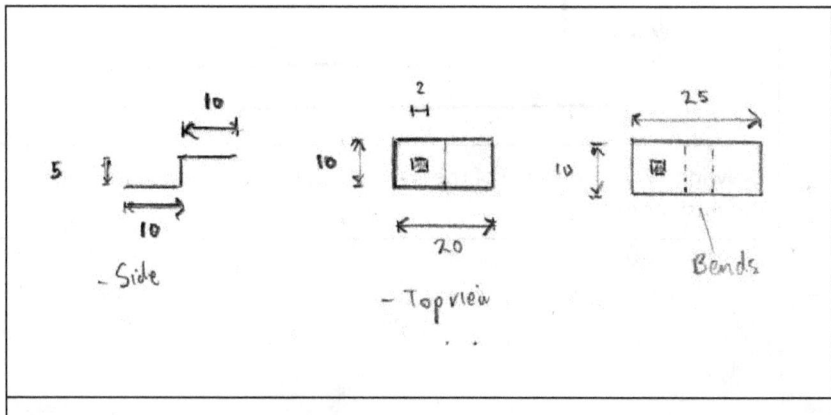

Drawing 18. Basic ward. Dimensions in mm.

Ward plate (attach to lock plate). Define arc of key.

1. Mark the extent of the keys arc on the lock plated.
2. Place the ward on the lock plate where the upper section of the ward will strike the key, make where the attachment point is.
3. Drill the hole for the rivet, place the rivet through the holes in the lock plate and then peen the rivet. See fitting the key to the wards.

Lock Slide.

1. Mark out, cut out and file to shape.
2. Mount slide (temporarily to see where and how the key engages the slide (the arc of the radius).
3. Cut 'V's' in bottom of slide, file to shape with triangular file. You may want to cut the 'V's in the slide after the slide is mounted in the lugs so you can see precisely where the key engages the slide.

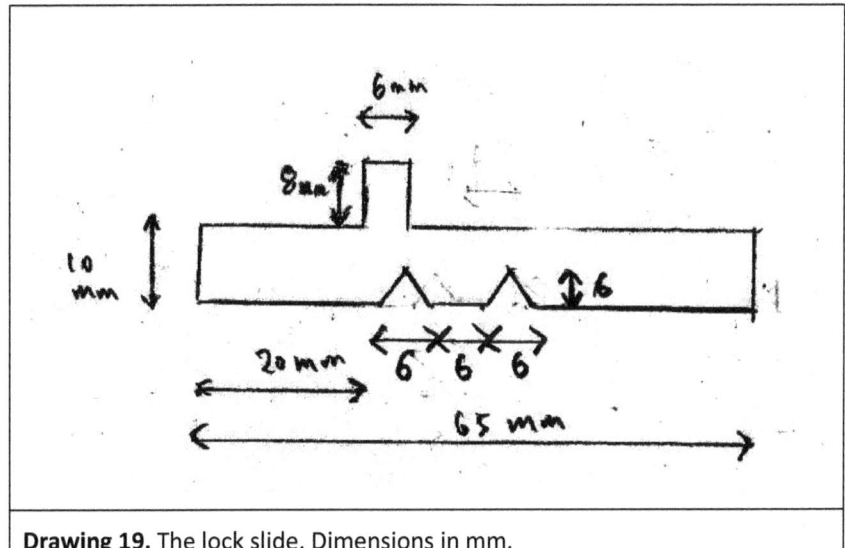

Drawing 19. The lock slide. Dimensions in mm.

Spring.

1. Mark out, cut out and file to shape from spring steel (I used a band saw blade).
2. Mark out, and anneal area for rivet holes (use a heat source that is available i.e. forge, butane or propane torch), pouch and drill holes. You may have to anneal the end for the rivet holes a number of times, or repeatedly use the punch from either side to pop out the divot.
3. Using heat bend spring to shape, allow the rivet end to lie flat on the lock plate, the tail of the spring turns round and the tip of the tail lies on the top of the slide bar, pushing down and applying pressure to the slide (so it resist sliding due to gravity or being shaken).

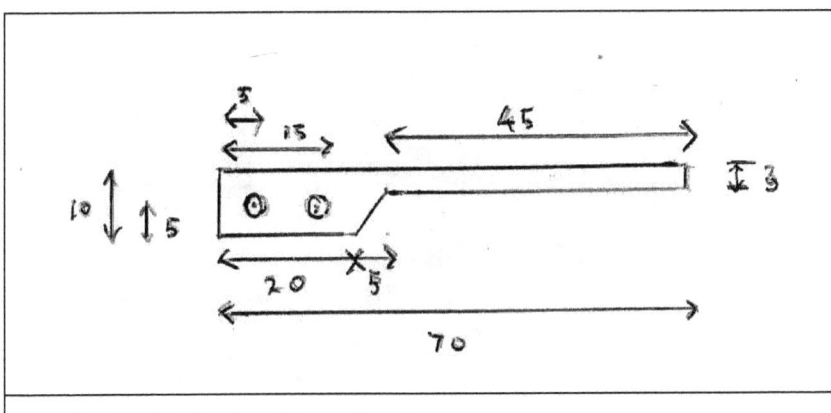

Drawing 20. The Spring. Dimensions in mm.

Fitting key to wards.

1. Cut and file the key to pass the wards.

This may take a bit of trial and error to get right. You may want to only add one ward on your first lock.

Mark where the key makes contact with the ward as it rotates. Cut key and file to fit, turning clockwise and anti-clockwise.

Lock Assembly.

Working on the back or inside of the lock plate.

1. Mark out the horizontal centre line on the back of the lock.
2. Mark out the keyhole on the centre line.

Photo 27. The key's swivel point is fitted to the top of the key hole.

3. Punch holes[31] down the keyhole (i.e.'.....') and drill with 3 mm ($\frac{1}{8}$") drill bit.
4. Cut the remainder of metal using a cold chisel, hammer and anvil. Turn the piece over and hit from the other side until a cut is made and that you can fit a file in the hole.
5. File remainder of keyhole with file to fit key.
6. Line up the centre hole of the ward plate with the top of the key hole and ark out attachment holes for the ward plate. Punch and drill 3 mm holes. Countersink the lug holes on the front of the lock plate.
7. Attach the ward plate in place with nuts and bolts. Mark out the top arc of key rotation on the lock plate.
8. Line up the slide with the zenith of the key so the top of the key reaches the top of the cut out on the slide.
9. Mark, punch and drill attachment holes for lugs.
10. Counter sink lug holes on front of lock plate.
11. Mark lugs '1' and '2' and mark which lug goes where on the back of the lock plate. Positioning of lugs must allow full movement of slide, so as to reach the 'locked' and unlocked position. Lug no. 1 is between the 'stop' on the slide and the hasp lug hole. Lug no. 2 supports the other end of the slide.
12. File lug holes to fit the legs of lugs with a small square file. Fit lug no. 2 in place, slide 'slide' into the lug and attach lug no. 1. Modify with a file until the slide moves freely when moved by turning the key.

---

[31] Punching holes using a punch, hammer and an anvil (or a handy block of steel) stops the drill bit wandering.

Photo 28. The hole in the ward plate lines up with the top of the key hole.

Photo 29. The slide lugs support the slide, the slide slides into the lug of the hasp.

13. Rivet lug No. 2 in place, ensure lug is secured in vice when riveting.
14. Mark out, punch and drill the top hole (countersink outside of hole) for attachment of spring, rivet in place. While the slide is removed, rotate the spring so that it is 5 mm (¼") below the level of the slide.
15. Drill the second rivet hole through the second hole on spring (countersink outside of hole) and rivet in place.
16. Slide the slide in place and rivet lug No. 1 is placed against the pressure of spring. Ensure lug is secured in vice when riveting.

Photo 30. Front of the lock.

Notes:

The *'stop'* on the far end of the slide is formed by the cut out of the timber of the front of the chest.

Photo 31. Back of the lock, all in place.

Making the lock work.

1. Lubricate the mechanism with a spray on lubricant (CRC / WD40) or beeswax.
2. Ensure that both keys work which may include filing the key to fit through the keyhole or to miss the wards but should still in gauge the teeth of the slide.
3. Filing the lug on the hasp to fit in the hasp hole or the hole in the lug of the hasp where the slide slides through.

Notes: Jeweller's files come in sets with a range of cross sectional shapes. The spring provides friction to the slide to stop it sliding to the locked or unlocked position if the chest is tilted or shaken.

Attaching the hasp and lock to the chest.

1. Centre hasp on the front of the chest.
2. Ensure hasp can reach the lock.
3. Chisel out the front of the chest to fit the inner workings of the lock.
4. Attach hasp to lid, pre-drill holes, hammer the nails in place.
5. Ensure lock works.
6. Cleat the nails of hasp to lid.
7. Ensure lock works before permanently attaching the lock.
8. Attach the lock plate, pre-drill holes, hammer nails in place.
9. Cleat nails of lock plate.
10. Ensure that the lock works.
11. Finish off with providing the chest wood work with a coating of linseed oil, see recipe.[32]

---

[32] Recipe: 3 parts turps (mineral or gum turpentine) to one part boiled linseed oil. For one litre use 750 ml turps and 250 ml boiled linseed oil (an imperial quart

Photo 32. The completed chest with corner brackets.

---

contains 3 Imperial cups of white spirit and one cup of boiled linseed oil/ /32 US fl. oz.contains 3 US cups of mineral spirits and one cup of boiled linseed oil. Look, it's a 3:1 ratio, don't you dare tell me metric is too hard). Linseed oil treatment should be carried out annually to add longevity to the woodwork by reducing crack and warping, warding off insect attack.

The Santa Croce Sitting Bed.

By Stephen Wyley.

The Santa Croce Sitting Bed.	**Where:** Florence, Italy	**When:** 1385-87 CE
Fresco by Agnolo Gaddi, Preparation of the cross, Santa Croce, Florence, Italy.		

Photo 33. Close up of a man in a sitting bed. The original. Fresco, Preparation of the cross, Santa Croce, Florence, Italy. (Scala Archives).

Photo 34. The replica with plywood panels to support a mattress, other mattress supports would include ropes or slats. The panels are resting on noggins along the inside of the side beams. The side rails have long through tenons so they can be wedged tight.

Introduction.

The type of bedding in the medieval period depended on your status and wealth. For the poor it was some straw, or a *'tick'* (a cloth bag filled with straw), the well-off could afford wooden beds which kept you off the ground and was usually provided with a mattress, pillows and bedding.

The original for this project is based on Agnolo Gaddi's fresco *'Preparation of the cross'*, in the Santa Croce Basilica, Florence, Italy. The fresco shows a hospice in the top left hand corner with a number of men sitting in beds. The beds appear to show the head boards with edging and plain square legs at the foot of the beds. Examples of other similar beds can be found in Table 11.

The fresco shows the men in the sitting position which comes from the theory based on *'Galenic'* medicine which is based on the four *'humours'*, superstitions that lying prone was reserved for the dead.[33]

---

[33] See Hippocrates (ca. 460 BCE — ca. 370 BCE).

Table 11. Example of similar beds.

Source	Bed detail	Dated
The Birth of Mary by Pietro Lorenzetti, 1342 The Nativity of the Virgin is a painting by the Italian late medieval painter Pietro Lorenzetti, dating from around 1335-1342, now housed in the Museo dell'Opera del Duomo of Siena, Italy.	Rectangular head and foot boards, black (ebony?) moulded on top of head and foot boards, in contrast to the lighter wood of the head and foot boards. The foot of the bed is similar in construction to the head but shorter. Both the head and foot of the bed show edging or cut out in the main part of the structure. Along with the ubiquitous long rectangular wooden chest beside the bed.	1335-1342 CE
Fresco by Giotto, St.Francis appears to Fra. Agostino and the bishop, upper basilica of San Francesco, Assisi, Italy.	Only the side of the bed is shown. 'X's under side rails and lines on side beams could indicate mattress support.	Early 14th century CE
Illuminated manuscript of Phinehas thrusts a spear through an Israelite man and Midianite woman in the midst of copulation (Numbers 25:1-9), Add MS	The illumination appears to show a headboard with corner posts with multiple cross planks between the posts, and plain square legs at the foot. Along with the ubiquitous long	1400 CE

Table 11. Example of similar beds.

Source	Bed detail	Dated
15277, f. 51v, British Library.	rectangular wooden chest beside the bed.	

I have not yet been able to find any extant beds from the period, I do live in hope. I have made a number of assumptions when working with this manuscript, which include:

The joints are not shown, so I have assumed the use of halving joints or mortise and tenon joints;

The support for the mattress is not shown. It could be planks or roped support, based on evidence from Giotto and Gaddi himself, see Table 11 above.

I have provided drawings for a sitting bed based on the original. The drawings for a longer version, based on the bed I made for myself, are in Appendix 7.

Materials.

Timber (oak preferably but Pinus radiata will do).

Table 12. Timber cutting list in cm (inches).

Timber	Length	Width	Depth
2 Side rails	120 (47")	10 (4")	4 (1½")
2 Planks for headboard	100 (40")	28.5 (11½")	2 (¾")
1 x Plank for foot	100 (40")	10 (4")	2 (¾")
2 x Corner posts - head	90 (36")	10 (4")	10 (4")

2 x Corner posts - foot	40 (16")	10 (4")	10 (4")
2 x Edgings for head	48 (19")	30 (12")	2 (¾")
1 x Edging for head	94 (37")	30 (12")	2 (¾")
6 x Noggins for ply mattress supports	20 (8")	4 (1½")	4 (1½")
1 Plywood boards for mattress support.	120 (47")	80 (32")	2 (¾")
Or 4 Planks of timber	80 (32")	24 (9½-10")	2 (¾")

Tools.

Tool list: rulers (30cm, 60cm, and 100cm (12", 24" and 36")), set square, chisels (25mm (1") and 7mm (¼"), plain edge), files (Coarse - flat bastard, fine - square bastard), tenon saw, hand saw, plane, 'G' clamps, scrap wood (for holding work without damaging it), claw hammer, wooden mallet, bench vice, pencil, hand drill (with 4mm (5/32") bit).

Construction process.

Head board.

1. Mark out and cut posts to length.
2. Mark out and either drill and chisel out the mortises, or just use a chisel to make the mortises.
3. Mark out and cut the head boards.
4. Attach the head boards to the posts.
5. Cut the pieces of edging to length, with a 45 degree cut for the corners.
6. Glue and nail edging in place.

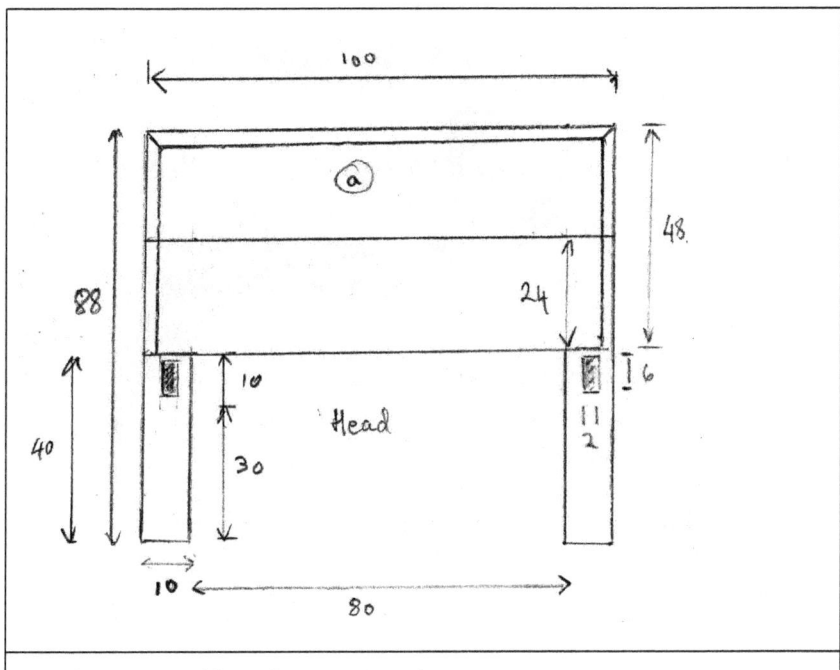

Drawing 21. Head board. Dimensions in cm.

Photo 35. The headboard with edging around the outer edge.

Photo 36. The detail on the corner of the edging on the outer edge of the head board.

Note. For permanent fitting, insert dowels into the side beam through posts. For a flat pack, rasp out to the point where it moves in and out freely.

Foot board.

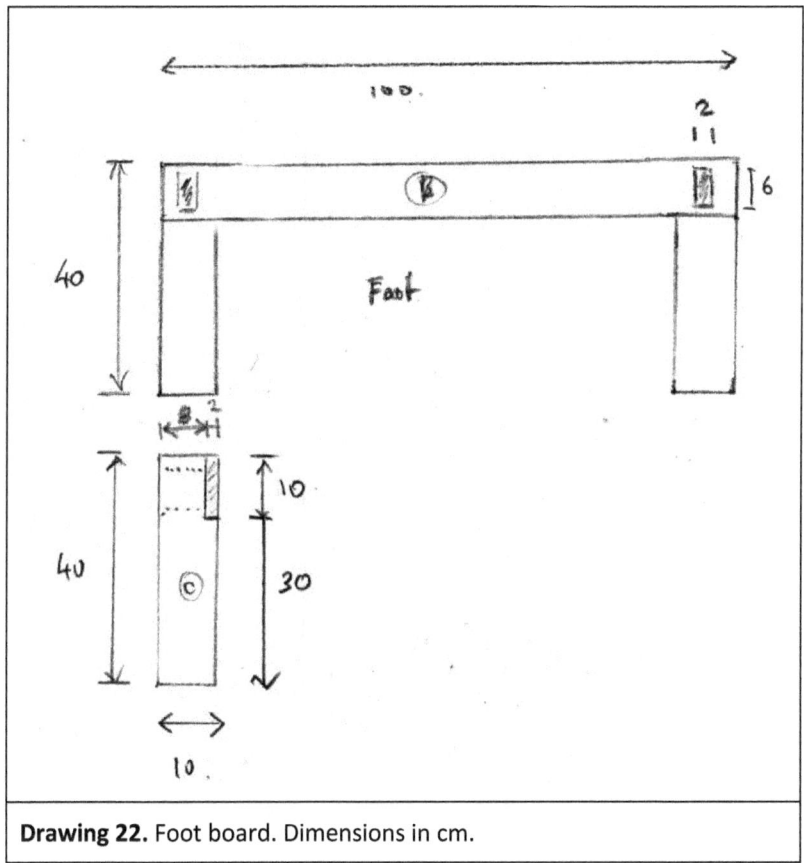

Drawing 22. Foot board. Dimensions in cm.

1. Mark out and cut posts to length.
2. Mark out and cut the ledge for the side rails.
3. Attach side rails to posts. Use glue and either dowels or nails.

4. Mark out and either drill and chisel out mortises through post and side rail, or just use a chisel to make mortises.
5. For permanent fitting, insert dowels into the side rails through posts.
Side rails.

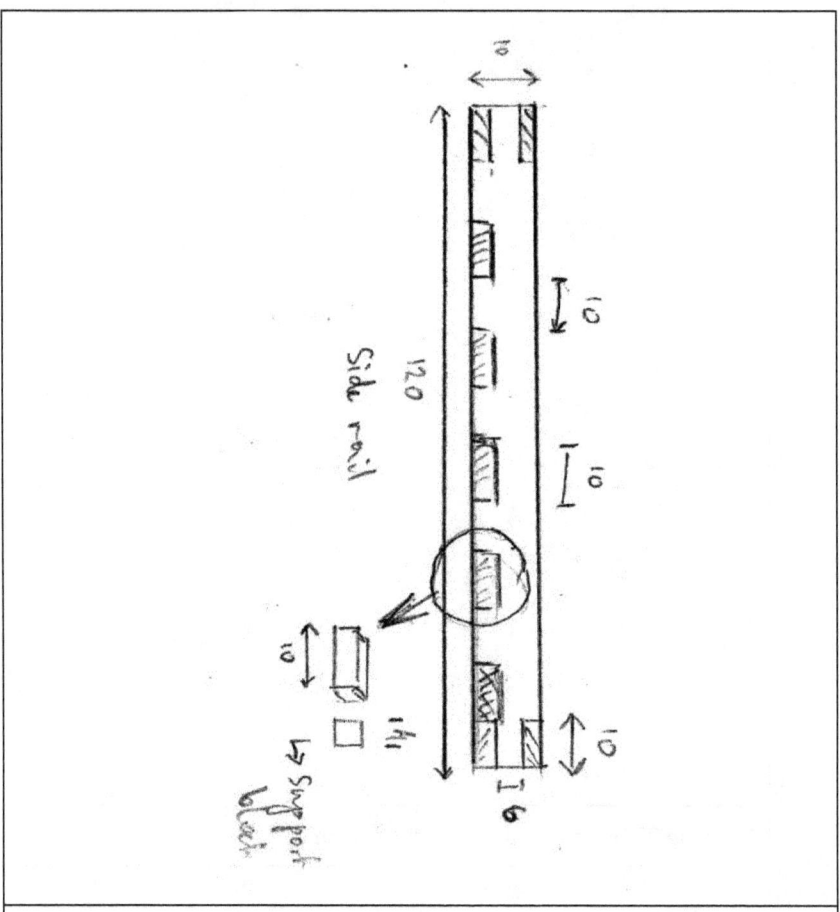

Drawing 23. Side Rails. Dimensions in cm.

1. Mark out and cut 2 side rails to length.
2. Mark out and cut supports for mattress support (planks or plywood panels), or drill holes in side rails to attach rope netting.
3. If using supports, attach supports to the inside side rails. Use glue and either dowels or nails.
4. Ensure tenons fit mortises in head and foot boards.

Plank mattress support.

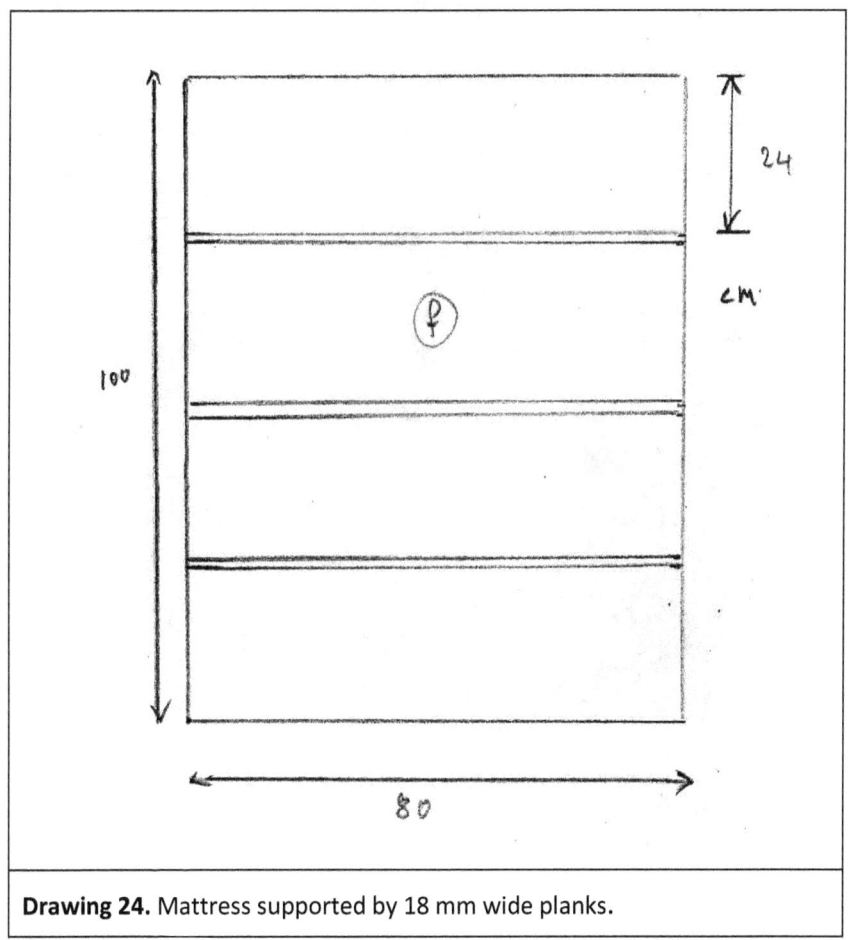

Drawing 24. Mattress supported by 18 mm wide planks.

1. Mark out and cut 24 cm (9½") wide planks to fit on side rails supports, see Drawing 22, or mark out and cut pieces of plywood to fit on side rails.
2. Drill holes in side rails to attach rope netting, for examples of possible cross woven support, see Table 11.

Note: You could use 8 mm ($\frac{3}{8}$") thick plywood sheet for re-enactment purposes, no one would see it…

Proposed rope support (not the usual woven cross hatched pattern) but the rope passes through each hole in the side of the bed, four times over the top and twice underneath, based on Gotti's St Francis fresco. See Photos 37, 38 and 39.

Photo 37. The proposed rope mattress support. See Giotti and Gaddi for examples of possible cross woven support, see Table 11.

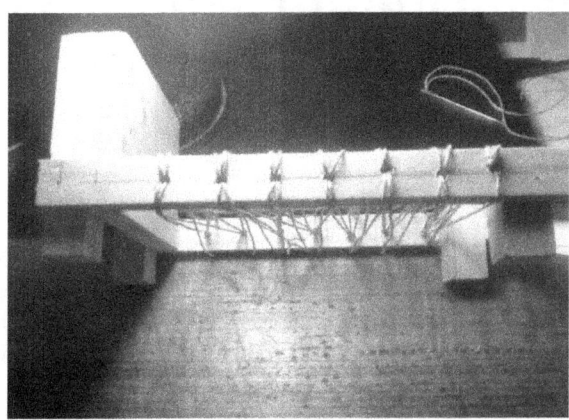

Photo 38. Side view of bed showing the rope supports.

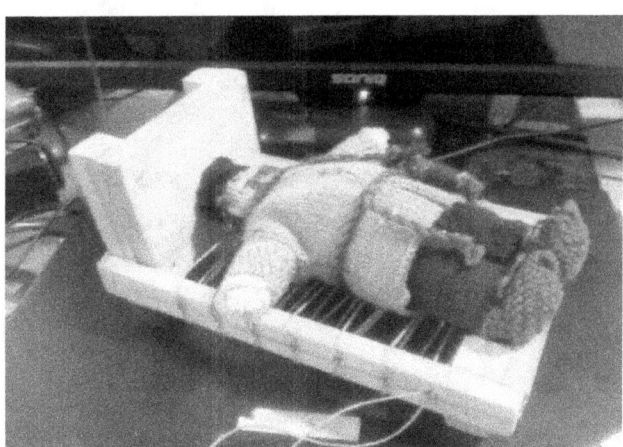

Photo 39. Sven the Merchant on the bed. Thanks to a big fan for the life-like crocheted figure (yes, the bed is a bit short for lying down on) of Sven the Merchant.

The Taciunum Sanitatis table - Making Spaghetti.

By Stephen Wyley.

Taciunum Sanitatis - Making Spaghetti.		**When:** 1390 - 1400 CE
Stored: Bibliothèque Nationale de France (BNF), France.	Nouvella acquisition Latine 1673 Folio 50 (Milan or Pavia, Italy).	Illuminated manuscript

Figure 4. The original. A woman prepares spaghetti. There may be a tray on top of the table.

Introduction.

Tables were used for a range of activities from feasting, trading and also as work tables. Work tables were used in a wide range of trades as well as in domestic and farming settings. It is rare for a table of the 14th century to survive, so we must study the manuscripts. According to a source there are only two surviving 14th century tables: *"one in a museum in Paris (France) and the other in Onze Lieve Vrouwe ter Potterie Museum in Bruges (Belgium)"* [34]

Table sizes varied from the long table for feasts of the nobles (i.e. Luttrell Psalter, 208r) to the those smaller tables used to prepare food (i.e. cutting up an oxen - Luttrell Psalter, 207r) or the tailor making clothes (Paduan Bible Picture Book[35]). Table supports varied from 'A' shaped trestles to legs that were mortised into the table top. Some table legs appear to be spayed outwards with the legs tapering from the bottom to the top, which would add to the stability of the table.

The original for this project is from an illuminated manuscript entitled *'Taciunum Sanitatis'*, an instructional text on health and wellbeing. The illumination shows two women making spaghetti on purpose-built boards with edging. One rests on the ground sloped in front of the woman on the left and the other on top of a table. The table has two sets of legs at either end of the table top. Both sets are connected by a shaped and carved stretcher with multiple raised points along the top edge with a circular design on the main body of both the inner and outer faces of the stretcher. See Table 13.

---

[34] Master Marijnus (2012)
[35] British Library Add Ms 15277

Photo 40. The replica table, end on.

Table 13. Examples of similar tables.

Source	Description	Dated
Maciejowski Bible / Morgan Crusader Bible, MS M 638, Folio 23r, Piermont Morgan Library, New York, USA – cutting up oxen.	Only the front of two 'A' shaped trestles with the stretcher are shown, two square mortises poke through the table top. The ends of the straight stretcher show as squares on each side piece of the trestle.	Between 1244-1254 CE
Luttrell Psalter, British Library Add. MS 42130. Folio no 208r - English feast in a family home.	8 people dining at a long table with two trestles supporting either end. Only the front of trestles shown, flat top, 'A' shaped, with support at top with an inverted 'U' cut out.	Between 1325 and 1335 CE
Luttrell Psalter, British Library Add. MS 42130, Folio no 207r - Carving the meat.	2 three legged tables, one rectangular, the smaller square, legs tapper from bottom to top. Circle on the top on the left of each table top would indicate the legs have a circular cross section where the legs insert through the table top.	Between 1325 and 1335 CE
Tacuinum Sanitatis (ONB Codex Vindobonensis, series nova 2644) fol. 25r -	Rectangular table top, 4 legs, legs tapering from bottom to top, circles that	1390-1400 CE

Table 13. Examples of similar tables.

Source	Description	Dated
Leeks.	correspond to the legs on the left hand side are circular in cross section.	
Tacuinum Sanitatis (ONB Codex Vindobonensis, series nova 2644) fol. 104v, - Cutting linen.	Square table, 4 legs, legs tapering upwards to rounded block on front legs.	1390-1400 CE
Paduan Bible Picture Book, British Library, Additional 15277, fol. 16r - A Tailor's table.	Rectangular table with two trestles with end, trestle with cross beam across width of table.	1400 CE

Materials.

Timber (oak preferably but pinus radiata will do).

Table 14. Timber cutting list.	
Table top	114 x 57 x 2 cm (45 x 22½" x ¾")
4 Legs	75 x 4 x 4 cm (29½ x 1½ x 1½")
2 Cross bars	39 x 16 x 2 cm (16" x 6¼ x ¾")

Paper, cardboard and graph paper.

Tools.

Tool list: rulers (30cm and 100cm(12" and 24")), set square, chisels (25mm (1") and 7mm (¼"), plain edge), files (coarse - flat bastard, fine - square bastard), tenon saw, hand saw, plane, 'G' clamps, scrap wood (for holding work without damaging it), claw hammer, wooden mallet, bench vice, pencil, scissors, and a drill with 4mm ($\frac{5}{32}$") bit.

Construction instructions.

Leg Stretcher (Crossbar) template.

1. Make up a cardboard template as per measurements.
    a. Photocopy template from book (or draw up based on measurements and draw curves).

b. Scale up using graph paper or a computer program like '*paint*' to bring the scale bar up to 5 cm (2").
c. Print a copy and glue to cardboard.
d. Cut out the shape of the template.
e. Punch centre holes for the circles.

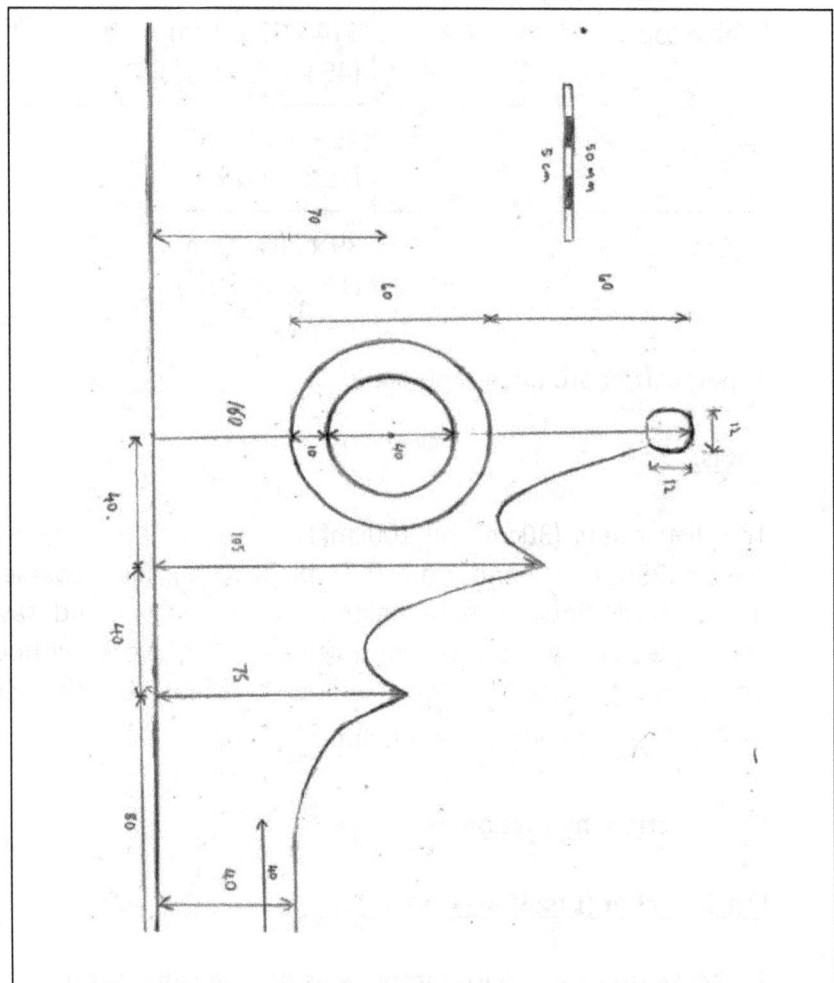

Drawing 25. This is only half of the stretcher template, with detail of where to put the circular carving. Dimensions in mm.

Leg Stretchers (Crossbars) - make 2.

2. Centre the template on the timber. Mark up using cardboard template and pencil
3. Cut to length.
4. Cut to shape using a coping saw or jigsaw.
5. Carve the apex point into a knob with a knife or rasp.
6. Carve out the donuts shapes on each of the four faces of the stretchers with a *'shallow gouge,* about 3 mm ($\frac{1}{8}$") deep in the centre, sloping up to the sides.

Photo 41. Cutting out one of the stretchers with a jigsaw.

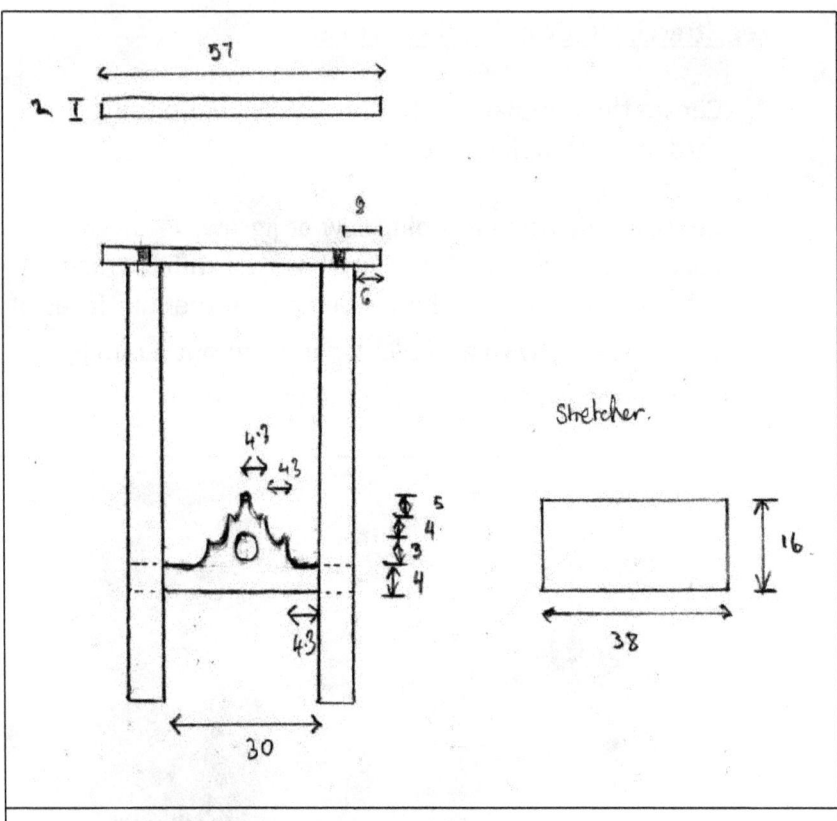

Drawing 26. Table legs – Stretcher. Dimensions in cm.

Legs - make 4.

1. Mark out and cut timber to length.
2. Drill or chisel out mortises for the tenons. Drilling can mean drilling lots of small holes around inside the perimeter of the marked mortise. Or drilling can mean using a spade bit less than the 20 mm (¾") wide mortise to drill out most of the wood, allowing access for a chisel, rasp or file to finish off the mortise.
3. Test out mortise and tenons as you go to check for a snug fit.

Photo 42. The tenon at the top of one of the legs.

Note: If the tenons are going through the attached cross beams (added to the table top to aid stability), increase the length of the tenons to the thickness of the cross beam (i.e. 4 cm (1½")).

Photo 43. The legs and stretcher.

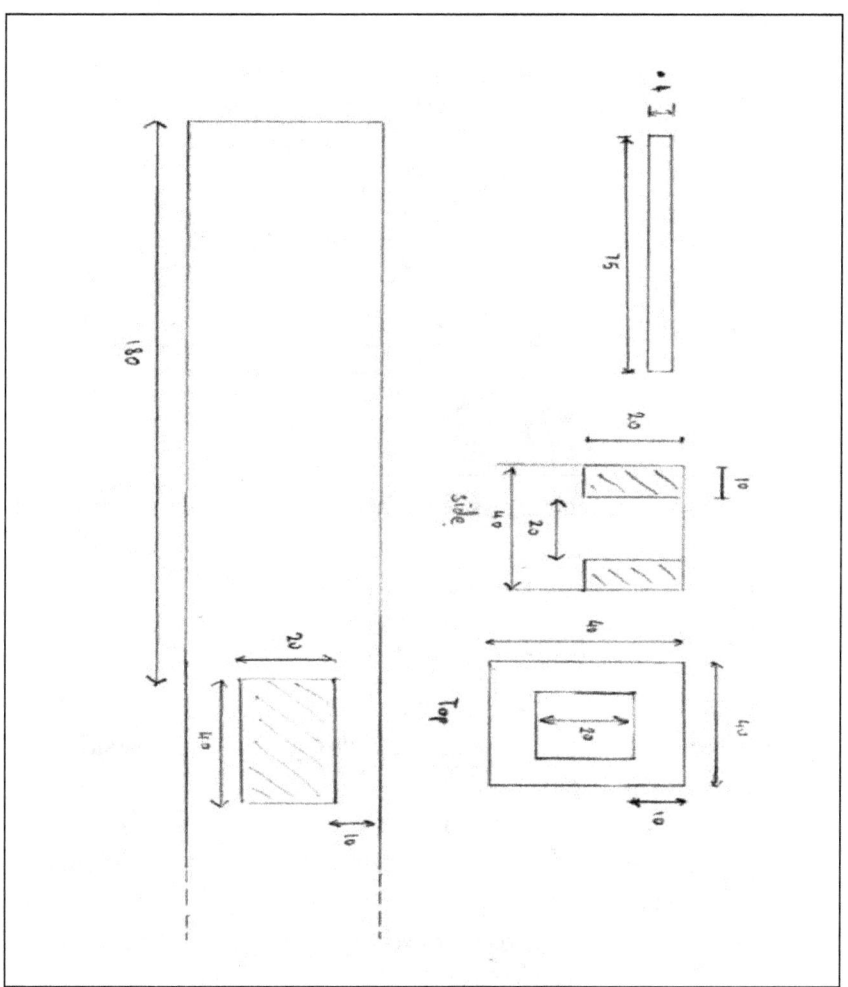

Drawing 27. Table legs, tenon and mortise. Dimensions in cm.

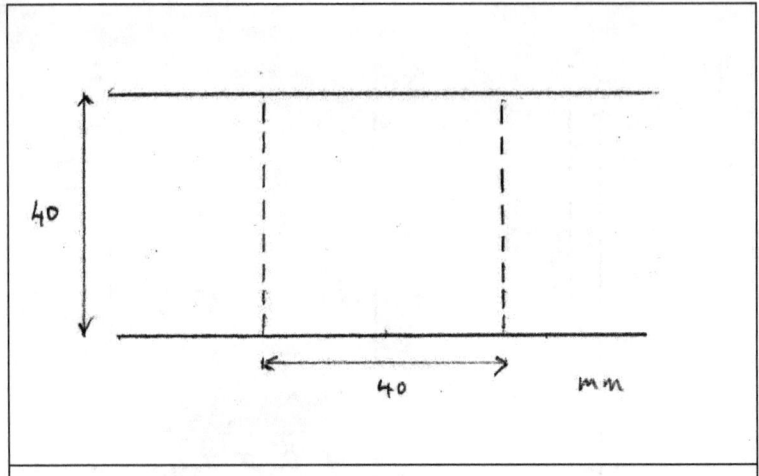

Drawing 28. Table leg – side elevation of through tenon. Dimensions in mm.

Table top.

1. For a sturdy table top I would use 3-4 cm (1¼" - 1½") thick timber, then you can mortise holes into the underside of the table for the top of the legs.
Since thick boards are hard to come by you can attach to boards together with a dowel or two cross beams. See Appendix 2.
2. Mark out and cut two boards 28.5 (11") wide to length.
3. Dowel the two boards together and/or step 5.
4. Cut two cross beams to length. Line up two wide boards, lay the cross beams at 10 cm (4") from each end, clamp together and attach with glue and skew nails.
5. Drill or chisel mortise holes through table or through table top and cross beams for the tops of the legs. Ensure that it is a snug fit.
If this table is not going to be moved around a lot the stretchers can be permanently glued and dowelled in place.

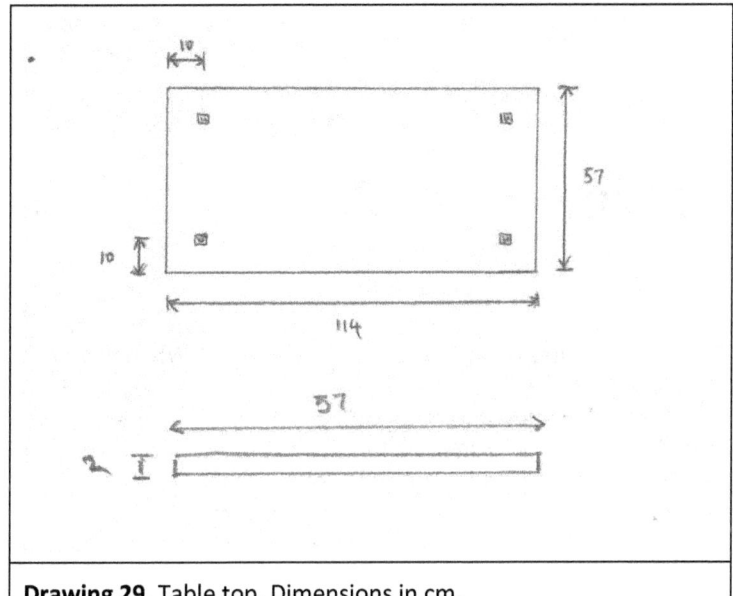

Drawing 29. Table top. Dimensions in cm.

The Luttrell Psalter Trestle Table.

By Stephen Wyley.

The Luttrell Psalter Dining Table.		**When:** Between 1325 and 1335 CE
Stored: British Library, England.	Luttrell Psalter, British Library Add. MS 42130. Folio no 208r	Illuminated manuscript

Figure 5. The original. Sir Geoffrey Luttrell at dinner. British Library.

Introduction.

Similar to today, tables were used for a range of activities such as feasting, trading and work. In this case the family sits along one side of the trestle table, with the family and guests sitting to the left and right of the leading person of the household. The table top sits on and is separate to the trestles, which makes it easier for dismantling, storage and transport.

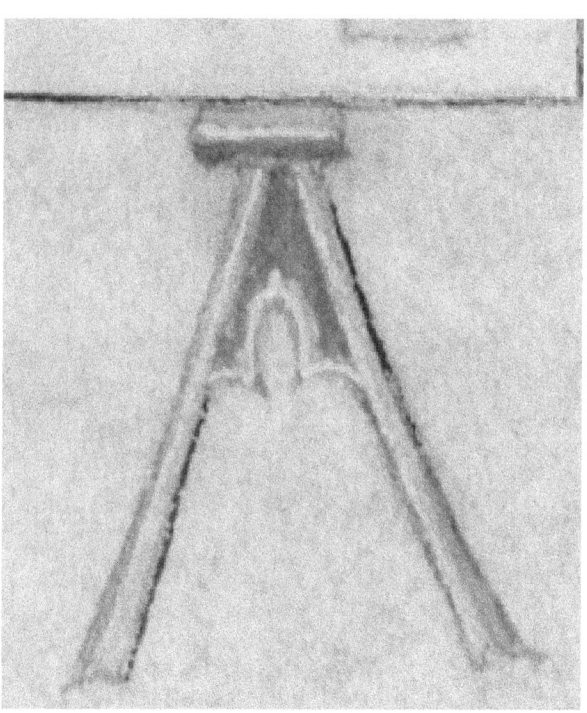

Figure 6. One of the trestles, which just shows the front. British Library.

Photo 44. The replica table. Legs in Pinus radiata and table top in Huon pine.

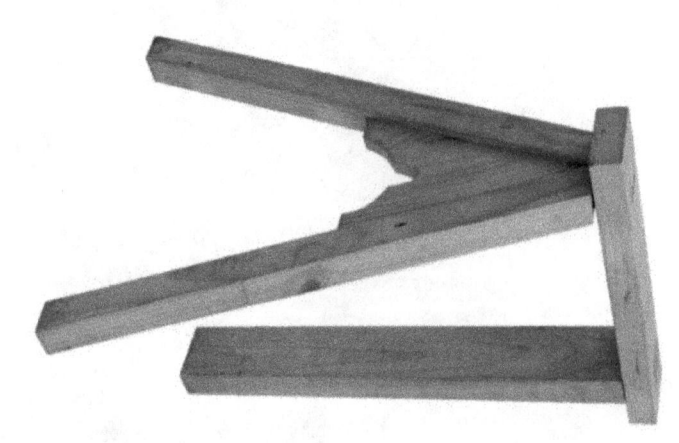

Photo 45. Close up of the legs of the replica.

Table sizes varied from the long table for feasts of the nobles (i.e. Luttrell Psalter, fol. 208r) to those smaller tables used to prepare food or the tailor making clothes (Paduan Bible Picture Book).

Table legs and supports varied from a trestle with an 'A' shaped front to simple legs that were mortised into the table top. In the case of the *'Making Pasta'* table from the Taciunum Sanitatis (in the previous section), each set of two legs is connected by a horizontal piece of wood known as a stretcher. This is carved in a distinctive shape, possibly with a *'G'* carved into it. On some tables (i.e. the Luttrell Psalter, British Library Add. MS 42130, fol. 207r *'Carving the meat'*) the legs appear to be spayed outwards and the legs taper from the bottom to the top, which would add to the stability of the table. See Table 15.

The table for this project is from the Luttrell Psalter which depicts an English feast in a family home, with 7 people dining on one side of a long table with two trestles supporting either end. Only the front of trestles is shown, with a horizontal 'A' shaped beam at the top, with a brace at the top with an inverted 'U' cut out. I have assumed that there is a stretcher at the top connecting to a back leg.

Table 15. Example of similar trestles.

Source	Description	Dated
Maciejowski bible / Morgan Crusader Bible, MS M 638, Folio 23r, Pierpont Morgan Library, New York, USA – cutting up oxen.	Illuminated manuscript, showing only the near side of two 'A' shaped trestles with a thin horizontal stretcher between the two legs of the 'A' are shown. The tops of the trestle are shown as two square mortises protruding through the table top. The ends of the straight stretcher show as squares on each side piece of the trestle.	Between 1244-1254 CE
Paduan Bible Picture Book, British Library, Additional 15277, fol. 16r - A tailor's and a carpenter's workshops	Illuminated manuscript. The tailor's workshop shows a rectangular table with trestles at either end, trestle with cross beam across the width of the table at the top. The trestles in the carpenter's workshop are used more like *'saw horses'*.	1400 CE
Onze Lieve Vrouweter Potterie Museum, in Bruges, Belgium.	Extant table top is 8.4m (27½") long, 84cm (32¼") wide and 5.5cm (2") thick,	1425 CE

Table 15. Example of similar trestles.		
Source	Description	Dated
	which has a date of '*1425*' chiseled on one of the short sides. The 4 oak trestles are undated but probably date from the 15th C. The brace in the top of the 'A' of the front leg is small at 1cm ($\frac{3}{8}$") thick and is pierced by a leaf shaped hole. There is a stretcher across the lower part of the 'A' of the front leg and another crossbeam across the top. The tops of the front and back of the trestle are connected by a crossbeam. Both front and back legs slope backwards, the back by 4 degrees and front legs by 15 degrees. Dowels are used to hold the various parts of the trestle together.	

Materials.

Timber (oak preferably).

Table 16. Timber cutting list.	
Table top	400 x 57cm (13' x 22½") (2 boards 28.5cm (11¼") wide joined together), Use 30mm (1¼") thick if you can, or you may need a third cross beam in the centre.
2 Table top cross beams	57cm x 45mm x 18mm (22½" x 1¾" x ¾")
4 Front Legs	85.5cm x 40mm x 40mm (33¾" x 1½" x 1½")
2 Back Legs	81.5cm x 90mm x 55mm (32" x 35½" x 21½")
2 Cross bars	57cm x 18cm x 18mm (22½" x 7" x 7")
2 Braces	35cm x 20cm x 18mm (13¾" x 7¼" x 7")
Dowel	24cm x 6mm diameter (10" x ¼")

If you can hew the timber to sizes all the better. If you can only get bigger timber you can cut or shave down to sizes. If you can only get smaller timber, use what you can get or use that to glue together to make bigger boards.

Cardboard and tracing paper for a brace template.

Tools.

Tool list; bench vice, chisels (25mm (1") and 7mm (¼"), plain edge), bevel square, clamps (sash or 'G'), claw hammer, coping or jigsaw, files (coarse - flat bastard, fine - square bastard), drill with 4mm and 6mm (¼" and ½") bits, hand saw, pencil, scissors, plane, rulers (30cm and 100cm (12" and 36")), scrap wood (for holding work without damaging it), set square, tenon saw, bench vice, pencil, wooden mallet, or maybe even a biscuit joiner.

Construction process.

This trestle is designed to be demountable and flat packed. If you want to make the trestle permanent it is recommended that you glue and dowel the cross beams to the legs.

Table top.
See Drawing 30 & 31.

1. If you can find a 4 meter (13') long board at 57 cm (22½") wide you don't have to go through the following process, just clean up edges, sand and linseed oil.
2. If you can't find a suitable wide board choose 2 of the widest boards you can, and about 3 - 4 cm (1¼-1½") thick timber.
3. You may only find thinner boards which will need to be joined together with dowel and/or two cross beams. See making '*Wider boards*' in Appendix 2.
4. Dowel the two boards together with dowels (6 cm (2½") long, at ends and 50 cm (20") apart) or use a biscuit jointer.
5. Trim off timber at the ends so both boards line up.

6. Cut two cross beams to length. Join the two wide boards, lay the cross beams at 5 cm (2") from each end and attach with glue and by skewing the nails.
   Note: You may consider a third cross beam in the centre of the table for added strength.
7. Plane off any excess timber from the join.
8. Round corners (reduces splitting from impacts) and break sharp edges (fine file) (or chamfer) of table top again to reduce minor damage from being used.
9. Apply linseed oil (3 parts mineral turpentine / (UK) white spirit / (USA) mineral spirits to 1 part boiled linseed oil) and repeat on an annual basis.

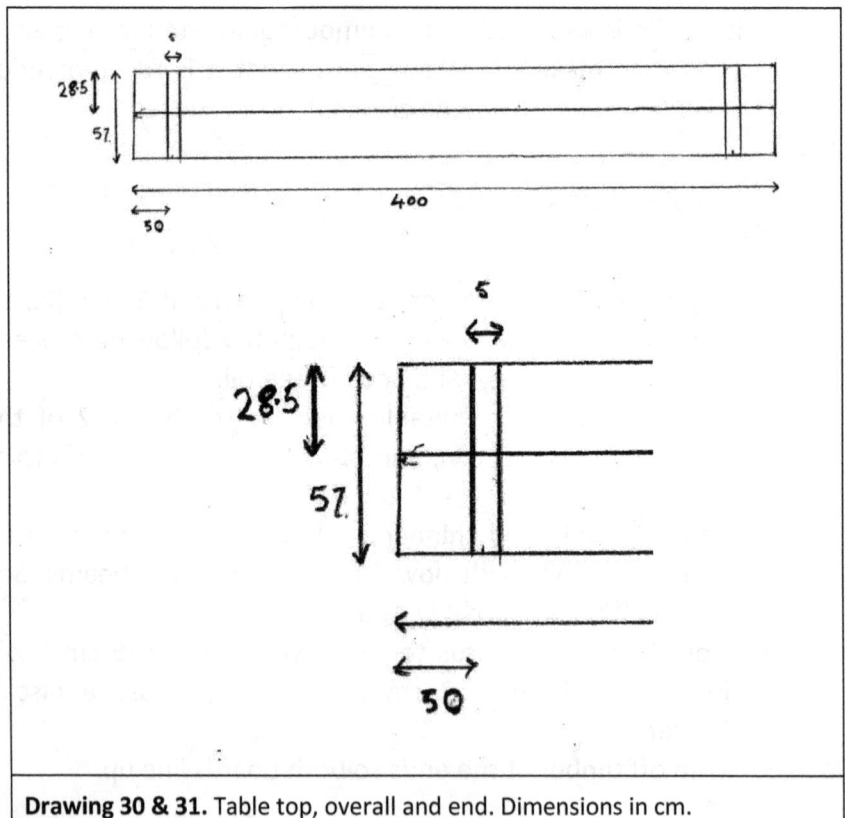

Drawing 30 & 31. Table top, overall and end. Dimensions in cm.

Leg brace template. See Photo 46 and Drawing 32.

1. Make up the cardboard template as per measurements.
a. Photocopy template from book (or draw up based on measurements and draw curves).
b. Scale up using graph paper or a computer program like *'paint'* to bring the scale bar up to 5 cm (2").
c. Print of a copy and glue to cardboard.

Note: The crossbeams act as stops for the trestles when they are placed on the inside of the cross beams.

d. Cut out the shape of the template.

Photo 46. Brace cardboard template (not to scale).

2 x Braces. See also Figure 6.

1. Mark and cut out the triangle of the braces.
2. Draw up a stencil on cardboard for the shape of the brace.
3. Use the stencil to mark out the lower end of the braces.
4. Secure timber and cut out the bottom with a coping or jigsaw.
5. Clean up work and sand smooth bottom end.

Note: Store stencils in flat and dry place for later use.

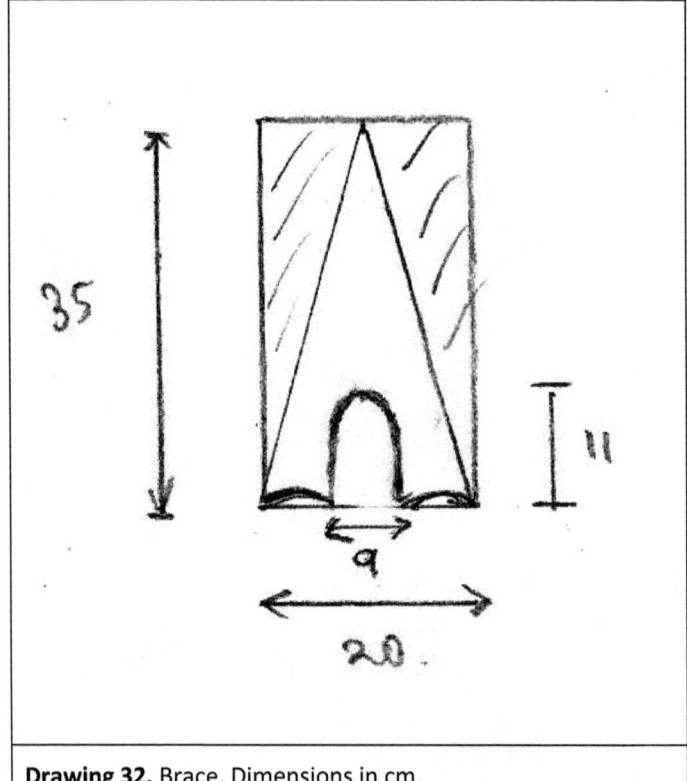

Drawing 32. Brace. Dimensions in cm.

Cross beams - make 2. See Drawing 31.

1. Mark out and cut to length.
2. Mark out and chisel mortises at either end.
3. Clean up mortises.

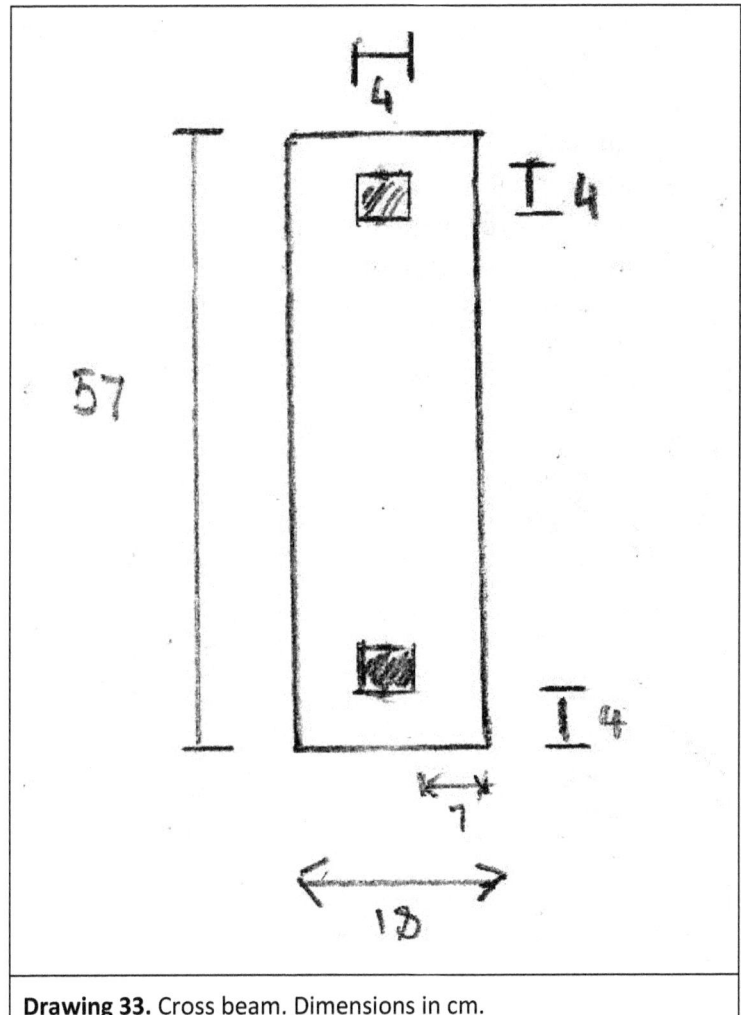

Drawing 33. Cross beam. Dimensions in cm.

Front Legs – Make 2 sets. See Drawings 34 to 37.

1. Mark out, and cut to length, including 10 degree angle top and bottom.
2. Mark out and chisel mortises along the inside of the leg for brace.
3. Test out mortise and tenons for a snug fit into the cross beam.
4. Glue and dowel legs and brace together with clamps.
5. Allow glue to dry.
6. Mark out the slope on both ends (a bevel square [36] and a protractor would be handy for marking out the angles) so the legs sit flat.
7. Mark out and cut the step in the top of the leg.

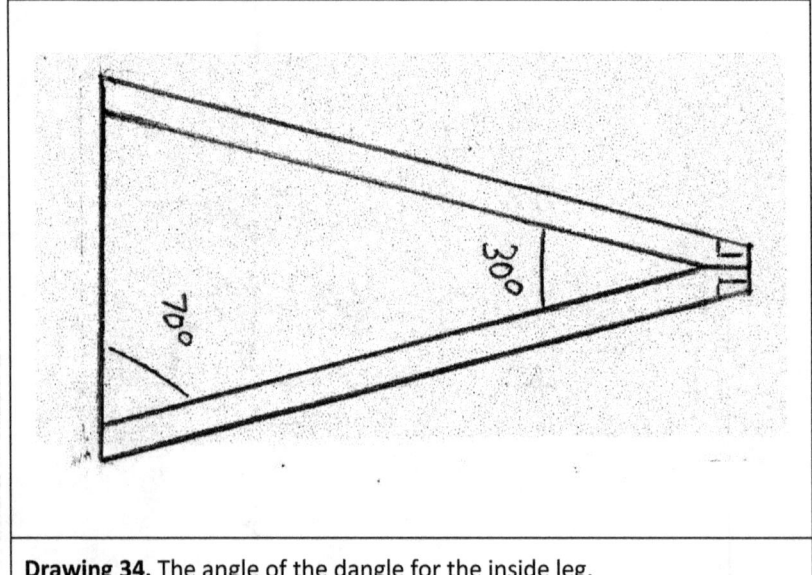

Drawing 34. The angle of the dangle for the inside leg.

---

[36] From Heelas p.40. A bevel square is like an adjustable try square, with an adjustable slotted blade, fixed to the stock by an adjustable screw. The blade can be changed to any angle, and is chiefly used for marking out dovetails.

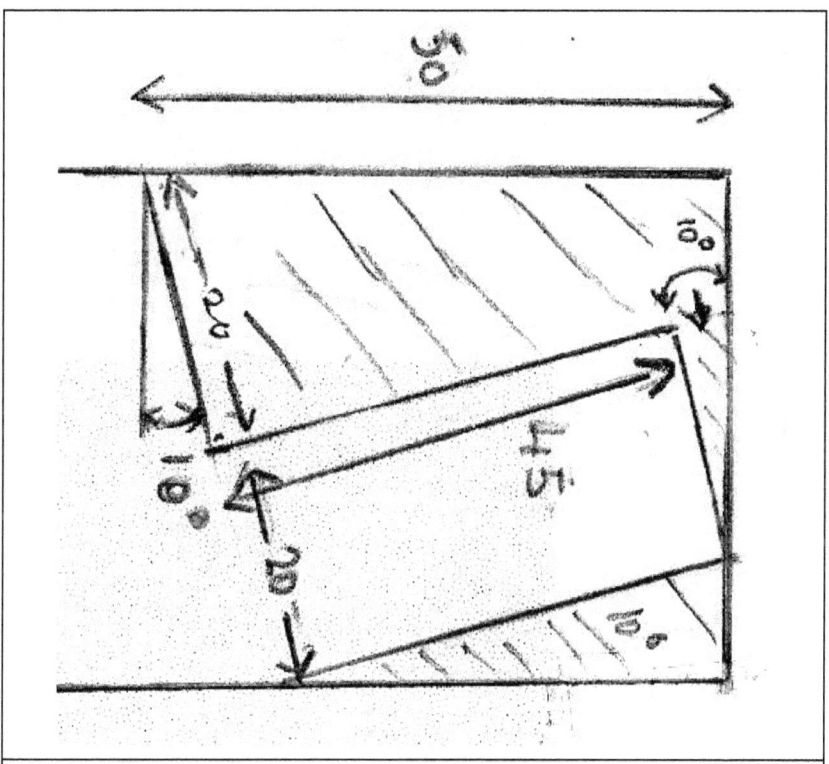

Drawing 35. The angle of the top of one piece of the leg.

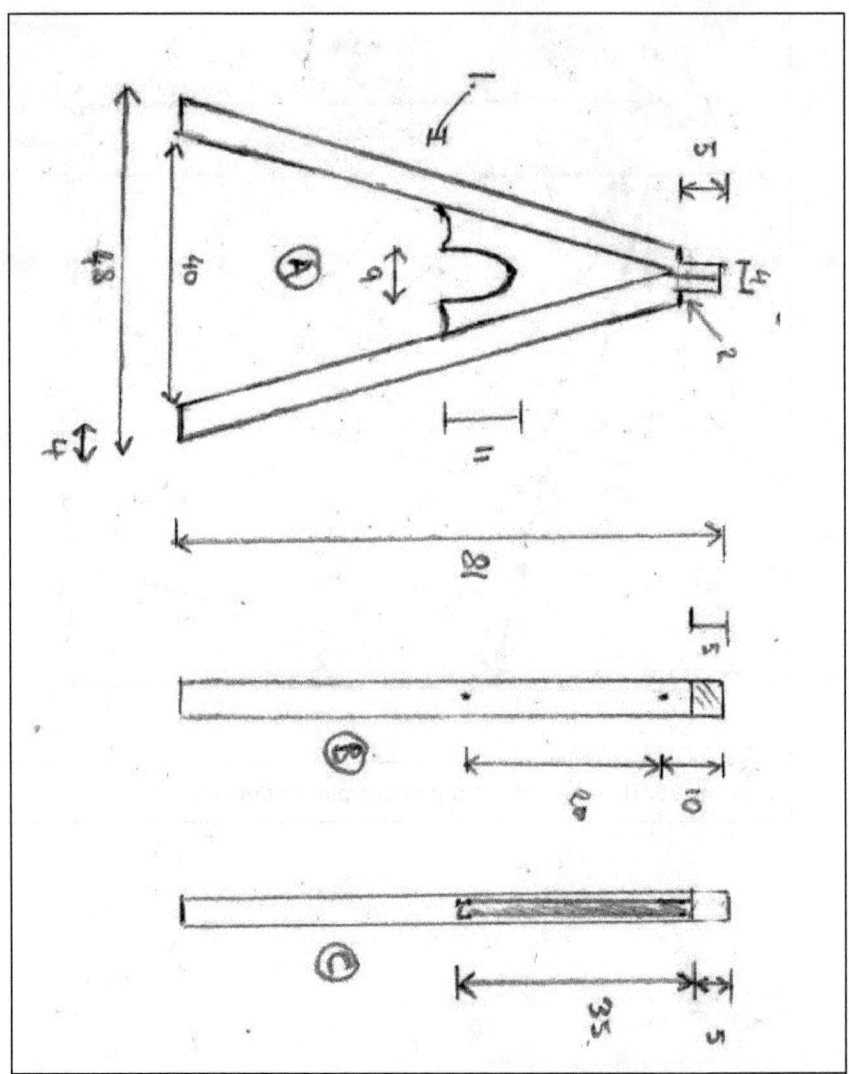

Drawing 36. Front legs. (A) front view, (B) outside view of side of leg with dowels through leg into front piece, (C) inside view of mortise for front piece, 1 cm ($\frac{3}{8}"$) deep.

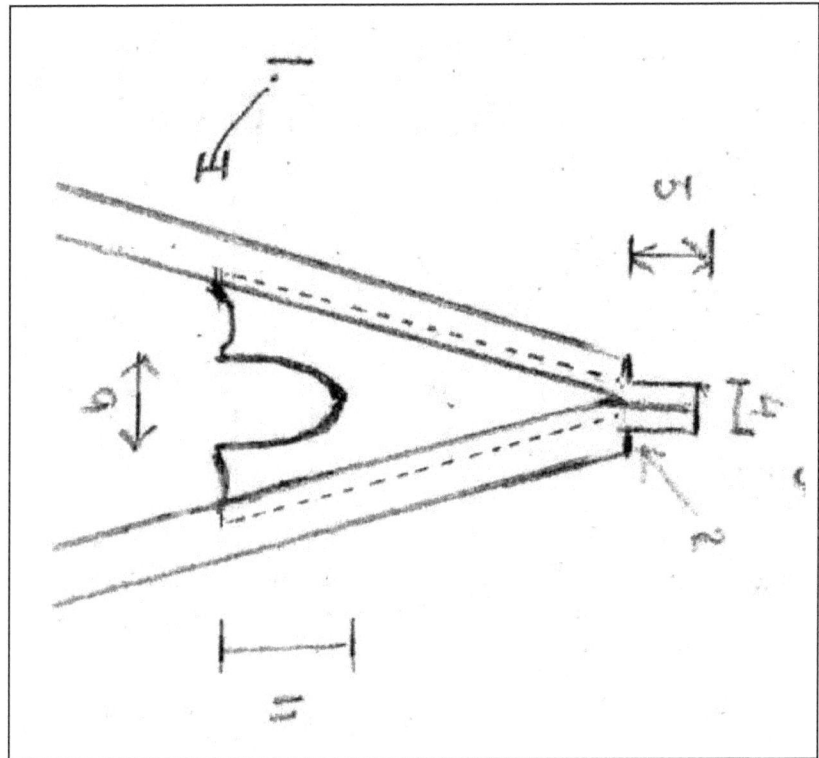

Drawing 37. Expanded view of front legs. The dotted line shows 1 cm deep mortise for the side of the front piece.

Back Legs – Make 2.

1. Mark out and cut to length.
2. Mark out and cut the tenon at the top of the leg.
3. Test out mortise and tenons for a snug fit.

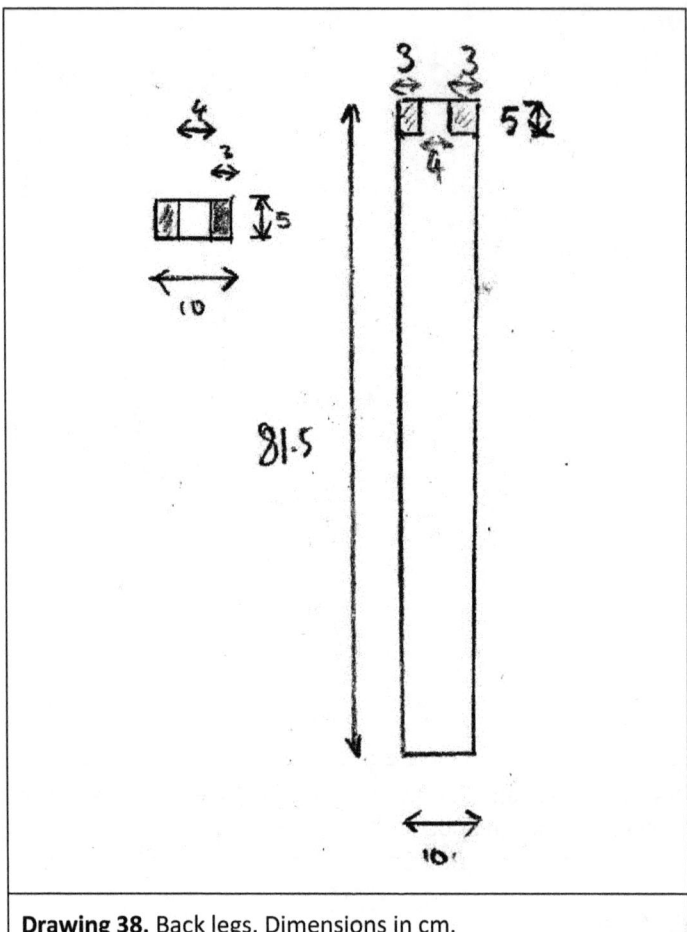

Drawing 38. Back legs. Dimensions in cm.

Levelling up.

If you place the trestle on a level surface and the top of the cross beam is not level, you can cut off the corresponding amount on the other longer legs, add some material to the leg that is too high (by gluing on a similar piece of wood), or just live with a slight unevenness.

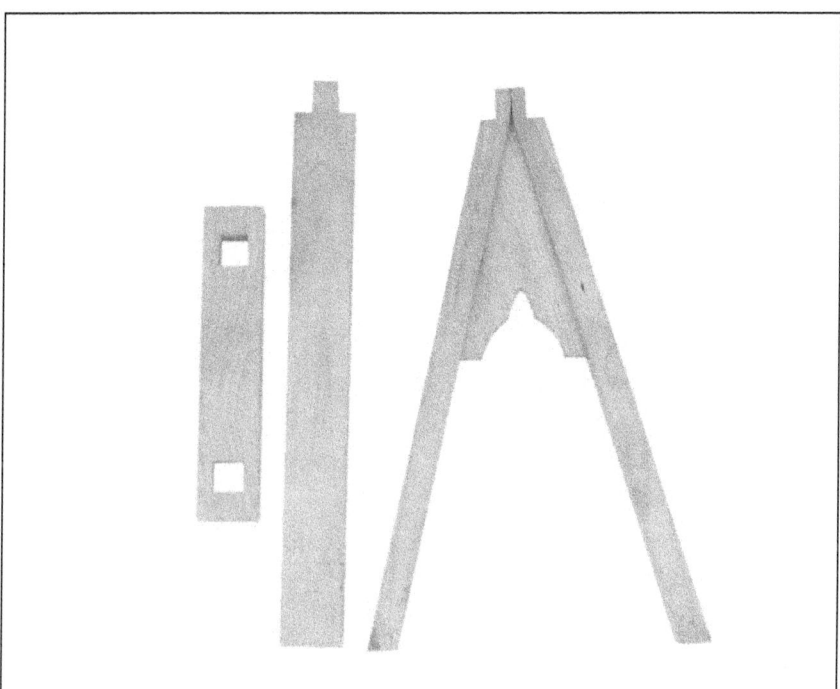

Photo 47. Trestle disassembled, the cross beam, the rear leg and the '*A*' frame.

Photo 48. The trestle from the back.

Hanging Salt Box of Buda, Hungary.

By Stephen Wyley.

The Hanging Salt Box.	**Find location:** Cellar Well, Buda Castle Hill, Buda, Hungary	**When:** 14th century CE
Stored: Budapest Historical Museum	**Collection no:** Unknown	**Material:** Timber - Unknown
Size: 14 x 10 x 16 cm (5.5 x 4 x 6.29")		

Figure 9. The original picture is from 'Mittelalter liche Funde aus einem Brunnen Von Buda [Medieval finds from a cellar well on the Buda Castle Hill], Holl (1966) p47.[37]

Introduction.

Salt was a very valuable commodity in the Medieval period. It was used in the kitchen for seasoning and preserving food. During a 1954 archaeological dig of a cellar well of a house (Disz Square No. 10) in the middle section of Buda Castle Hill (Buda, Hungary), extensive finds were made, including a hanging salt box dating from the 14th century.

---

[37] Thanks to Thies Grendahl for the copy of the book and photos.

Photo 49. The replica was made from 12 mm (½") thick pine.

A hanging salt box was hung on the wall of a kitchen near the cooking fire to keep the salt dry and clump-free. A salt box is different to the salt cellar[38] used for serving the diners on the feasting table. Those 'below the salt' were on the other end of the table to their betters.

Table 17. Example of similar salt boxes.

Source	Description	Date

---

[38] There are a lot of extant salt sellers made from various metals, glass and pottery as these materials are more likely to be preserved.

Speculum humanae salvationis. Date d'édition: British Library. Harley Ms2838 Folio 36r.	Flat rectangular box, lid front edge forms a point, triangular hole in back for hanging, the back curves up to a round apex.	1301-1500 CE
'Klauenmartyrium des Hl. Georg' altarpiece [trans. Claw Martyrdom of St. George], from Austria. [39]	Rectangular box, simple lid, circular hole in back for hanging, back has cut out top corners.	1460-1470 CE
Speculum humanae salvationis, Latin manuscript on parchment. British Library Harley MS 2838. Fol 38r.	Flat rectangular box, simple lid, small circular hole in back for hanging, the back is tall with long sloping sides to the top of the back.	1485-1509 CE
Die Narrenbeschwörung (Appeal to Fools) by Thomas Murner.	Square box, front of lid curves up to point in the middle of the front edge, back a small circle cut out for hanging, and curved edges to top.	1512 CE

The top of the back is damaged on the original and the shape and size of the hanging hole is speculative. The drawing of the original shows a curved topped rectangle. I have used a semicircle as the example shown in figure 9 is circular. If a circle was used on this box the circle would be about 25 mm (1") in diameter.

The tab at the front of the lid appears to be bifurcated and I suggest that this is also damaged and the tab originally formed a round tab with a circular hole in the centre of the tab.

---

[39]Landesmuseum Kärnten, Klagenfurt Austria Inventory number IN 27a.

The material used for the pivot point is unknown. Pins are usually made of wood or iron, but as iron rusts in the presence of salt, I am using wooden pins. I pushed two 30 mm (1½") long 4 mm ($\frac{5}{32}$") chopsticks through the sides so the lid can travel to the open position parallel to the back of the box.

The interior of the box is large enough to contain about two and half cups of salt at a pinch.

Materials.

Table 15. Timber cutting list.	
Back	160 x 100 x 12mm (6¼" x 4" x ½")
Front	90 x 75 x 12mm (3½" x 3" x ½")
2 Sides	120 x 120 x 12mm (4¾" x 4¾" x ½")
Bottom	110 x 75 x 12mm (4¼" x 3" x ½")
Lid	140 x 75 x 12mm (5½" x 3" x ½")

Other materials: Treenails 4 mm ($\frac{5}{32}$". See Appendix 11. Or similar dowel, in this case I used bamboo chopsticks, wood glue.

Tools.

Ruler (30cm (12")), set square, chisels (25mm (1") and 7mm (¼"), plain edge), files (coarse - flat bastard, fine - square bastard), hand saw, plane, G clamps, scrap wood (for holding work without damaging it), wooden mallet, bench vice, pencil, drill (with 10mm, 6mm and 4mm ($\frac{3}{8}$", ¼" and $\frac{5}{32}$") bits) and jigsaw or coping saw.

Construction instructions.

Lid.

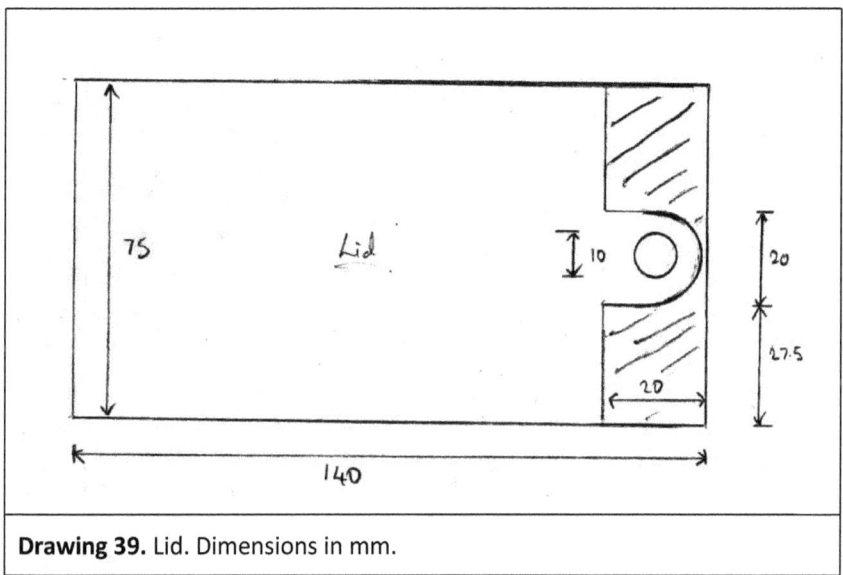

Drawing 39. Lid. Dimensions in mm.

1. Mark out and cut to length and width.
2. Cut out the lifting tab using a jig or coping saw.
3. Drill 10 mm ($\frac{3}{8}$") hole in the centre of the tab.
4. Clean up with sandpaper.

Sides.

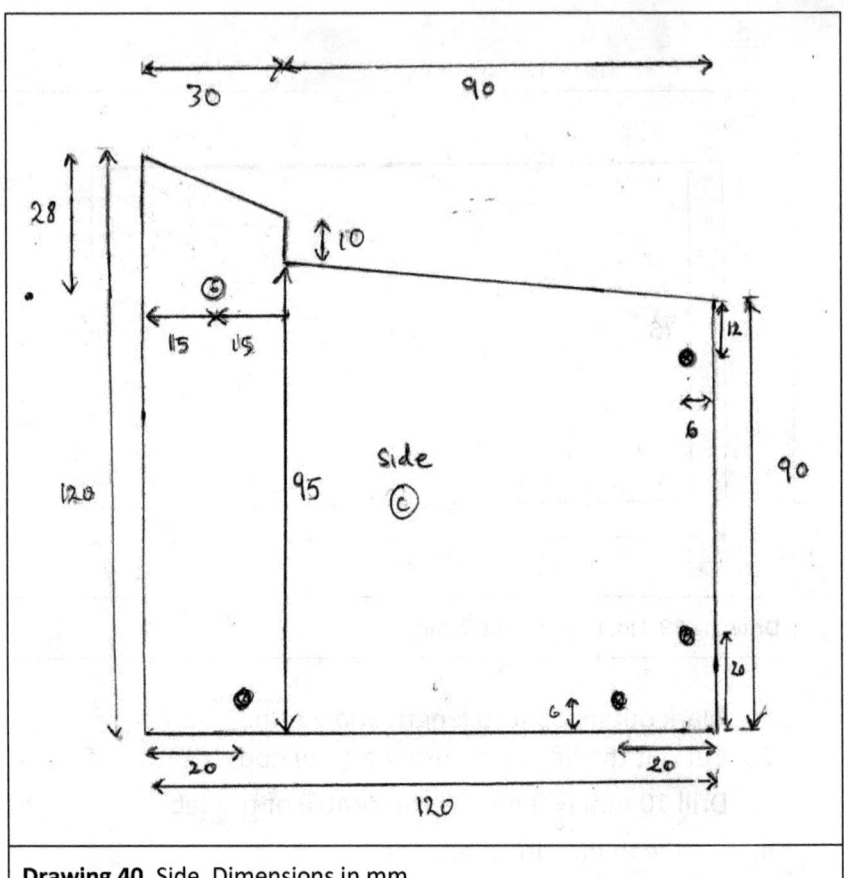

Drawing 40. Side. Dimensions in mm.

1. Cut to length and width.
2. Cut out detail at the top of the sides.

Back.

1. Mark out and cut to length and width.
2. Cut out the detail of the hanging hole. Since the area is damaged it is a matter of supposition to the shape and size of the hole. Drill a hole a bit bigger than the size of the blade of the coping or jigsaw.
3. Secure piece to bench, cut out with a saw and clean up with sandpaper.

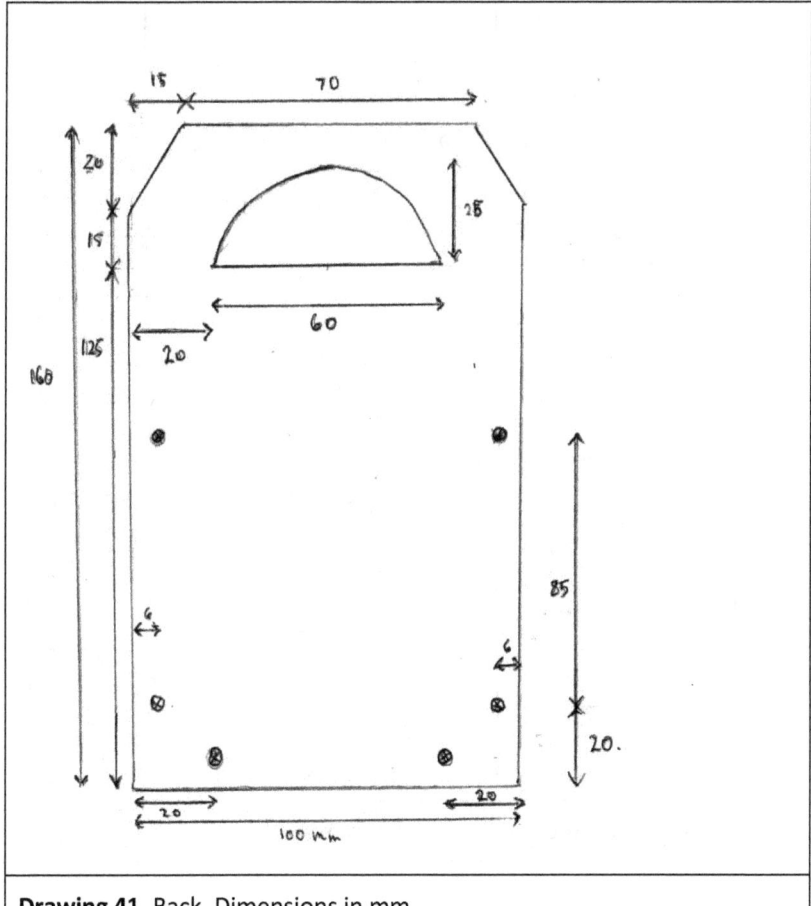

Drawing 41. Back. Dimensions in mm.

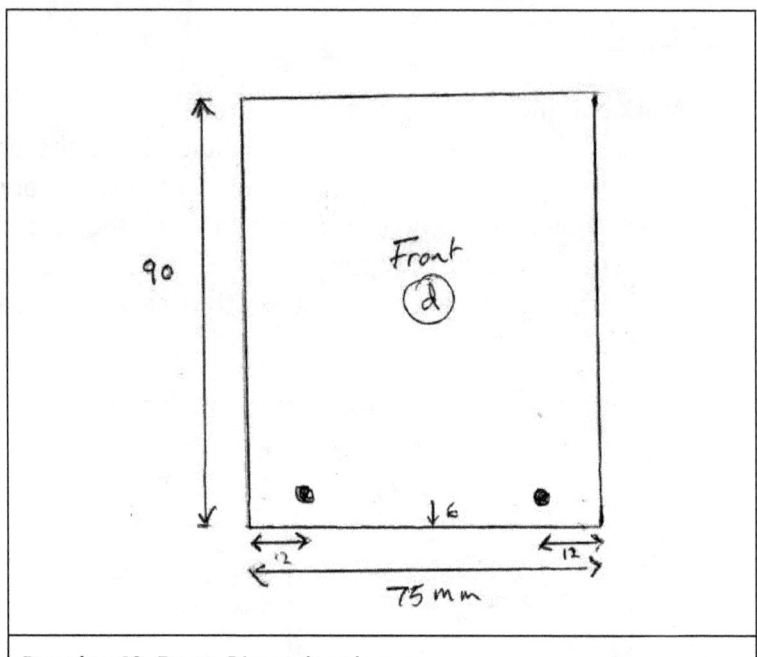

Drawing 42. Front. Dimensions in mm.

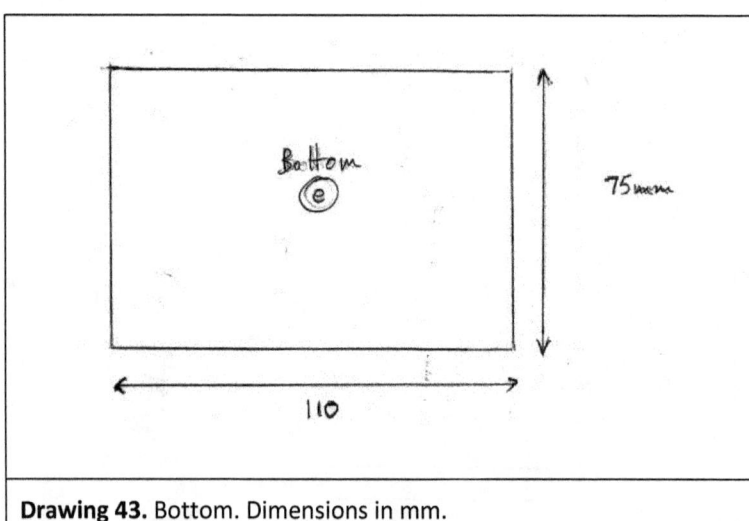

Drawing 43. Bottom. Dimensions in mm.

Front and Bottom.

1. Mark out and cut to length and width.

Assembly.

1. Butt join front to bottom with glue and treenails or dowels.

Photo 50. The bottom and front glued, dowelled and clamped.

2. Butt join sides to bottom and front with glue and dowels.
3. Butt join back to bottom and sides with glue and dowels.
4. Slide the lid into place between the raised sections of the sides, drill through the side and into the lid. Drive in dowel, repeat for opposite side. Pivot should enable the lid to be moved to the upright position parallel to the back.

Photo 51. The 4 mm holes predrilled in the sides.

Notes: The dowels are shown on the drawings as a circle with a cross inside. I only used linseed oil on the outside of the box so it doesn't spoil the salt.

Photo 52. The back of the box.

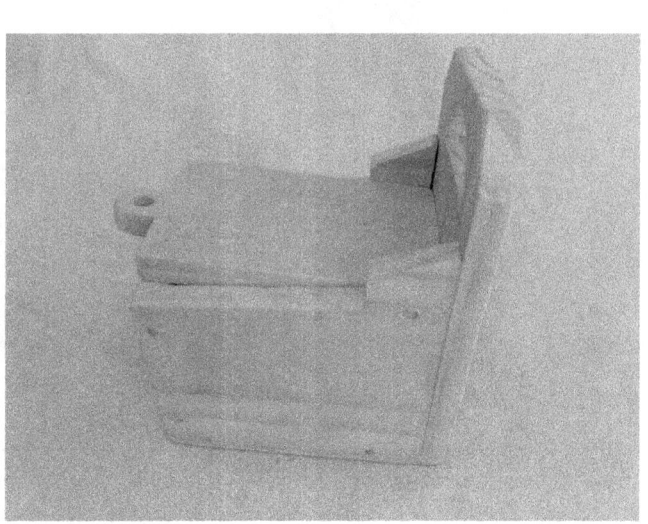

Photo 53. The side of the box.

The Bellows from the Smithfield Decretals.

By Stephen Wyley.

The Bellows from the Smithfield Decretals.		**When:** 1300-1340 CE
Stored: British Library, England.	**Collection no:** Royal 10, EIV, Fol. 142R	Illuminated manuscript
Size: Body 52 x 52 cm (20½ x 20½"), Pipe and throat 24 x 8cm (9½ x $3\frac{1}{8}$").		

Figure 7. Fanning the fire under a three-legged cooking pot in the Smithfield Decretals.

Introduction.

The bellows was a tool for adding more air to a fire to increase the amount of oxygen available to the fire triangle. This is great for starting or increasing the temperature of a fire. They can be used for cooking, forging, smelting and casting metals, glass blowing, pottery kilns and even musical organs. Bellows could be powered by either hand or foot action. For industrial use a water wheel can turn a cog to power the bellows. Bellows also appeared as dual bellows, where one side draws in as the other blows out. This supplies an almost continuous air flow.

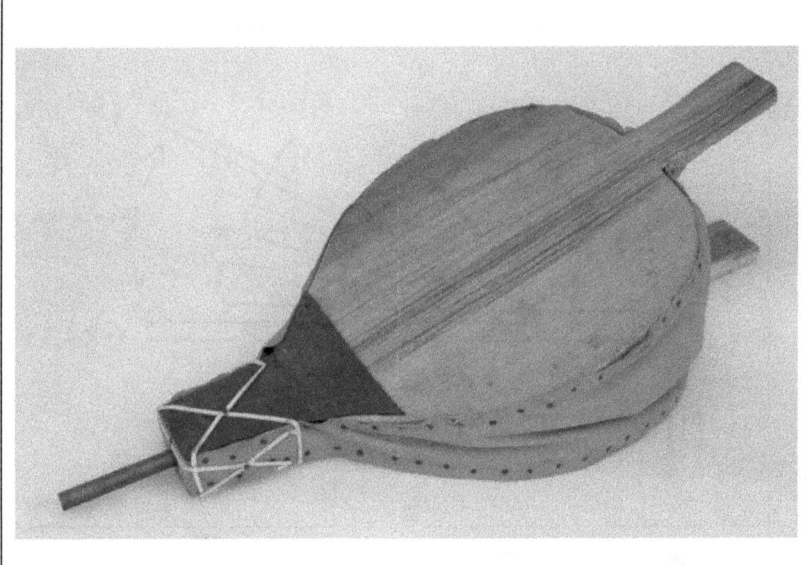

Photo 54. The replica bellows.

A primitive bellows was just a leather bag with two openings[40], one to suck the air in and the other to blow the air out. Later bellows had two boards on top of each other with leather tacked onto them, and one or two valve or breath holes in the body to either the top or bottom panel. The nozzle was the conduit that supplied the air to the fire, usually made of a non-combustible material. The vent(s) had a piece of leather attached on the inside of the hole, to stop the air escaping when the bellows was closed. And the air rushed out the nozzle adding air to the fire. A bellows with the vent on the bottom closes with more efficiency, and handles make the bellows easier to operate.

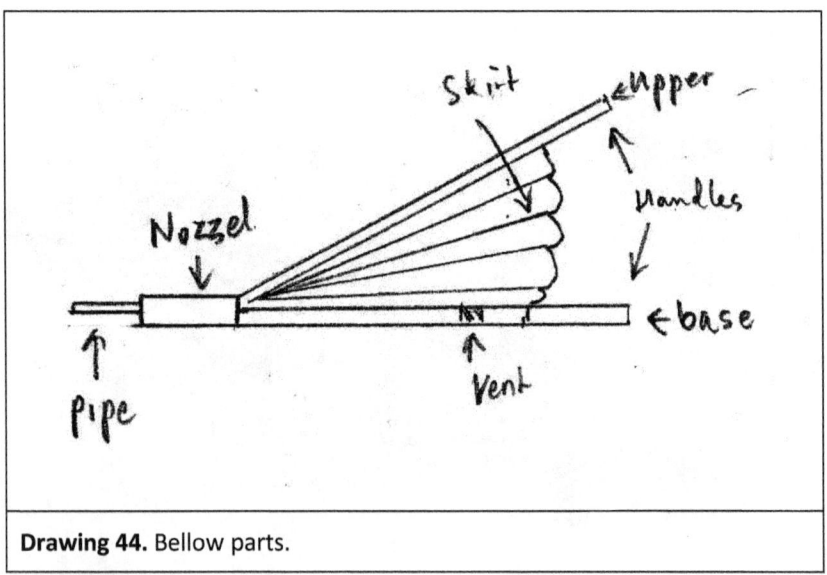

Drawing 44. Bellow parts.

Other forms of bellows were:

---

[40] Forge and bellows from the Stuttgarter Psalter, Cod.bibl.fol.23, dating from 801-850 CE.

- Pot bellows, consisting of a ceramic pot with a loose leather hide attached to the top, were used in ancient Egypt[41] and the Levant [42].
- Box bellows, consisting of a rectangular box with a moving partition, controlled via a wooden handle which was pulled in and out of the box. This design came from China and Japan.[43]

Later bellows got larger, with multiple compartments, closed by a pole lever. This lever was used to pull the bottom of the bellows up, allowing gravity to open the bellows and draw more air in.

Table 18. Example of other similar bellows.		
Source	*Detail*	*Dated*
Extant remains of a bellows - cellar well of a house (Disz Square No. 10) in the middle section of Buda Castle Hill (Buda, Hungary) Holl (1966), pp 47-48	body = pear shaped with wood throat, flat head nails used to hold leather in place.	14th Century CE
The martyrdom of St Barnaby (fol. 183) The Lives of the Saints (BNF Francios 183).	body = egg shaped, breath hole not shown, cross cord over throat (similar to project).	first half of the 14th Century CE
Herr Jakob von Warte, Manesse	body = pear shaped, long	1300-

---

[41] Metal casting shown in a Theban tomb of the Eighteenth-Dynasty vizier Rekhmira (TT10o).

[42] Ancient near eastern pot bellows by Christopher J. Davey (1979), in *Levant*, 11, 101 – 111.

[43] For examples of Japanese box bellows, see Yoshihara et al (1987). The schematic diagram is also reproduced in the Anvilfire book review at https://www.anvilfire.com/bookrev/kapp/oriental_box_bellows.htm.

Table 18. Example of other similar bellows.

Source	Detail	Dated
Codex (UBH Cod. Pal. germ. 848, fol. 46v), Universitätsbibliothek Heidelberg, Cod. Pal. germ. 848 Große Heidelberger Liederhandschrift (Codex Manesse) — Zürich,	thin handles, throat shown but detail poor. Black throat is the same black at the cauldron, both could be iron.	1330 CE
Fols 70v of the Luttrell Psalter (British Library Add 42130).	body = egg shaped, breath hole = circular and patterned, nozzle cone shaped different colour to throat and body of bellows, simple rectangular handles.	1325- 1340 CE
Extant remains of a bellows - Mary Rose, Tudor ship wreck, No. 82A0100, L 48.6cm x 25cm (19.14" x 9.8") Gardiner et al. (2005)	body = rough oval, extent of opening 12cm, triangular breath hole.	1545 CE

Materials.

Table 19. Material list.

2 x Bodies of the bellows	L 64 x W 52, 2cm thick. (L 25" x W 20", T ¾")
Pipe (brass, copper, iron, steel).	L 26 x 1.6cm diameter (L 10" x $\frac{5}{8}$" diameter)
Cord (hemp, jute, linen) or rawhide strip	About 1.2m long x 6mm wide (4' x ¼")

Leather	Skirt – 140 x 35cm wide, 1- 1.2mm thick (55" x 13¾" x 3oz) Vent flap – 10cm square, 3mm thick (4" square x 8oz) Hinge – 20 x 8cm, 3mm thick. (8" x 3" x 8oz)
Tacks	Lots of 25mm (1") long tacks for attaching leather
Nails (bullet heads)	4 nails for attaching the top of throat to bottom section
Glue	PVA will do, unless you want to make up some fish bladder glue.[44]

Tools.

Saw, ruler, tack hammer, needle nose pliers, pencil, set square, plane, drill and drill bits.

---

[44] Theophilus, Chapter 28 – Milling Gold for books: casting the mill. "*Now take the bladder of a fish called Sturgeon, wash it three times in warm water, cut it up in pieces, put them into a very clean pot with water and let them soften overnight. On the next morning cook them over the fire without letting them boil, and test with your fingers to see if they stick together. When they stick fast, the glue is good*". (Hawthorn & Smith 1979). My question: How do you unstick your fingers?

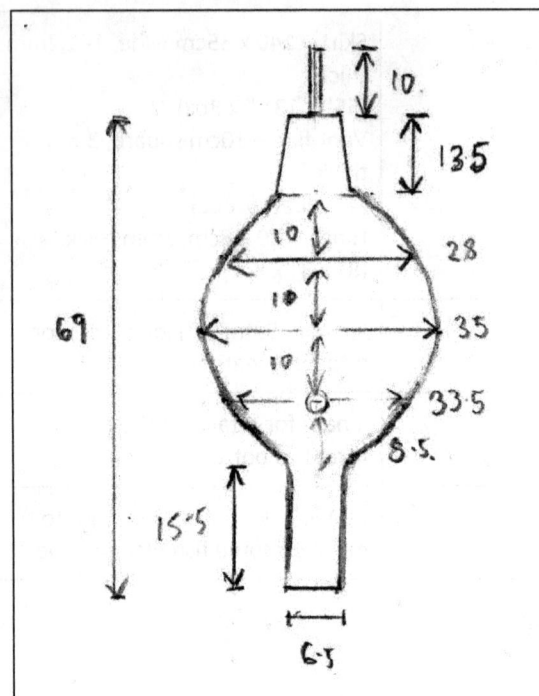

Drawing 45. Plan view of bellows.

Dimensions in cm.

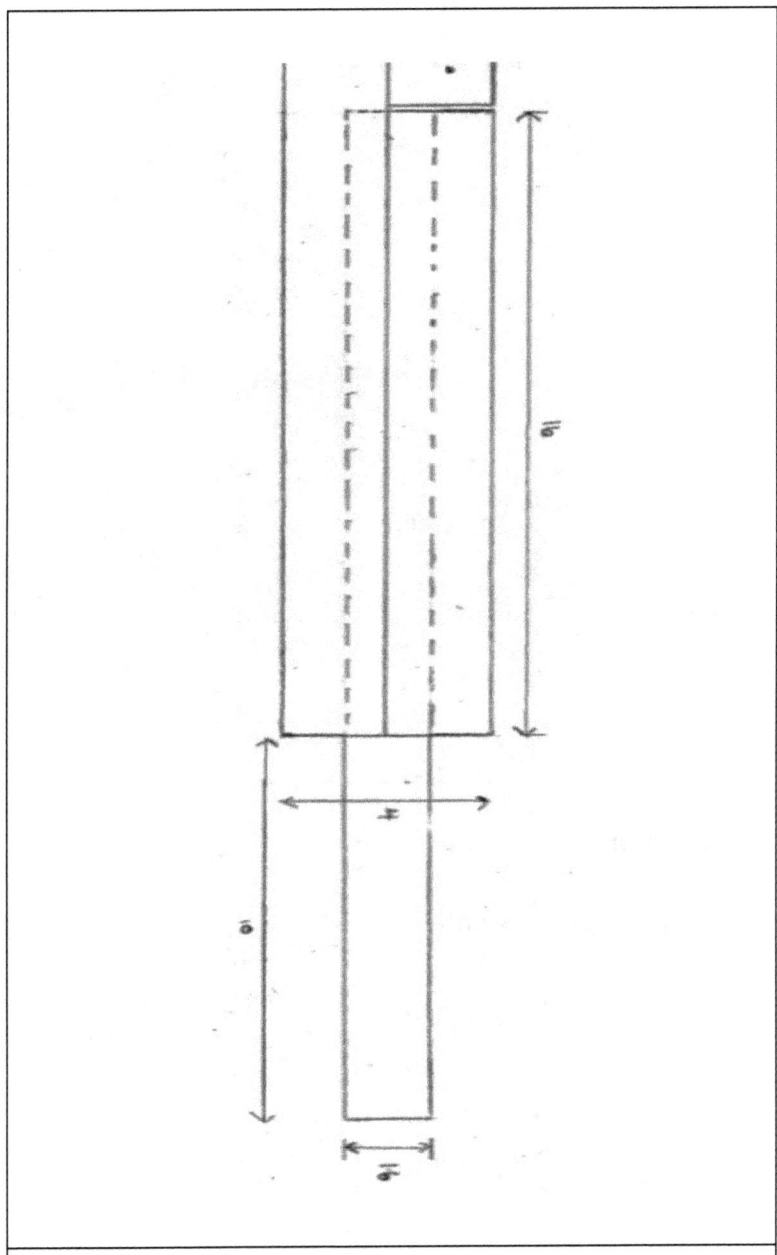

Drawing 46. Side plan of the nozzle. Dimensions in cm.

Photo 55. Bottom view of cord cross over.

Instructions.

Body (top and bottom).

1. Mark out and cut to shape (jigsaw or coping saw).
2. Cut the breath hole 25 mm (1") diameter in the bottom with a hole cutter or spade bit, use waste timber on the other side to stop timber splitting.
3. Attach a leather flap (10 cm (4") square in 3 mm (8 oz.) leather) so that the breathing hole is in the centre of the flap, on the inside of the leaf, with the flap opening towards the handle.

Photo 56. Top view of cord cross over.

Throat.

1. Mark and cut out the timber in the shape to match the front end of the throat of the bottom leaf of the bellows.
2. Attach to base by dowels or nails and glue.
3. Drill out a hole in the block running through the centre of the throat, emerging at the end of the internal end of the throat, adjust with a round file to fit the pipe.
4. Gouge out flared a channel in top and bottom plates where the pipe exits the throat.
5. Attach the top leaf to the bottom leaf with a leather hinge (in at least 3 mm (8 oz.) leather) using tacks (the original

size of such a hinge is unknown). See photos for more details.

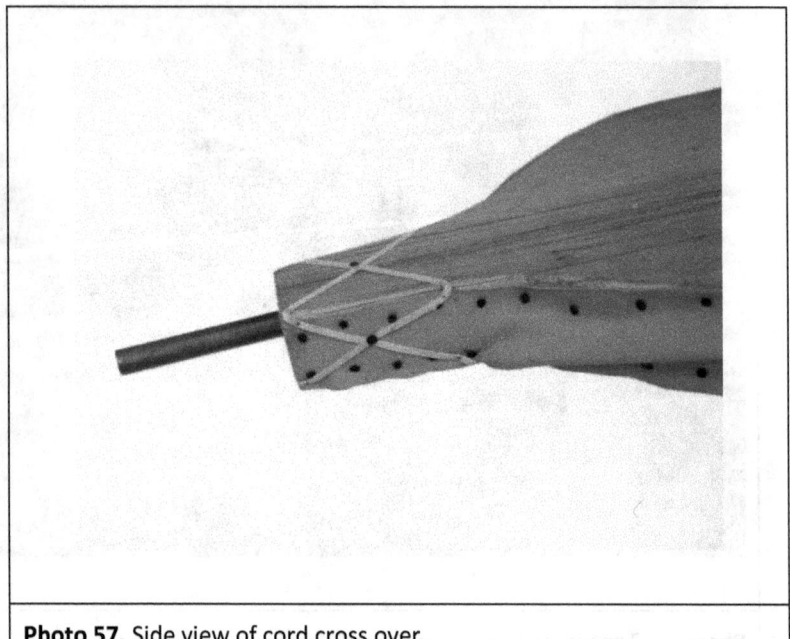

Photo 57. Side view of cord cross over.

Pipe.

1. Cut pipe to length with a hacksaw, clear any burs with a round file.
2. Apply glue to pipe and hole, insert into throat and allow to dry.

Skirt.

1. Cut out the skirt of 1-1.2 mm (3 oz.) leather (roughly) into a rectangle 140 x 32 cm (55" x 13¾").
2. Hold the bellows in the open position by hanging from above the bellows (i.e. rafter in the shed).

3. Apply PVA glue to the bottom leaf and tack bottom edge starting from the handle working around to the throat, spacing tacks every 25cm (10").
4. Apply PVA glue to the top leaf and tack edge starting from the handle working around to the throat, spacing tacks every 25cm (1").
5. Trim excess leather with a sharp knife. Check for leaks.

Crossover.

1. Attach cord/strip cross ties to secure the throat to top and bottom. Tack start, crossovers and corners. If using raw hide, I recommend that the rawhide is soaked in warm water before attaching with brads or tacks, then allowed to dry. See photos 55, 56 & 57 for details.

The Frame Saw (Santa Croce).

By Stephen Wyley.

The Santa Croce Frame Saw.	**Location:** Florence, Italy.	**When:** 1385-87 CE
Fresco by Agnolo Gaddi, Preparation of the cross, Santa Croce, Florence, Italy. (Scala Archives).		

Figure 8. The carpenters using a frame saw on the cross.

Introduction.

A frame saw consists of a framework with two sides separated by a spacer bar. The spacer bar is joined by tenons at either end, placed into mortises in the centre of the two side bars. The saw blade is attached to the bottom ends of the sides by rivets or pegs. Tension on the saw blade is supplied by a twisted twine strung between the tops of the two side bars. The twisting of the twine is assisted by a strip of wood poked through the twine. As the toggle is rotated the twine twists, increasing the tension, pulling the tops of the sides and increasing the tension on the blade.

The earliest reference I found for use of frame saws was by the Romans[45]. The frame saw allowed a long thin saw blade to be used to cut timber, it produced a finer cut and less metal was needed for the saw.

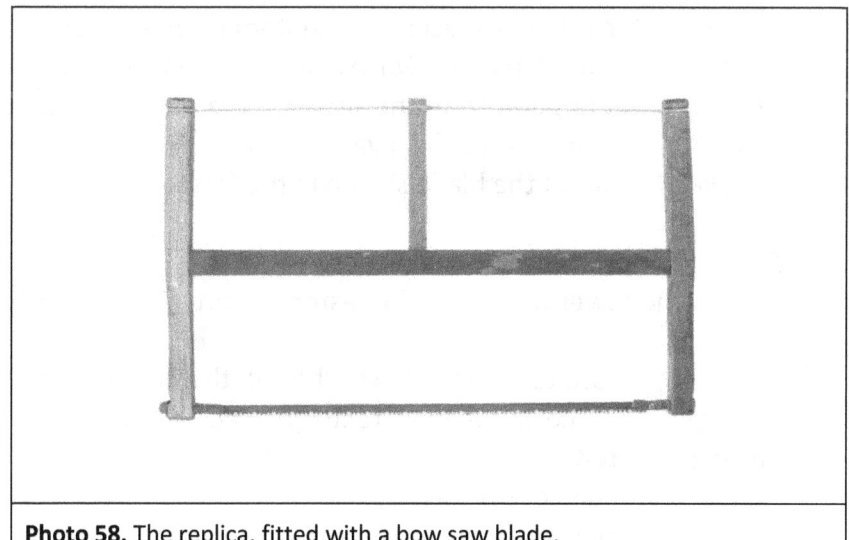

Photo 58. The replica, fitted with a bow saw blade.

Are there any extant frame saws? Well, so far I have only been able to find one that was found during the excavations of Whithorn and St Ninian from (1984-1991)[46], dating from

---

[45] Mercer (2012), pages 152-153;. Mols (1999), p. 89. – painted façade of a workshop in Pompeii (V1, 7,8), Museo Nazionale in Naples (inv. 8991) – Alter dedicated to Minerva, Capitoline Museums in Rome (inv. 2143).

[46] Hill (1997), p. 510. The Whithorn Trust may have more details on the frame saw remains.

between 1000 and 1300 CE. It was made from yew and consists of one of the ends of a possible frame saw, but on examination it is more likely to be a rip saw with the blade in the centre of the handle. Goodall lists the remains of two extant blades, both in the UK, one from Pinsley in Hampshire (11th century) and the other from Goltho in Lincolnshire (an unstratified find which could be anywhere from late Saxon to early 15th century).[47]

It is always difficult to discern detail from a fresco or an illuminated manuscript. As a secondary source it should be viewed with caution, especially if the item of interest is just a small part of the depiction. For example, it is hard to see the number of teeth per inch or the shape of the teeth on the saw blade. Looking at saw blades available today we can guess at the likely details of the blade shown in the fresco.

Some basic principles of saw blades:
- The fewer the teeth, the faster the cut, the courser the finish;
- The more teeth, the slower the cut, the finer the finish.

So a guide to the number of teeth per inch for the type of cutting required:
- 3-5, rough or rip cutting;
- 6-8, universal for both dry and green wood;
- 9-11, fine carpentry;
- 12+, very fine carpentry.

The other consideration is the set of the teeth, which is how far the teeth are bent sideways, which helps to free the blade of chips and produces a certain size of cut. For making the

---

[47] Goodall (2011), p38. B93 and B94.

replica I used a store-bought blade with a bow saw pattern, able to cut on the push and pull.

Table 19. Frame saw survey.

Date	Collection /site details	Type of Saw (Rip or Plain)	Comment	One or two users
1023 CE	Carpenter and blacksmith, miniature from De universo by Rabano Mauro. Biblioteca Statale del Monumento Nazionale di Montecassino Cod. Casin. 132	Plain	Ripping a log. Toggle has a circular tab at the top. The tourniquet goes through holes in the top of the sides and the large teeth on the saw go just one direction.	Two
1200 CE	Augsburg UBA Cod.I.2.4.15 - Pamplona Bible, Spain.	Plain	Torture. Circles on the end of the blade where they join the sides show circles which could be rivets or dowels holding a blade in place.	Two
1230 CE	France, AMIENS, Bibliothèque municipale, No. 0023	Plain	Torture. Blade appears to extend past sides with a black dot on the left semicircle which could be a fastening rivet or dowel.	Two

1250-1275 CE	Italy, Biblioteca comunale di Trento MS 10424	Plain	Torture. The terminals of the left side could be turned knobs.	One
1290-1310 CE	France, Chantilly, Bibliothèque du château de Chantilly, 0005 (1045 bis)	Plain	Torture. Detail of rope, stick, rivet to hold blade on right. Large teeth going one way on blade.	Two
1425 CE	Joiners in the Mendel Hausbuch - Karl Schreyner Amb. 317.2° Folio 21 recto (Mendel I)	Plain	Convex sides with recurve ends on tops. Circle on outside of the side could be through the tenon for the cross bar. Handle at right angles to blade	One
1589 CE	Joiners in the Mendel Hausbuch - Georg Han Amb. 317b.2° Folio 50 recto (Mendel II)	Fret	Extended handle in line with blade	One

Materials.

Wooden frame (choose a hardwood), steel for the blade and twine (linen / hemp etc.) for the twist or toggle stick, rivets or wooden pegs (if the pegs are removable, it makes it easier to pack down for travel / storage)

Blade: Use commercially available bow saw blades (between 3 to 4 teeth per inch), see your local supplier. I am not about to go into how to make a saw blade, that is well beyond my bailiwick.

Tools.

Saw, ruler, pencil, square, plane, drill, rat tail file, mallet, chisels, knife.

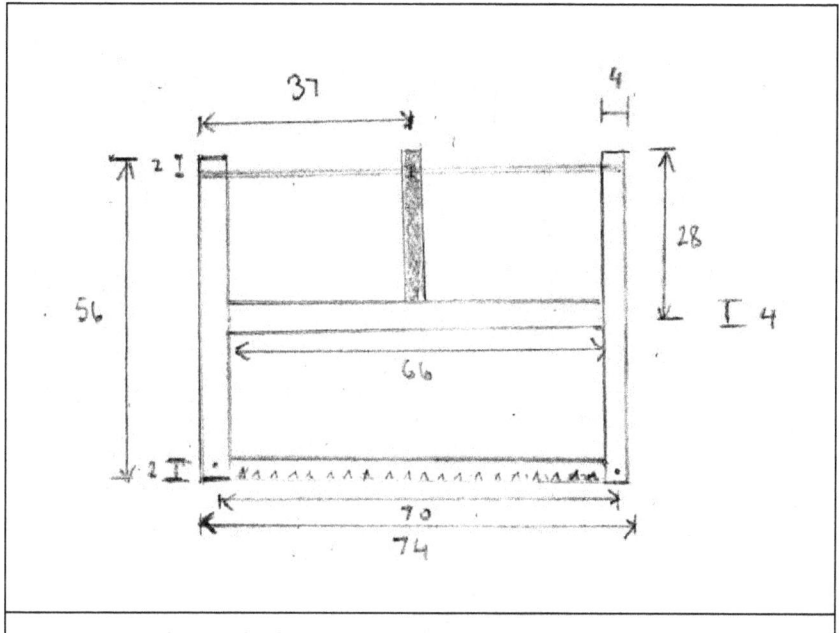

Drawing 47. The whole thing. Dimensions in cm.

Construction instructions.

Sides.

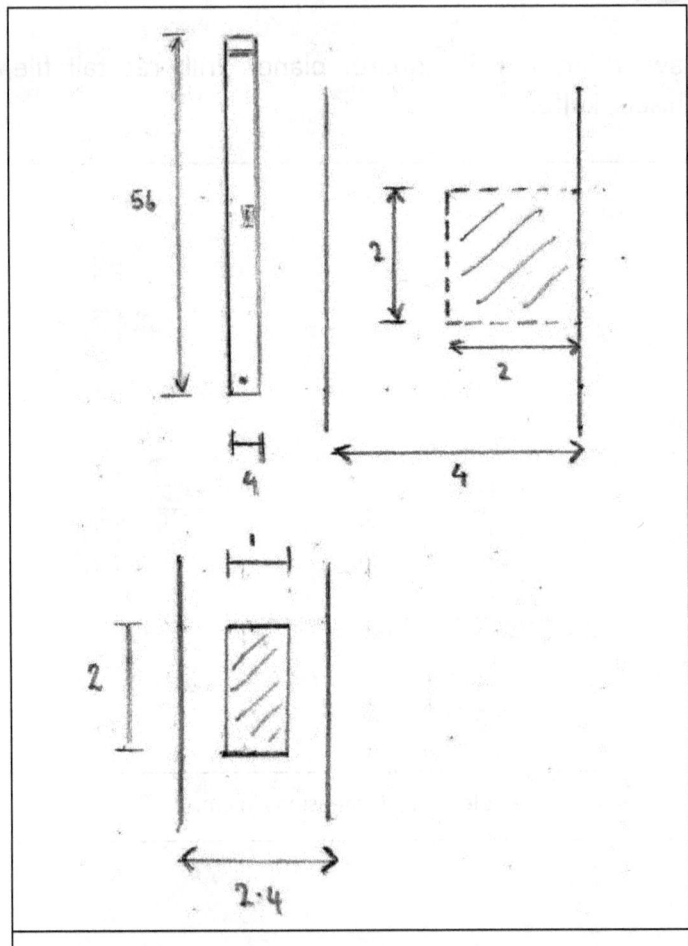

Drawing 48. Side and close up of mortise. Dimensions in cm.

1. Mark out and cut ends to shape and length.
2. Drill holes and chisel out the mortise for the ends of the spacer bar.

3. Cut slot in bottom end of ends to take the ends of the metal saw blade.
4. Drill holes in the ends of the ends to match up with holes in the end of the metal saw blade.
5. File in the groove around the top of both sides, about 2cm (¾") from top. The groove is for the tourniquet cord so it does not slip off.

Crossbar.

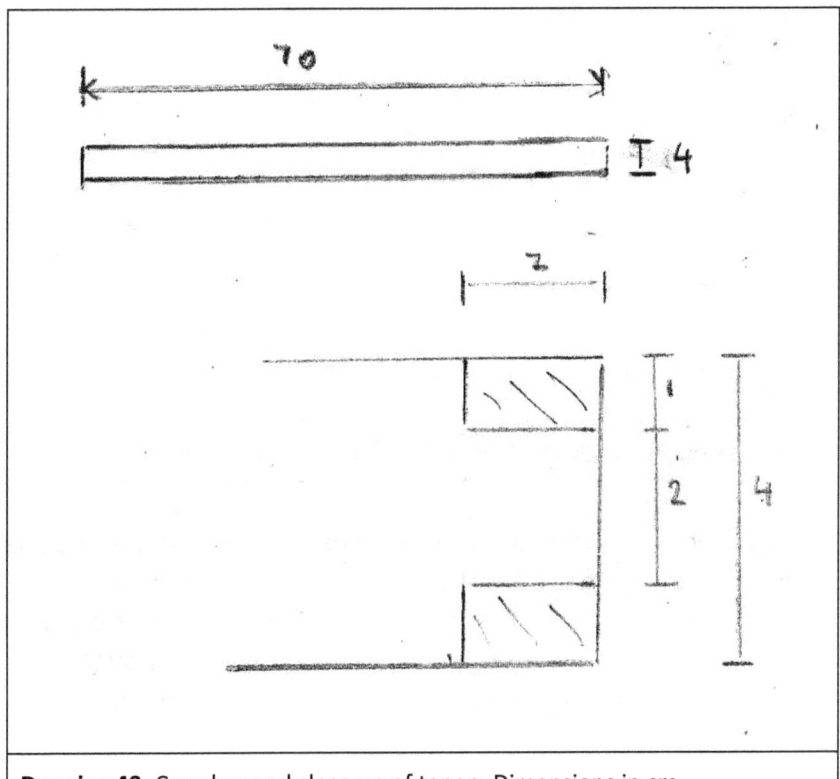

Drawing 49. Crossbar and close up of tenon. Dimensions in cm.

6. Cut the spacer bar to length.
7. Cut the ends of the spacer bar to fit the mortise holes in the centre of the ends.

8. Fit the tenon of the spacer bar to the mortise holes in the centre of the ends (forms an 'H').
9. Cut and file a notch in the outer side of the top end of each of the ends, to ensure the twice does not slip off.

Make a twist or toggle stick.

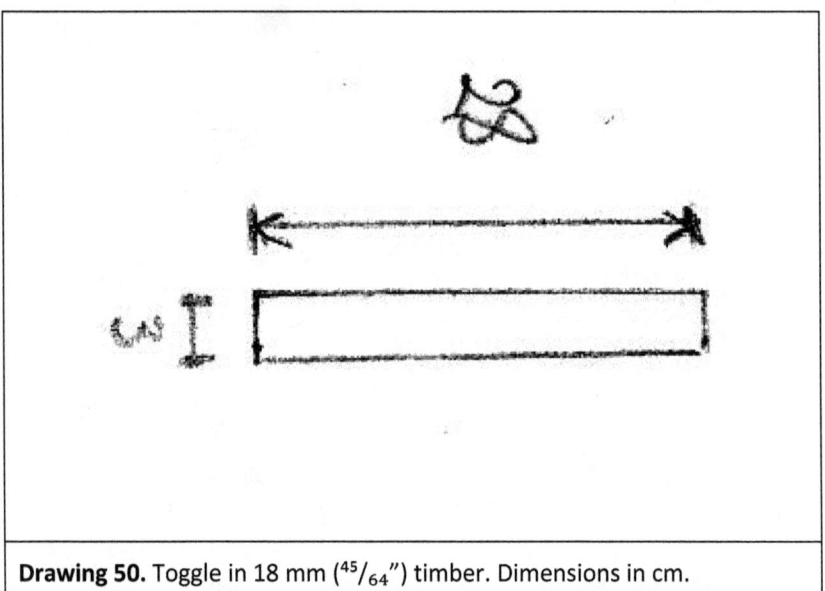

Drawing 50. Toggle in 18 mm ($^{45}/_{64}$") timber. Dimensions in cm.

10. Loop the twine around the tops of each end, place a stick/small rod between the loops of the twine and rotate at right angles to the frame, increasing the tension of the twine, to the point until the tension is high enough to hold the blade in place and stiff enough to saw the wood.

Assembly.

11. With a spacer bar in place, place the blade in the slit in the bottom ends of the ends, in line with the holes and rivet or peg the blade in place.
12. Tie off the cord around the top of one of the sides, and then loop the cord around the tops of both sides (using the grooves so it does not slip off) about 4 or 6 times of a 6 mm (¼") thick linen (depending on the breaking strain of the cordage).
13. Insert toggle stick between loops and rotate the stick to cause the cordage to twist. Twist until the saw blade is firmly fixed in position and does not wobble when cutting.

Photo 59. The replica fitted with a saw blade riveted through a hole in the side of the frame saw.

14. Oil blade and sharpen on an annual basis. Store in a dry place where you are unlikely to brush or hit the blade.

15. Slide the toggle down so that the cross bar impedes the toggle from unwinding (beware that the toggle stick flips back while twisted up; it could cause you an injury if it hits you).

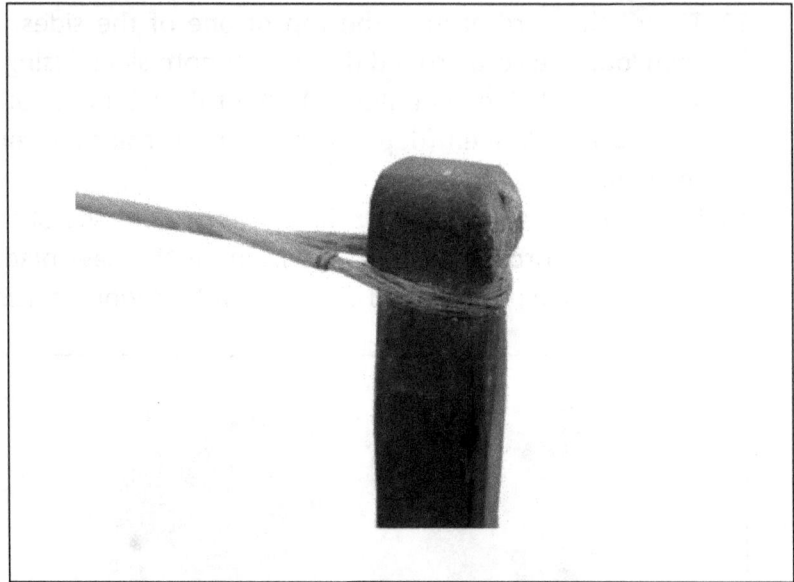

Photo 60. The replica, showing the top of one of the sides with a grove for the tourniquet.

Photo 61. The replica, showing the toggle stick twisted up in the tourniquet.

The Costrel from Baynard Castle Dock, City of London.

By Wayne Robinson.

Baynard Castle Dock Costrel.	Location: Baynard Castle Dock, City of London. (Baynard House, Queen Victoria Street).	When: late 14th century CE
Stored: Museum of London (MoL)	Collection no: BC72[83]<1996>	Material: Leather, linen thread, pitch.
Size: L 195mm, H 180mm, W 80mm, leather up to 7mm thick. (L 7¾", H 7", W 3¼", leather up to $\frac{9}{32}$" thick)		

This is an advanced project that needs both woodworking and leatherworking skills. The jigs can make a number of different costrels, so you could do this as a group project and make a few costrels from one set of jigs.

There's a strong tradition of making costrels from leather, wood, or pottery across southern and Western Europe. The costrel shape is the most efficient use of materials for a given volume. The barrel shaped costrel remained largely unchanged from the 14th century until the 19th century, with evidence of earlier forms existing back to the 11th century[48].

---

[48] Baker (1921), pp55-56

You could just stick to the woodwork or the leatherwork and share the work with someone with talents in the other craft, making one costrel for each of you.

Photo 62. Original costrel (used with the kind permission of the Museum of London).

Many examples have a documented use of 400 years or more. One costrel made for either Henry VIII or his brother Arthur, spent a considerable amount of its life until late Victorian times, carrying water for harvesters working in fields around Oxford.

Photo 63. A replica costrel.

Leather examples, both extant and depicted in various works of art, are decorated with anything from two to five perpendicular ridges, with three being the most common. They only occur on one side of the costrel, the bottom being flat. One ridge is always in the centre and usually flares out as it reaches the top to be the same width as the mouth. The others are parallel to the end seams and fade out about 25mm (an inch) from the top seam. Costrels with bands invariably have elongated slots for leather carrying straps. Frequently, foliage or heraldic shields are incised between the raised bands. The advantage of this shape of costrel is that the ribs or other decoration can be embossed while the leather is still flat.[49]

Stitching is invariably double rows of saddle stitch, a practice attested to in Article 13 of the statutes of the sheath and scabbard makers of Paris, dated 12 September 1560. It states that it is forbidden for the trade to make leather bottles with any other leather than cow or ox, and that bottles must be stitched with double-seams sewn from both sides.[50]

Examples from the late 16th century onwards have embossed decoration, again on one side only, the most common being a single large fleur-de-lys in the centre of the front. Pomegranates and Tudor roses also feature. These later costrels commonly have a round hole for the carrying cord.

Leather vessels require periodic maintenance, normally by patching, relining and re-blacking with ink.[51] Baker (1921) and Waterer (1944) both state that once made, jacks and bombards were hung in the smoke from the fire to cure. Waterer attributes some magical preservative qualities to the smoke[52], but to me it seems more likely that the combination of heat hardening the waxed leather and allowing any hair-line cracks in the pitch lining to reflow and seal.

I've been a bit picky about which costrels I've included of the seven from the Mary Rose in the table below. The raised rib examples are likely to be from a long time before the date of the wreck, and from the style of decoration they may have

---

[49] *"Ornament... can also be incorporated in hollow moulds, being carved intaglio so that it stands out in relief on the surface of the finished article..."* Waterer (1981) p62

[50] Roland de la Platiere (1788) in *Encyclopedie Methodique*. Paris, 1790.

[51] Baker (1921), p73

[52] Waterer (1944), pp35-36

been from well into the previous century. While the wreck finds skew the data, it shows how common costrels would have been across the middle and lower classes. I've noted a 15th century transition between the ribbed medieval style and the embossed early modern style.

Table 20. Comparison of Extant Costrels.

Place	Date	Collection	Description
London	15th C CE	Museum of London A10640	MoL gives height 80mm ($3\frac{1}{8}$"); width 85mm ($3\frac{11}{32}$")[53]. Three raised bands with incised foliate decoration between. Oval ends. Slots for carrying.
Oxford	Tudor period	Ashmolean Museum	406mm (16") long, 330mm (13") tall. Five raised bands, two raised shields incised with Tudor rose on the left and pomegranate on the right. S-scrolls in the flat fields between bands. Triangular ends. Slots for carrying. Published in Baker (1921), pp34, 56-57.
Portsmouth	1545 CE	Mary Rose Museum 81A0881	Undoubtedly earlier than the find date. Three raised ribs, a double zigzag pattern between the ridges and to either side. Several pairs of parallel tooled

---

[53] Baker (1921), p56 gives the dimensions as 4 × 3¾ inches (100 x 95 mm). Having seen this one in the flesh in London, I think Baker is correct. I've calculated the volume from Baker's size to be about 300 ml/2 gills (0.5 pint). The MoL has also been a bit flexible with the date, with some mid-20th C guidebooks providing a 14th C date.

Table 20. Comparison of Extant Costrels.

Place	Date	Collection	Description
			lines including a large inverted V and various rectangles on the base and back. Associated with a stopper and showing signs of an organic sealer.
Portsmouth	1545 CE	Mary Rose Museum 81A2034	Decoration on both front and back. Front has three raised ribs, with a shield above two oak leaves within scrolls in the space between the ribs. The design is mirrored about the centre rib. Saltire crosses are cut into the shields, as on our feature bottle from the MoL. There is a small shield on the back near the neck with the letter "W" (really V V for *Virgo Virginium* in 1545). Flat strap holes and stopper with leather wrap. The find context makes it likely that this costrel belonged to an officer.
Portsmouth	1545 CE	Mary Rose Museum 82A5009	Evidence for painted shields on an otherwise very plain costrel. Three moulded ribs, with a small stamp on the middle rib just below the neck, no other decoration. Teardrop ends.
Portsmouth	1545 CE	Mary Rose Museum 81A5749	A transitional costrel between the medieval and early modern styles, the ribs are vestigial, only suggested by the spaces between the four fields

Table 20. Comparison of Extant Costrels.

Place	Date	Collection	Description
			of hatching. Irish harp on reverse. It retains slots for carrying. This was probably nearly new when lost. It is the largest of the Mary Rose costrels, 190 x 164 x 80mm (7½ x 6½ x $3\frac{1}{8}$").
Portsmouth	1545 CE	Mary Rose Museum 81A1214	Another transitional costrel. Front and back are decorated with five pairs of parallel lines from top to bottom, framed by a horizontal line at the base and two parallel lines across the shoulders and neck. There are two asterisks on the base, with a saltire cross (X) diagonally between them, and a saltire cross on each end. There are reinforcing pieces in the shoulders/lugs and a gasket piece around the inside of the neck. There remains a waterproof coating on the inside surface. This costrel was found in a chest containing woodworking tools.
London	17th C CE	Museum of London 82.149	Height 210mm (8¼") width 180mm (7") depth 155mm (6.102"). Undecorated other than stamped with its owner's initials *'TG'* and several crowns. Round holes for carrying strap.

When looking at manuscripts, it's important to work out what the costrel was made from as the shapes are similar but some of the details differ. Wooden costrels tend to be barrel shaped and often have lines going from side to side. Ceramic costrels are often shown in lighter colours and can have loops or tabs separated from the neck for hanging.

Table 21. Comparison of Costrels in Manuscripts.			
Manuscript	*Date*	*Collection*	*Description*
Maciejowski Bible (The Morgan Bible) Folio 27v.	mid-1240s CE	The Pierpont Morgan Library, New York, USA Ms M. 638	The War Effort. David delivers provisions to his brethren. (1 Kings 17:20-22). On the cart nearest to the viewer, a light brown barrel shaped costrel with three bands, the middle band decorated. https://www.themorgan.org/collection/crusader-bible/54
Livre du roy Modus et de la royne Ratio, qui parle des deduis et de pestilence, Henri de Ferrières. f. 163v.	1374-1377 CE	Koninklijke Bibliotheek van België, Brussels, Ms. 2018-2019	Fight at the cart. Third figure from the left is swinging a black costrel around by the strap, one band, teardrop shaped ends. https://uurl.kbr.be/1065691 (scroll to image 335)

Table 21. Comparison of Costrels in Manuscripts.

Manuscript	Date	Collection	Description
Livre de Chasse by Gaston Phoebus. f 65r.	1387-1389 CE	Bibliothèque Nationale, Paris, France Ms. fr. 616	The morning meal. Total of four costrels in illumination, three leather and one ceramic. From l. to r.: Ceramic armorial costrel cooling in stream under arch; figure in green near dogs drinking from black leather costrel, oval ends, three raised ribs, flat strap handle; figure in green at table drinking from smaller black leather costrel with two raised ribs; large black leather costrel on the table, oval ends, two raised ribs, textured fields between ribs and flat strap handle. https://commons.wikimedia.org/wiki/File:Gaston_Ph%C3%A9bus,_Livre_de_la_chasse._67r.jpg
Historia Plantarum, De' Grassi, Giovannino	1395-1400 CE	Biblioteca Casanatense, Rome, Italy	Figure carrying a brown costrel in one hand, three bands,

Table 21. Comparison of Costrels in Manuscripts.

Manuscript	Date	Collection	Description
De' Grassi, Salomone. f. 280v.		Ms. 459	strap handle and stopper. https://casanatense.contentdm.oclc.org/digital/iiif/miniature/9291/full/full/0/default.jpg
Des cas des nobles hommes et femmes by Giovanni Boccacio. f. 130v.	c. 1410 CE	Bibliothèque de Genève Ms. fr. 190/2	Radagaise, pagan barbarian chief, in his tent. Brown costrel with two raised bands and strap handle on ground next to figure in blue surcoat, ends appear oval. http://www.e-codices.ch/en/bge/fr0190-2/130v/0
Très Riches Heures du Duc de Berry.	1412-1416 CE	Musée Condé, Chantilly, France Ms.65, f.10	Calendar - October. Tilling and sowing are being carried out by the peaSantas, in the shadow of the Louvre, Paris. Black costrel in the foreground, teardrop shaped ends, turned wooden stopper, flat black carrying strap. https://commons.wik

Table 21. Comparison of Costrels in Manuscripts.			
Manuscript	Date	Collection	Description
			imedia.org/wiki/File:L es_Tr%C3%A8s_Riche s_Heures_du_duc_de _Berry_octobre.jpg

Materials.

Leather: The best leather is vegetable tanned harness butt, which is hideously expensive. The second-best leather is thick veg tanned carving leather somewhere around 5-6 mm (14-15 oz.) thick. Unsealed is ideal if you can get it. I managed to get a second quality double shoulder on special for $99 (AUS) recently. You'll need around 3 sq. feet. You'll also need a couple of small scraps of 1.2-1.6 mm (3-4 oz.) to form the neck gasket and the stopper

Linen thread: I use a 16/2 wet spun linen thread, but any heavy linen thread will do. I've used 18/3 and 20/5 on other costrels.

Beeswax: Enough to coat the outside, for the sealer below, and some for waxing the thread. I bought 1kg (2.2lb) from the local beekeeper for about $20 (AUS) and refined it myself.
Sealer: You'll have to work out what is available near you and what you want to use from the available options. I blended equal amounts of beeswax and rosin. The rosin came from a calligraphy warehouse. You don't need to pay a premium for sporting or musical instrument grade rosin.

Dye: Optional. Look up vinegarroon recipes if you want to do black.

Wood: 70 x 20mm timber (2¾" x ¾"), at least 120mm (4¾") long; 150 x 20mm (6" x ¾"), about 220mm (8¾") long; 45 x 90mm (1¾ x 3½") timber, at least 200mm (8") long; 20mm (¾") dowel; 300 x 20mm (12" x ¾") board, at least 400mm (16") long.

Other materials: Nails; string; glue; push stick; card for templates.

Tools.

Photo 64. The tools.

General: Pencil and ruler; sandpaper; scissors; PPE
Rib jig: Chisel; gouge; mallet; optional router
Shoulder jig: Coping, turning or jigsaw; backsaw or rip saw; drill and some large drill bits; rasp or files
End jig: Coping saw or jigsaw; drill and some large drill bits
Moulding: Four bar clamps; dowel or broom handle
Decoration: Bone folder; styli; knife
Assembly: Knife; saddle needles or bristles; awl; beeswax block
Sealing and finishing; saucepan; paintbrush; ladle; funnel

Construction Instructions.

The end jig.

Material required: 70 x 20mm timber (2¾" x ¾"), at least 120mm (4¾") long; 150 x 20mm (6" x ¾"), about 220mm (8¾") long; two nails; non-stretch string about 250mm (10") long.

Tools required: Hammer; drill and bits; coping saw, turning saw or jigsaw; rasp; files; rule; pencil (optional gouges, abrasive paper).

Egan et al (1998) on p239 suggests an oval end for this costrel. It's the simplest jig to produce, so we'll go with it for this reconstruction. I have some misgivings and suspect from the way the decoration is laid out on the front, the ends are shaped more like a rounded triangle than oval. You can choose to make a rounded shape if you like. One advantage of the triangle end is a flatter bottom, and it can be put down without falling over. You'll need to keep the perimeter about the same as the oval version or adjust the size of the body piece to fit.

Inside part.

1. To make the internal part of the jig, use a piece of timber at least 120 mm (4¾") long and 70 mm (2¾") wide. 20 mm (¾") thick is ideal but thicker works too.
2. Mark the centre lines on both the long and short axis.
3. Bang a couple of nails into the long axis, 45 mm (1¾") either side of the centre point. They should end up 90 mm (3 ½") apart.
4. Take a piece of non-stretch string around 220 mm (11") long and tie the ends together so the perimeter of the loop is 200 mm ($7\frac{7}{8}$") long.
5. Drop the string over both nails and using a sharp pencil, pull the loop taut and draw the oval. There are plenty of

YouTube videos showing the process if you need to see it being done.
6. Cut along the line with an appropriate saw.

If you'd like to draw the shape in a CAD package instead, the major axis is 110 mm (4.33"), the minor axis is 63 mm (2.48") and the eccentricity is 0.818. You could print that shape and glue it to the timber.

Outside part.

1. To make the outside part, take a larger piece of timber. I'm using 150 mm (6") wide and about 220 mm (8¾") long in the photos.
2. Lay the inner form on top, and trace a line about 4 mm ($\frac{5}{32}$") outside it. You can do this by keeping the pencil vertical – see photo 65.
3. Drill, chop, or cut to the line. I've used a drill, then coping saw and finished with a #7 and a #8 sweep gouge.

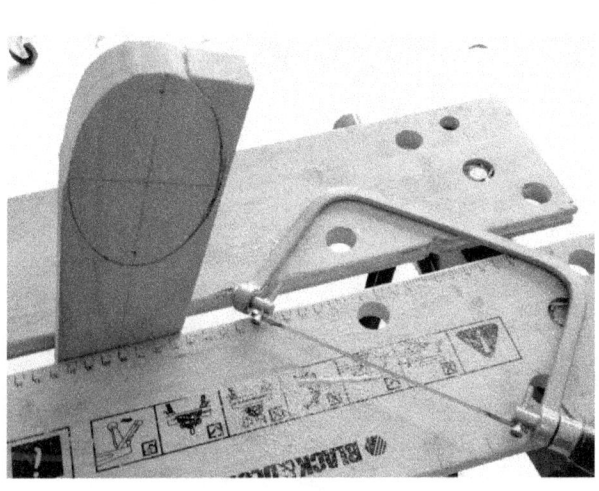

Photo 65. Remove everything that's outside. Clean up with rasp, files or sanding.

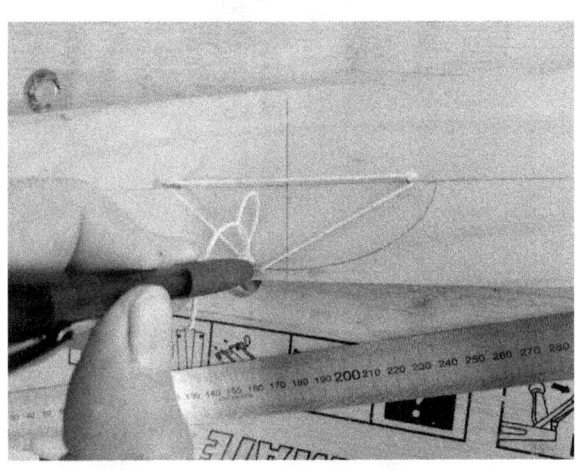

Photo 66. Mark the oval with two nails and a loop of string.

Photo 67. Mark the outside piece.

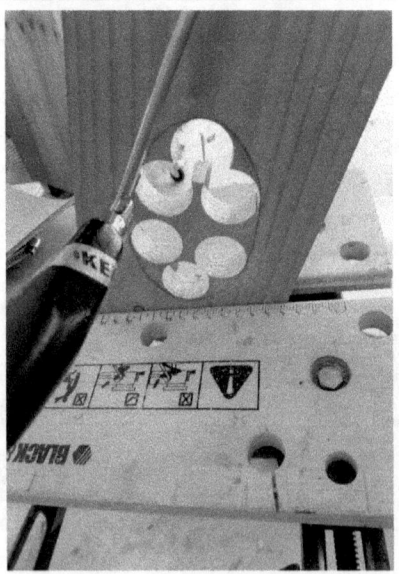
Photo 68. Saw close to the line.

The shoulder jig.

Material required: 45 x 90mm (1¾ x 3½") timber, at least 200mm (8") long; 20mm (¾") dowel.

Tools required: 25mm (1") drill bit and means of rotation; coping saw, turning saw or jigsaw; rasp; files (optional carving axe, abrasive paper).

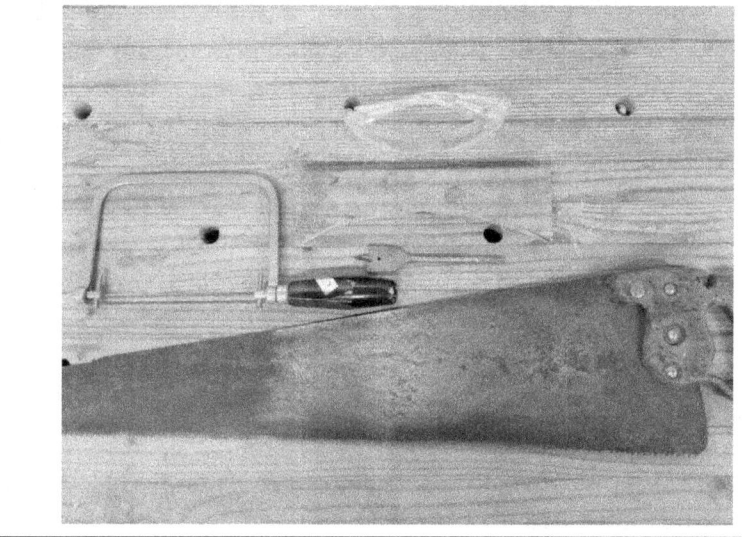

Photo 69. The tools required.

For shaping the shoulders and neck of the costrel you need another home-made jig. This will give a bottle neck internal diameter of about 18-20 mm (¾"). If you want a larger diameter neck than that, use thicker timber for the outer and inner pieces and go up a dowel diameter.

The Outside part.

1. Take a piece of 45 x 90 mm (1¾ x 3½") pine at least 200 mm (8") long.
2. Find the middle of the narrow side, mark the centre and also draw a line 100 mm (4") from the centre on one side so you have a mark to line up the leather.
3. At the centre of the narrow side, drill a hole 25 mm (1") in diameter to a depth of at least 50 mm (2").
4. On the wide side, mark and cut a curve that goes from 25 mm (1") up from the bottom corners to a point 63 mm (2½") up from the base in the middle and back down again. See Photo 68 for the shape you are chasing. Hang on to the waste piece, you'll need it for the part that goes inside the costrel.
5. Rip cut the piece down the middle so you have two equal sized pieces, centred on the hole.
6. Clean up the sawn surface, if required, so it doesn't leave marks on the leather.

The Inside part.

1. Take the lower part of the curve that you cut from the outside piece in step 3 above.
2. Using a rasp, file, or sander, completely round the top surface (see photo 68).

The Neck part.

1. Cut a 20 mm (¾") dowel about 100 mm (4") long.

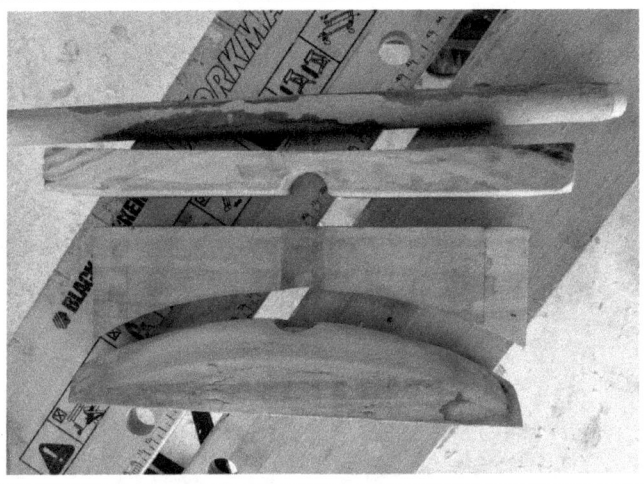

Photo 70. Here's one I prepared earlier. The pencil lines help align the pieces of leather.

Photo 71. Another angle, showing the depth of the hole in the inside piece.

The rib jig.

Material required: 300 x 20 mm (12" x ¾") board, at least 400 mm (16") long.

Tools required: Rule; pencil; knife; chisels; mallet (optional small gouge; router/routing plane).

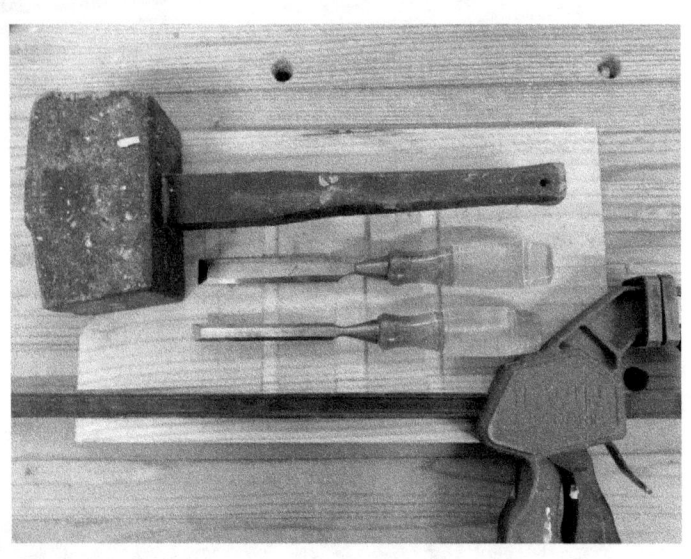

Photo 72. The tools required.

Making the jigs and raising the ribs will only add an afternoon to your project, and then you'll have the jigs to make more costrels in the future. Mine's made from a 300 mm (12") wide piece of pine, about 20 mm (¾") thick. I've carved three grooves, the outer two are 13 mm (½") wide and the inner is 25 mm (1") with a 31 mm (1¼") wide extension at the top. Offset the top edges of the outer ones to approximate the curve at the top of the costrel.

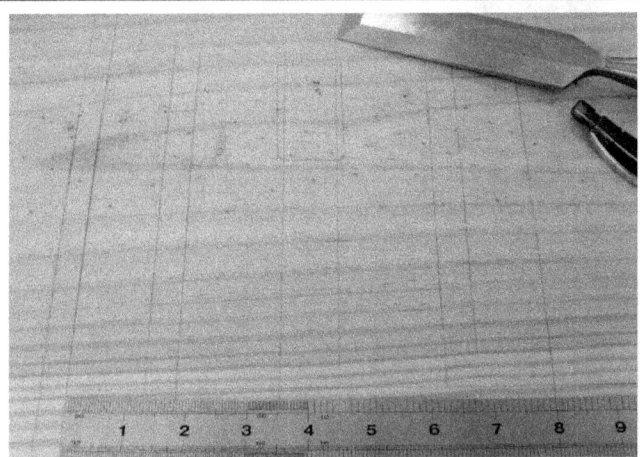

Photo 73. Jig for moulding ribs. All the trenches are outlined in pencil for this photo. I've also cut them with a marking knife.

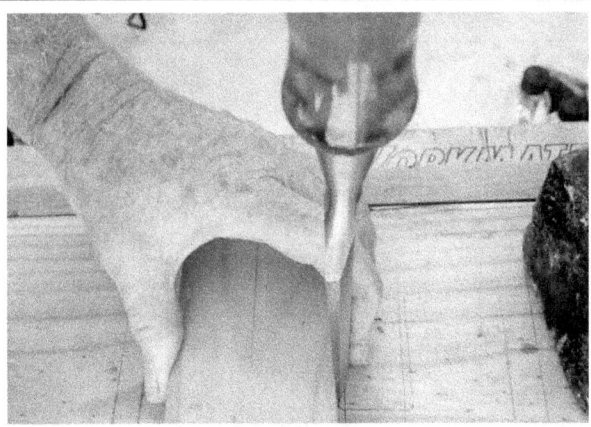

Photo 74. Defining the edges of the grooves with a broad chisel to keep a nice sharp edge and good definition when you're pressing the leather in. Holding a block of wood against the back of the chisel helps keep it vertical.

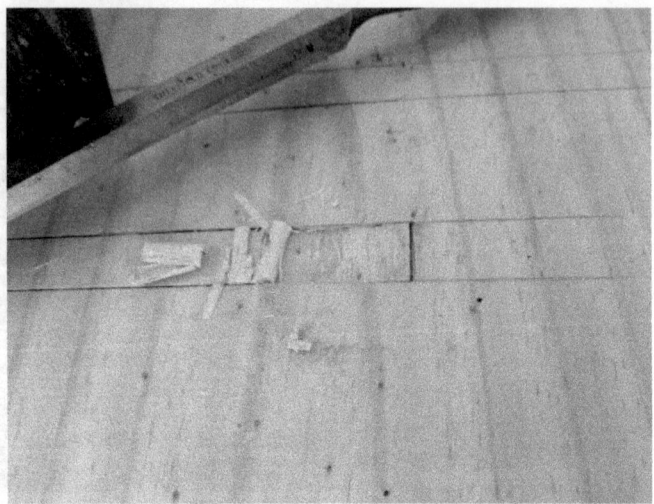

Photo 75. Trenching the grooves. The chisel is the same width as the groove, held with the bevel facing upwards. I'm tapping it with a mallet to get near the required depth.

Photo 76. A small router plane can help get it smooth, but you can get the same finish using a chisel with the bevel down and light hand pressure.

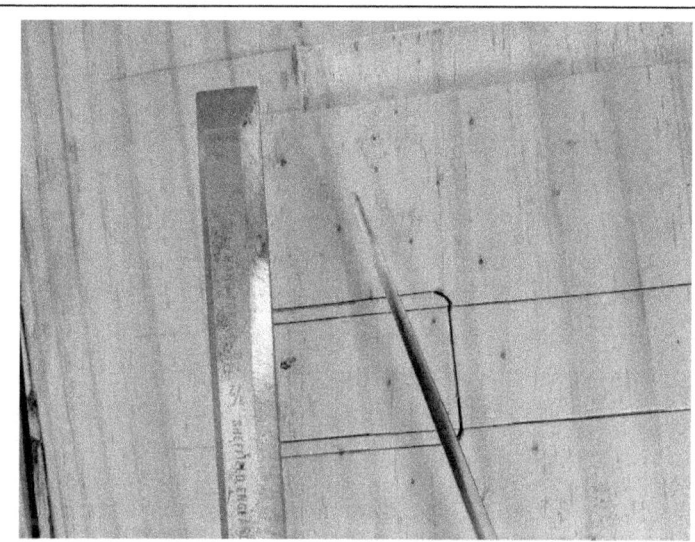

Photo 77. Easing the corners of the middle band with a 3 mm ($\frac{1}{8}$") number 5 sweep gouge. If you don't have access to a small gouge, you can just use a knife.

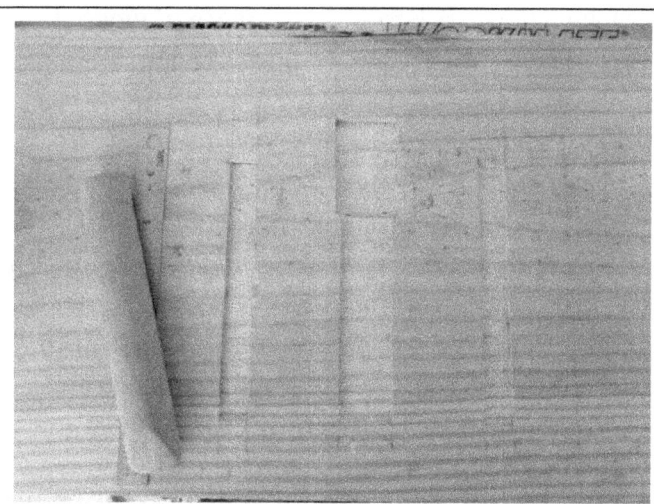

Photo 78. Finished rib moulding jig with push stick. The pencil lines show where to lay the edge of the leather.

1. Mark the long sides of the grooves in the wood with a knife or chisel.
2. With a chisel, cut the lines to a shallow depth of 3 mm (⅛"). The knife line should help guide the chisel.
3. Remove the waste with a chisel or router/router plane and ease the top end so that the corners are slightly curved. It may help to do the corners with a drill or gouge before removing all the waste at that end. I've used a #5/2 mm gouge in the photos.
4. Mark the outside of the wider, deeper part at the top of the middle band with a chisel and deepen it to 5 mm ($\frac{3}{16}$").
5. Draw a pencil line parallel to the ribs and 100 mm (4") from the centre line so you have something to line the leather up to.

Other tooling.

1. Make a push stick from a thin piece of wood. I've used a 20 x 9 mm (¾" x $\frac{3}{8}$") bit of silky oak and rounded one end slightly. It's used to push and stretch the leather into the grooves to form the ribs.
2. Make a shield and triangle pattern from light cardboard.[54] You may need to wait until you've finished the rib embossing on the leather to work out the size for your triangle.
3. Make a cardboard or paper template for the shoulder seams. Trace the curve from the shoulder jig outer piece and then trim it to match the cut edge of the leather on the original.
4. Make an embossing comb either from an old, broken wooden or plastic comb, or by cutting your own. It needs

---

[54] Don't use the good scissors... use the naughty scissors instead.

enough depth for you to hold comfortably, because there's a lot of comb work on this costrel. I used a 1.2 mm thick (18ga) piece of mild steel and cut some approximately evenly spaced notches along one edge with a sharp cold chisel and a hammer. I picked the best run of five and cut the others off with a hacksaw, then pointed them on the sides with a file. You can get the spacing from the life-size print of the MoL costrel photo.

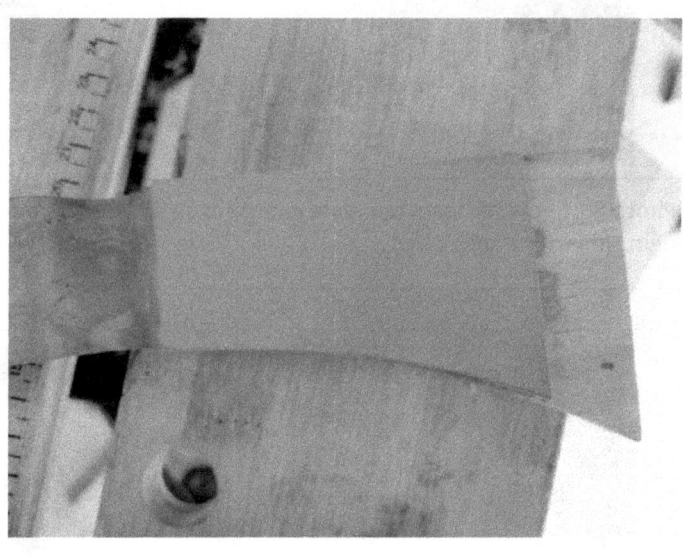

Photo 79. Making the shoulder seam templates from the shoulder jig. It goes from the edge of the neck to the pencil line you used for aligning the side of the leather.

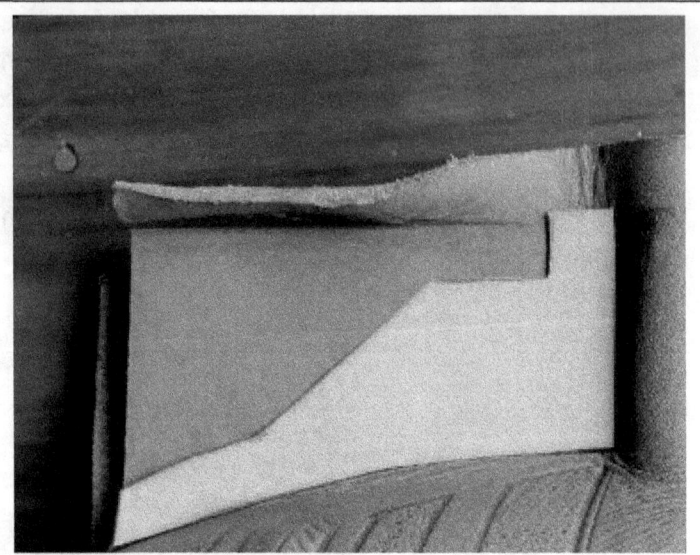

Photo 80. Shoulder seam template cut to shape and inscribed on the right side with a knife point.

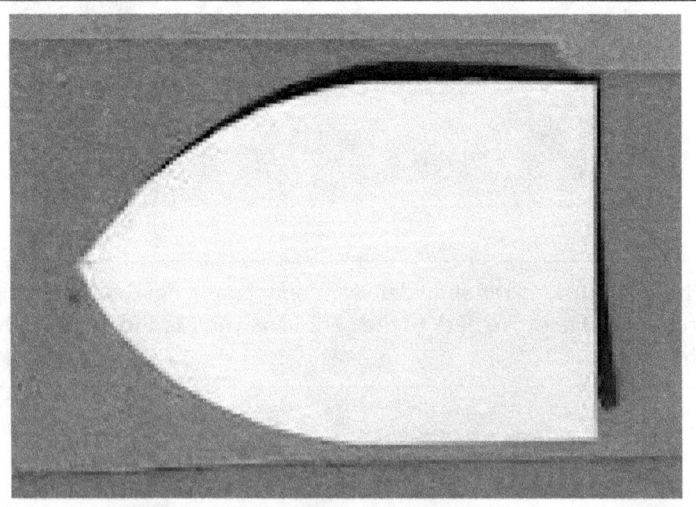

Photo 81. Shield template in card.

Photo 82. Triangle template in card.

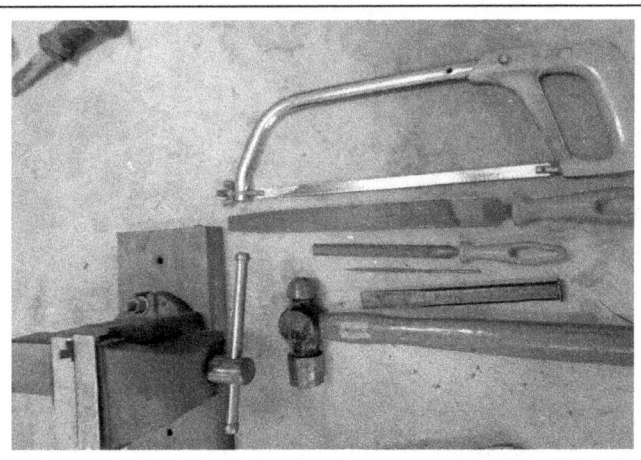

Photo 83. Tools used for making the embossing comb.

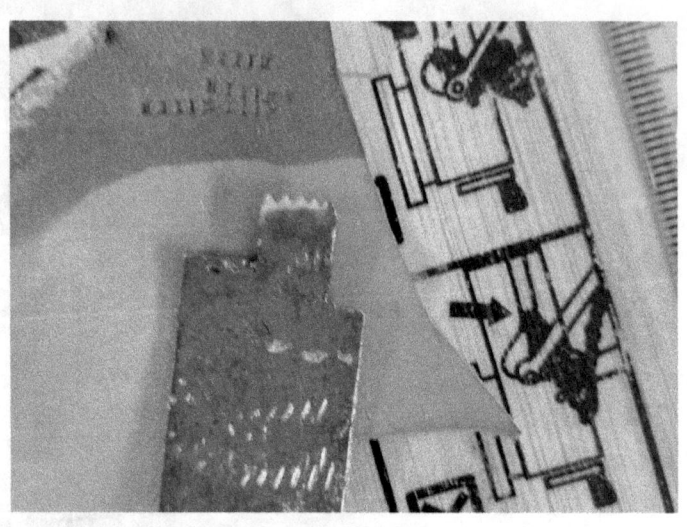

Photo 84. Finished comb and test impressions.

Total time for making jigs and tooling: 4-5 hours.

Making the Costrel Parts.

Two Ends.

Material required: 5.5-6.5mm (14-15oz) leather.
Tools required: End mould parts; knife; clamps; backing board; cut-proof gloves; bucket or basin of water (optional scissors, shears or snips).

1. Roughly cut two pieces of leather a good 20-25 mm (¾" - 1") larger than the inner part of the end mould.
2. Soak the leather for a few minutes in warm water until it is soft enough to take the impression of a fingernail with light pressure.

3. Place the leather, skin side up, on top of the outer piece of the end mould, making sure the overlap is approximately equal the whole way around the hole. Back the outer piece of the end mould with a piece of board or ply.
4. Feel the edges of the hole with your fingers through the leather. Try to place the inner part of the end mould as close to the centre as possible. If it's a little off, it won't matter because it will slip to the correct place as you apply pressure.
5. Tighten the clamps to compress the inner part and the leather into the outer.
6. Leave it to dry somewhere warm and in the shade for a couple of hours. Putting it in the sun will make it hard and brittle.
7. When the leather is just barely damp, remove the clamps and pop the leather out of the outer mould.
8. With the inner mould still in place as a support, cut the daggy outer bits away. It doesn't matter if this step isn't done perfectly, because you will be cleaning up with finishing cuts at the end of the assembly.
9. Remove the inner end mould piece, reshape any bits of leather that need it and put the leather aside to dry completely
10. Repeat for the other end.

Photo 85. Soaking the cut piece of leather.

Photo 86. Wet piece of leather between the outer and inner end mould. The skin side goes against the inner mould piece.

Photo 87. Clamping the end. The bench top behind it stops the inner part from being pushed too far in.

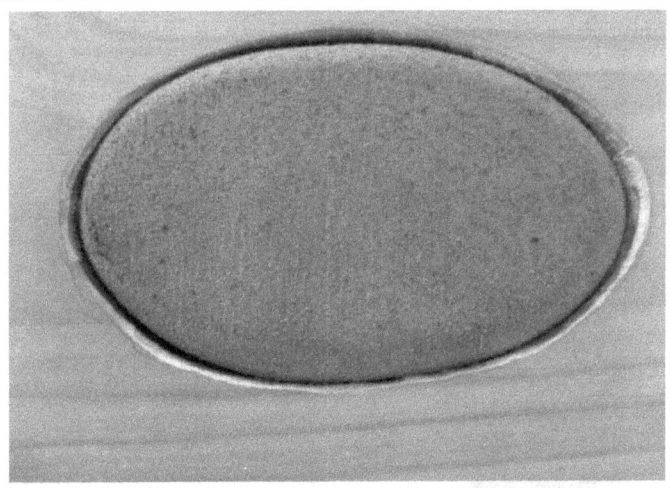

Photo 88. The moulded end with clamps removed, still in the outer mould.

Photo 89. Two moulded ends showing inside and outside. The inner part of the mould is still inside the right one.

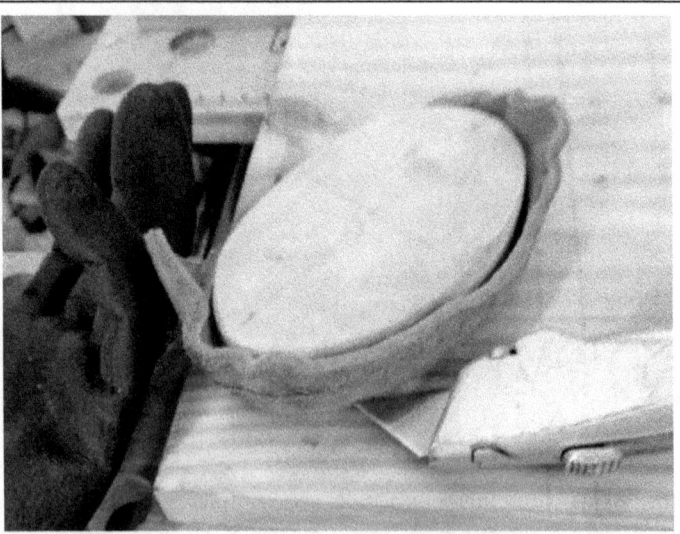

Photo 90. Cutting the end to the correct thickness. The inner part of the mould helps back the cut. Note the cut-resistant glove to the left.

Body, including raising ribs.

Material required: 5.5-6.5mm (14-15oz) leather.

Tools required: rib jig parts; sharp knife; straight edge; clamps; bucket or basin of water (optional bone folder; scissors, shears or snips).

1. Cut a piece of leather 200 x 420 mm (8" x 16½"). There will be plenty of scrap from the shoulders but this is used as welts when assembling.
2. Soak the leather for a few minutes in warm water, until it is soft enough to take the impression of a fingernail with light pressure.
3. Lay the leather skin side down against the rib mould, being careful to keep it square, and lightly clamp a board across the bottom to keep it in place. I like to use a taller board as a fence across the top.
4. Work the leather into each of the ribs using the calibrated stick you prepared earlier. Pay particular attention to the corners, and to making sure the leather doesn't move around while you're doing it.
5. When you're happy with the depth and evenness of the impression, release the clamps and turn the leather over. If the edges of the rib jig chipped while you were making the cuts, you'll have spots on the edge of the rib where they don't have a clearly defined crease at the edge. You can blend these in by pressing down with a fingernail.
6. Leave it to almost dry in the shade. It needs to be left until it looks dry, but still feels cool, before you move on to the embossing.

Photo 91. Soaking the cut piece of leather. The 25 mm (1") wide fence at the top sets the height, the clamps are lightly holding the wider caul on the rest of the leather. Don't clamp too tightly or you'll leave a line across the leather.

Photo 92. Working the leather down into the grooves. Due to the thickness of the leather, some fairly heavy pressure is needed to get a clear impression. You'll need to go over it a number of times.

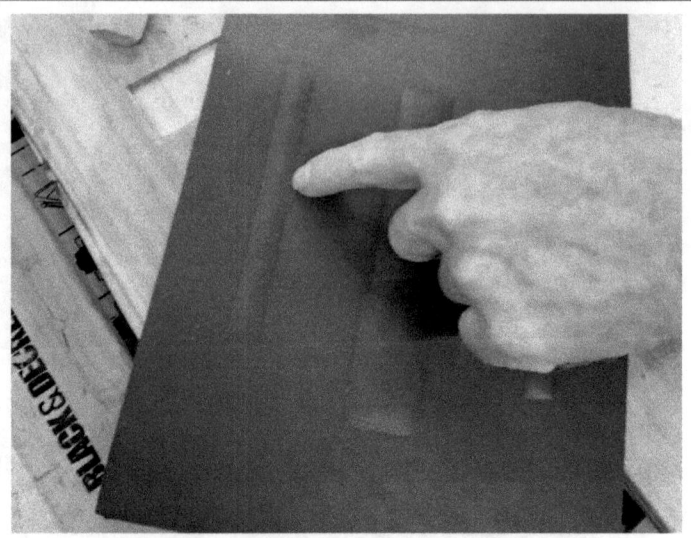

Photo 93. Pressing down a mark left from a chip in the rib jig.

Photo 94. The leather and I both needed to rest before moving on to the embossing.

Embossing.

Before you start embossing, jump on the MoL website at the linked address at the top of this chapter, grab a copy of the photo and print it out life size. It will help you make the layout decisions you didn't even know you would have to make.

Tools required: Shield template; triangle template; sharp knife; butter knife; straight edge; clamps; board at least 250mm (6") long; 5-point embossing comb; strips of 3mm (8oz) leather 10mm (⅜") and 20mm (¾") wide; steal the *'squirty'* bottle from the ironing board (optional bone folder; scissors, shears or snips).

1. Place the leather skin side facing up on the backing board. You'll need to apply moderate pressure so make sure the work surface is stable.
2. Start the embossing with the shields. They go with the tops just slightly above the point where the centre rib widens. Trace around it with your bone folder, paddle pop stick or back of the butter knife. Moderate pressure should leave a dark mark, if it doesn't, give the leather a light mist with water and wait a few minutes before trying again.
3. After the shields, do all the vertical lines on the flat areas using a straightedge and the bone folder. There are also horizontal lines across the bottom of the diagonally hatched fields that aren't shown in the official photo, but are in the Egan figure 187. See my photo if you can't get a copy of Egan.
4. With the bone folder, do the triangles. There are nine triangles on each end. Egan shows the bottom ones being halved but the drawing doesn't match the MoL photo.

5. Slide the thinner bits of leather between the ribs and backing board so the ribs are supported from behind, and do the vertical lines using the back of the butter knife and a straight edge, then do the diagonal hatching on the ribs – these radiate from the centre lines on each rib but generally don't quite meet the centre lines. I started from the outer edge and rolled the knife up onto the tip as I reached
6. With the embossing comb, fill the triangles nearest the ribs with dots in vertical rows. You can do just one or two dots in the points by angling the comb upwards. Next do the stippling in the alternate fields behind the shields. These all point from lower left to upper right on both sides of the costrel and are at a quite steep angle.
7. Finally, take a sharp knife and lightly cut the shields with one vertical line from the point upwards, and two diagonal lines. The right-hand shield gets an additional horizontal cut through the centre point, making the shield heraldically *'gyronny of eight'*.

It's thought that the heraldry was basically meaningless, just like on the contemporary knife scabbards or modern key rings.

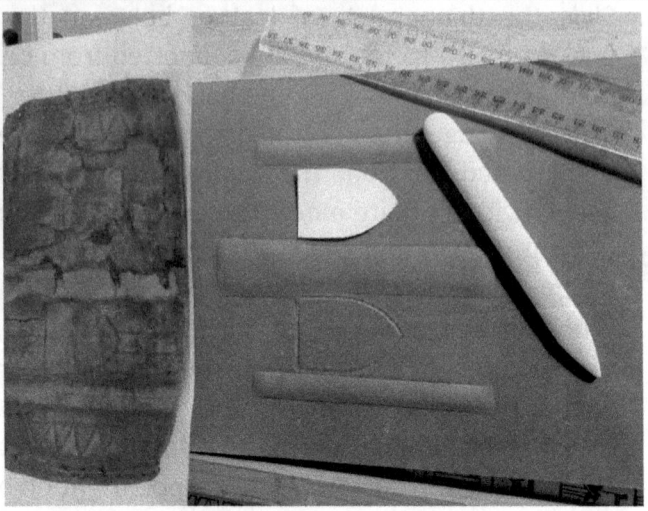

Photo 95. Embossing the shields with the point of the bone folder around the template. If you don't have access to a folder, a stylus or rounded pointed stick will do.

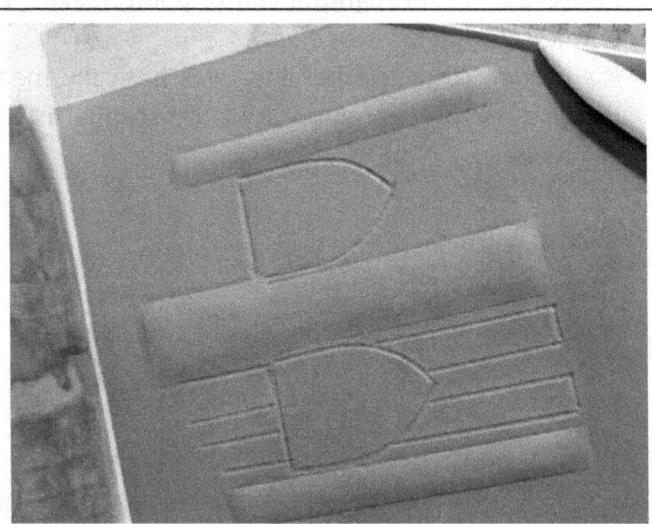

Photo 96. Both shields are done and starting the vertical lines. Keep referring to the MoL image for accurate placement.

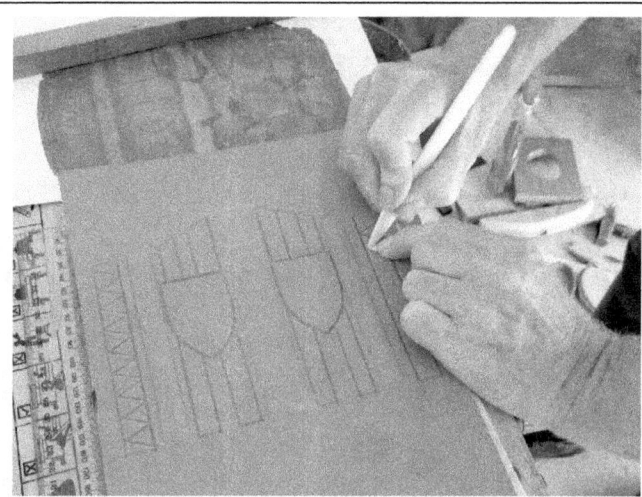

Photo 97. Embossing the triangles in the same way as the shields using the triangle template. I'm following Egan with the half-triangle at the bottom.

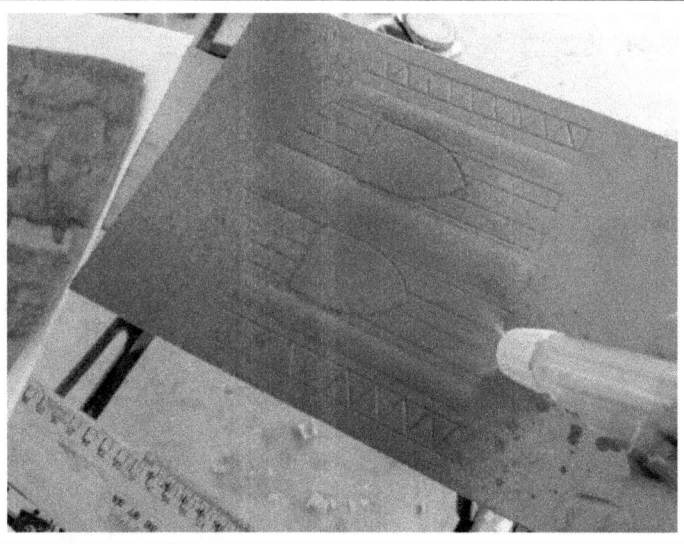

Photo 98. The leather was starting to dry out, so I added some more water and let it sit for 10 minutes.

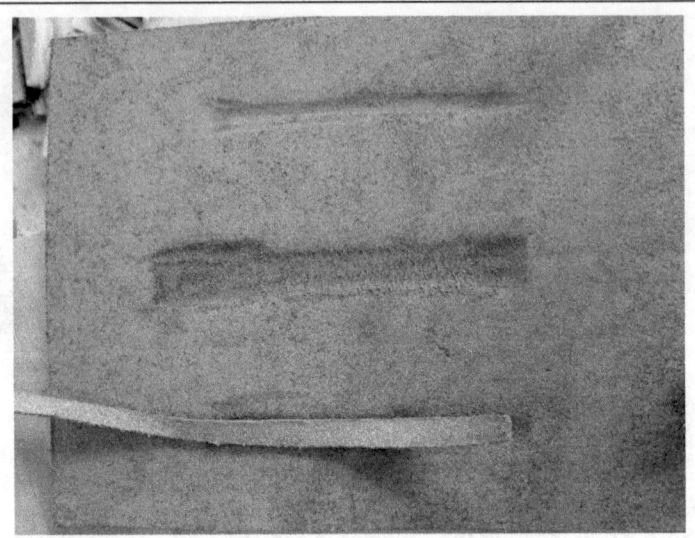

Photo 99. Backing the ribs with a temporary strip of leather for support during embossing.

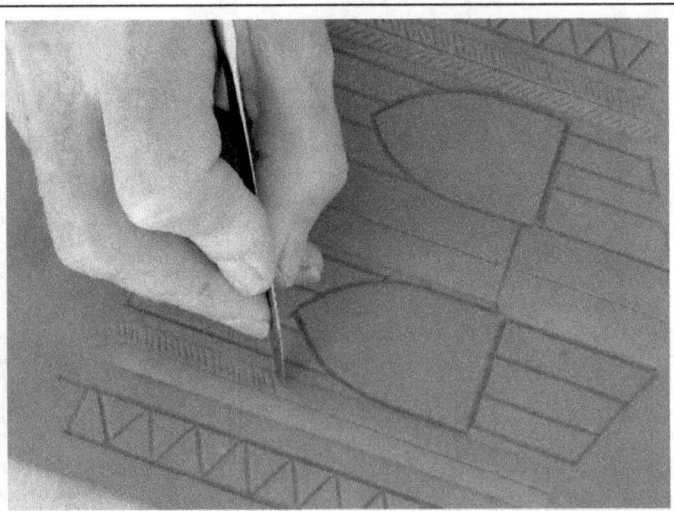

Photo 100. Embossing the diagonal hatching/feathering on the ribs with the back of a butter knife.

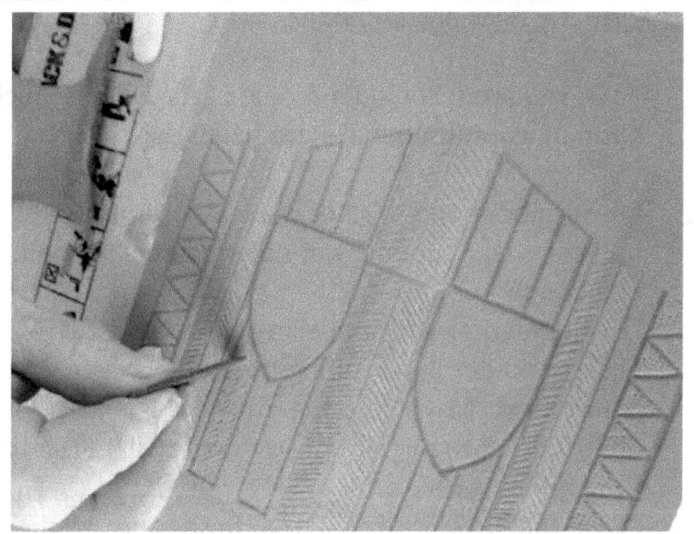

Photo 101. Embossing the inner triangles and the flat fields with the embossing comb.

Photo 102. Embossing complete and the knife cuts made on the shields.

Form the neck and shoulders.

Tools required: Shoulder mould parts; clamps; bucket or basin of water (optional extra hands)

1. Re-wet about one third of the leather in from the top and bottom. Make sure it's wet down to at least the top of the embossing.
2. Lay the leather with the skin side against one half of the outer shoulder jig, ensuring the edge is aligned with your pencil mark. Make sure the embossing is just clear of the underside of the jig. It doesn't matter if a little hangs out the top.
3. Place the dowel against the flesh side of the leather, aligning it with the neck groove in the outer jig piece. Give it a good push down with both thumbs to get it to sit comfortably.
4. Bring the other end of the leather up and align it with both the leather and the top of the jig. Put the other half of the outer jig in place, aligned on the neck and top edge of the other half and clamp either side of the neck. This step is easier with a friend.
5. Pass the inner shoulder jig through the opening in the costrel, align the hole in it with the end of the dowel and clamp from either end, while ensuring the whole thing remains square to the outer halves of the jig.
6. Allow to dry overnight and then remove the clamps.

I've made at least a dozen costrels with my jig and cracked it last time I used it so I've fixed it with the 3 mm mending plate you can see in the photos. Yours won't need it (probably...)

Photo 103. Wet leather being offered up to the shoulder jig. I'm aligning the edge at the top of the photo with the pencil line on the jig.

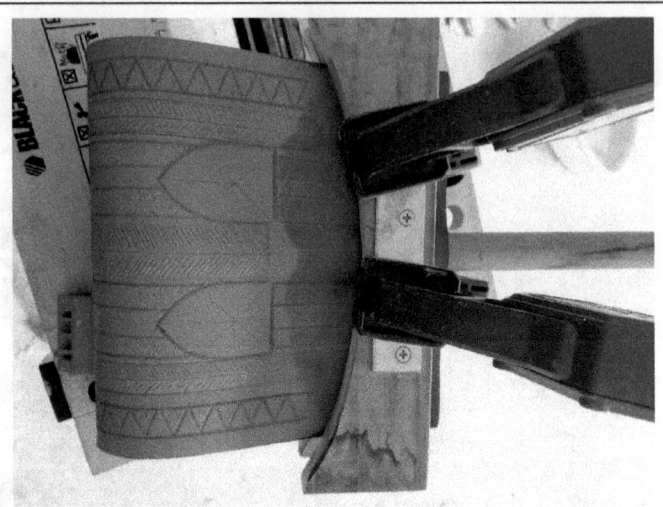

Photo 104. The dowel for shaping the neck is laid on top of the first layer, the other end of the leather is then bought up and lined up with the edges of the first end, the other part of the shoulder jig put on top and then lightly clamped.

Photo 105. Make sure the top edges of the leather and jig pieces align and tighten.

Photo 106. Slide the inner part of the jig to shape the shoulders and clamp.

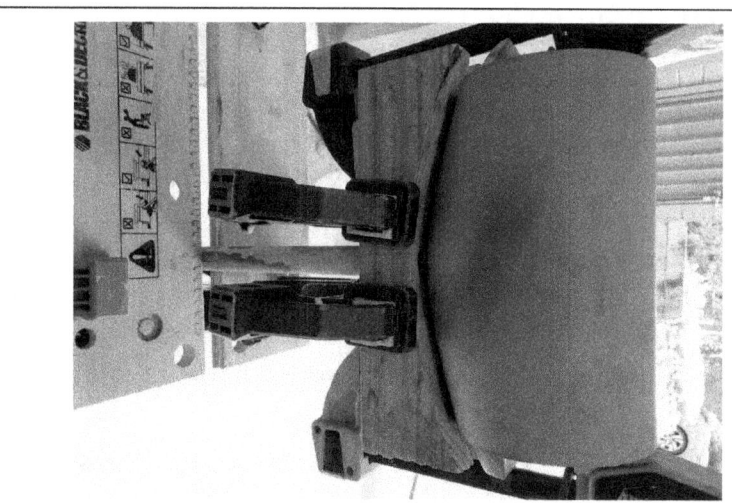

Photo 107. Back view with all clamps applied.

Photo 108. Next morning with the jig removed.

Cut the neck/shoulder gasket pieces.

An additional layer between the front and back of the costrel, they move the two surfaces slightly apart and make it much easier to seal. These weren't found with this particular costrel, but do turn up in every extant complete example. We don't even have the ends in this case, so there's no telling what is missing. Cut two pieces matching the flat areas of the body.

Total time for making costrel part: 4 hours excluding drying time.

Assembly.

Shoulder gaskets.

These gaskets are the one spot where an argument could be made for using glue (if anyone challenges me, I'll deny I said it). The other alternative is trying to control six different layers of leather while you stitch them together. For the first time ever, I'm using glue on a costrel. I'll use hide glue because it's basically liquid leather, the overspill can be cleaned off with warm water and a toothbrush and it doesn't resist dye, but you could use anything from rabbit size to PVA. I'd avoid anything that's not flexible when dry. Clamp it to ensure there are no gaps.

Photo 109. Shoulder gasket pieces. These are slightly wider than the templates you made for the shoulder seams.

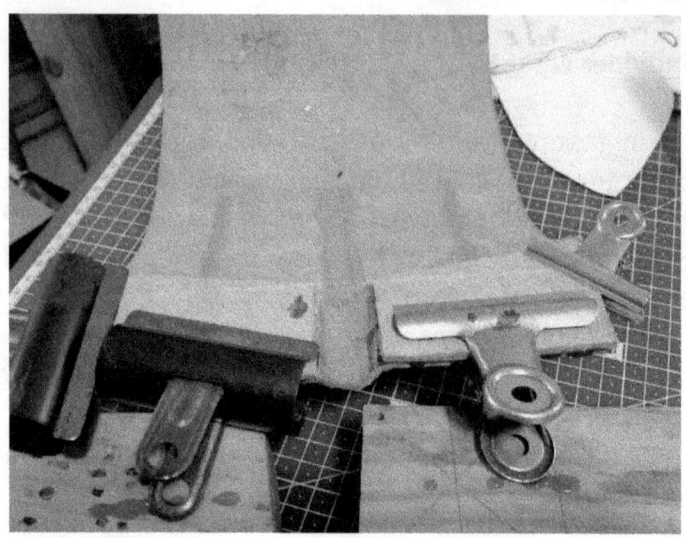

Photo 110. Gluing and clamping. I'm only doing one side because I'm not confident about lining the other side up accurately enough if it moves around a little when clamping.

Stitching.

Materials required: Pieces you prepared earlier; two strips of 3mm (8oz) leather for the end welts; small piece of 1.2-1.6mm (3-4oz) leather for the stopper gasket; pitch/beeswax/other for sealing; beeswax for stitching; heavy thread for sewing (18/6 or heavier waxed linen or hemp is ideal); dye, if you plan to use it (optional: coad[55] or rosin/wax mix).

Tools required: Awl; harness needles or boar bristles (optional: needle nose pliers; stitch spacer).

---

[55] Shoemaker's hand wax: to make your own, see Company of the Staple (2018) in the Bibliography.

PPE: hand leathers, finger tape or prophylactic Band-Aids. You'll know where to put the band-aid by about the fifth or sixth stitch.

Look at the photo of the original again. The holes are a long way apart; the fewer holes you have in the seam, the easier it is to seal. The holes are huge because the awl was pushed through 20-odd mm of leather (¾") and it takes a lot of effort.

Sharpen your awl and polish the blade, I use wax on mine to help it go through thick leather. Back each spot with a piece of rubbish softwood as you push the awl through, because if it hits your thumb, it's going to go a long way in and will take a couple of days for the bleeding to stop.

1. Start at the top of the neck, come down about 1.6 mm ($\frac{1}{16}$") and make your first awl hole. Make sure the holes stay aligned (I'll often pin the layers together with a harness needle), come down your stitch length and make the next hole. I'm using a bit of $\frac{5}{16}$" arrow shaft in the photos, but it doesn't matter if you do the spacing just by eye.
2. Once all the holes are done for the inner seam, it's time to stitch. Take a piece of thread three times the length of the seam, plus a bit. Thread your needles (I'll assume that you know what you're doing if you have boar bristles), wax or coad the thread and dampen the leather along the seam so the thread will sink into the surface when it's tight. Start a saddle stitch from the first hole near the mouth and sew to the end, tying an overhand knot in each hole as you go. There are some good tutorials on YouTube for how to do that.
3. Backstitch the last stitch and a half, leaving the needles inside the costrel. If you've used wax, tie the ends on the

inside and trim the ends, for coad, just cut the ends. Lay the loose ends along the seam so they get buried under the sealer.

4. Repeat the process for the second line of stitching, this time doing the spacing between the rows and the stitches by eye. Note how the original ones often don't line up after turning the corner onto the shoulder.

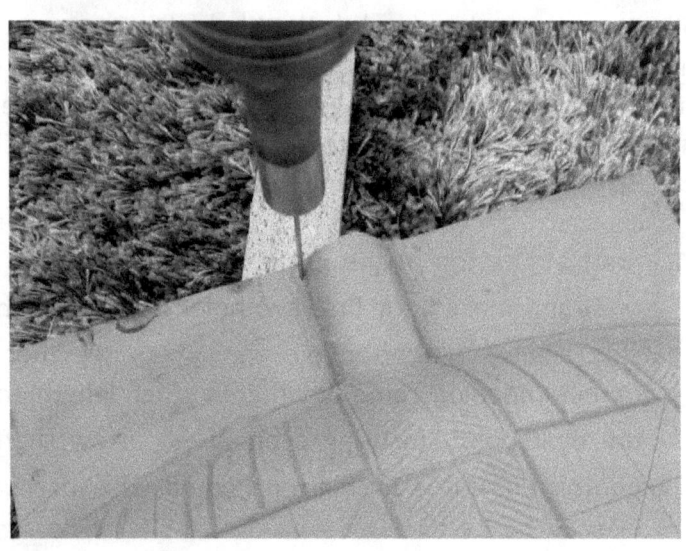

Photo 111. Start the awl from the side of the neck.

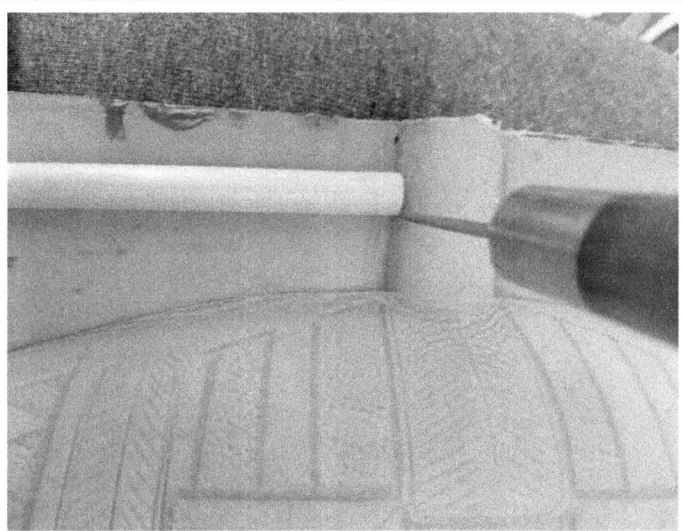

Photo 112. Using a piece of wood to space the stitches. In this case, it's a bit of an arrow.

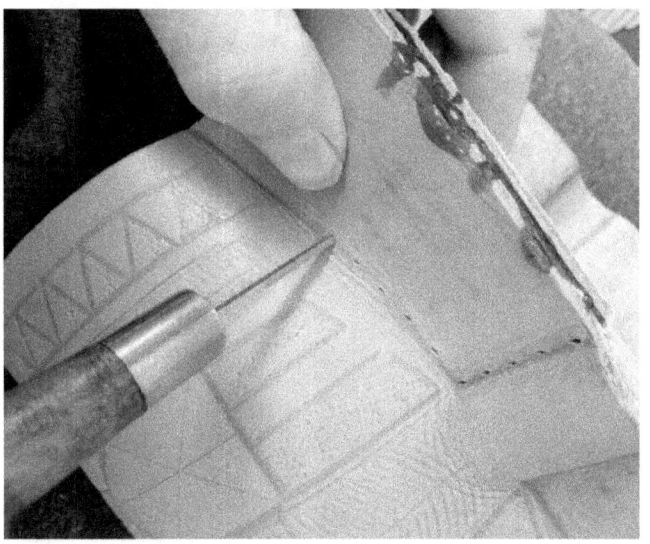

Photo 113. Continue making holes along the seam.

Photo 114. Start stitching from the neck. The leather is damp to help bury the stitches.

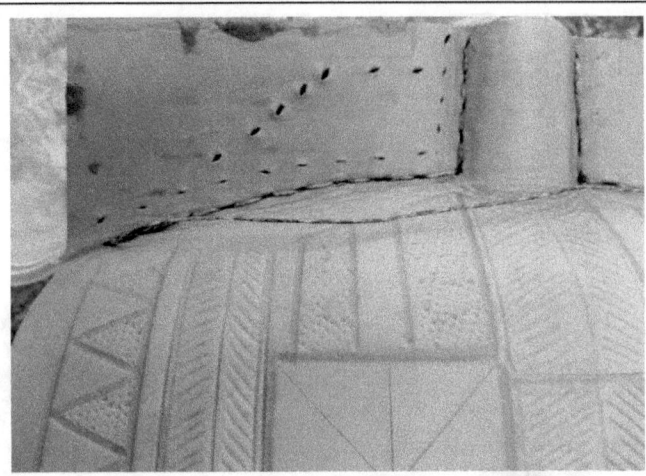

Photo 115. When you get to the end of the row, leave the ends long.

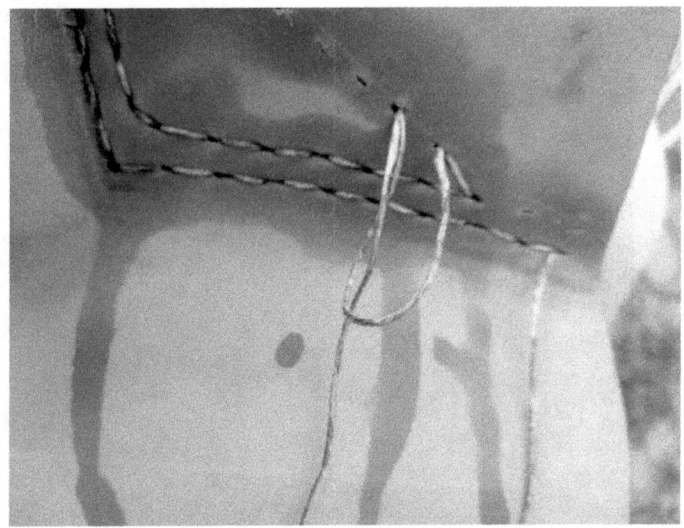

Photo 116. Outer seam with a new piece of thread. Don't worry about those last couple of holes, you can bring the end of the inner seam up and use it to finish.

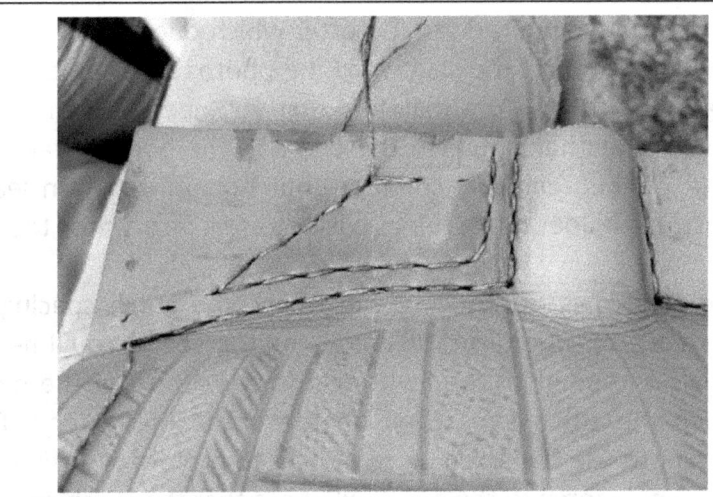

Photo 117. Stitch up to the neck. I've left myself short so I back stitched and started a new thread.

Photo 118. Finished side seam, now do the other.

Sew in the ends.

Push in one end. It doesn't matter which one, but I usually do the left end first (he said, with the photos showing doing the right end first...). You may find that you need an extra gasket layer of leather between the end and the body to take up a gap. This is relatively common, but not universal on leather costrels. It does make things easier to seal afterwards too.

Do two rows of stitching with the same stitch spacing and distance between rows as along the top seam. You'll need to angle the point of the awl towards the centre of the oval to keep the stitch sizes even on the inside of the end. Don't forget to use the scrap piece of pine to protect your fingers as you apply force to the awl. You'll note that the stitching on the original mostly aligns with the embossed decoration, but doesn't always quite line up.

Tie an overhand knot in each stitch as you push the needles through, and a double at the end of the thread, then back stitch one or two stitches. Pull the thread tight before you cut and align the cut ends with the main stitching. The wax will hold them in place.

Photo 119. The right end and gasket piece pressed into place.

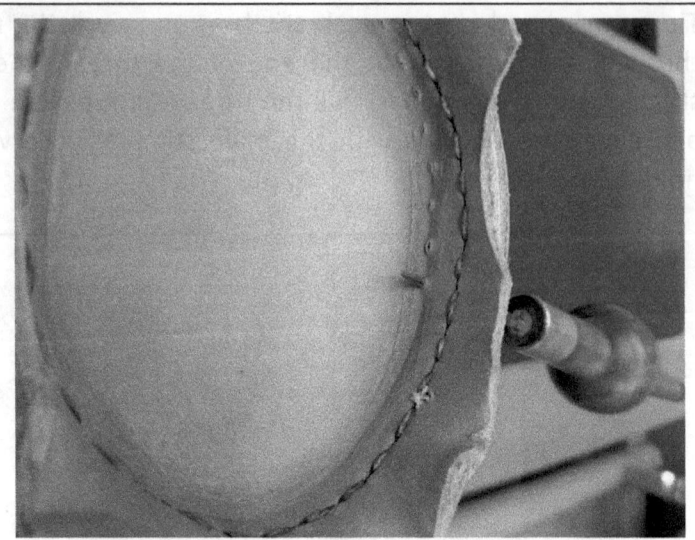

Photo 120. You have to watch the stitching on both the inside and outside.

Photo 121. I'm matching the spacing on both rows of stitching.

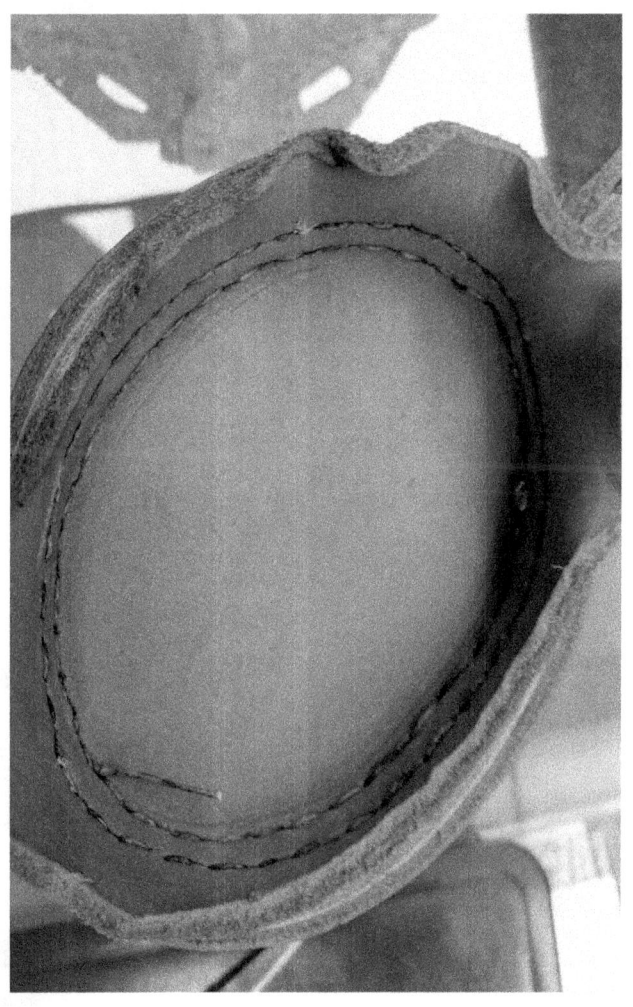

Photo 122. Stitching complete. Repeat on the other end.

Photo 123. It's obvious what needs to be trimmed. Cut it off with a sharp knife, backing the cut with a small block of wood. Use the cut-resistant gloves.

Photo 124. I had a small gap in the corner from cutting the gasket piece just too short. A wedge gets glued into place. The sealer will hold it in place.

Once finished, you need to trim the excess leather with a freshly sharpened knife (or new blade) and may need to dampen and remould the neck if it ends up flattened like mine.

Cut the carrying slots with a 19 mm (¾") and a 6 mm (¼") wood chisel, keeping the bevel of the chisel to the inside of the slot.

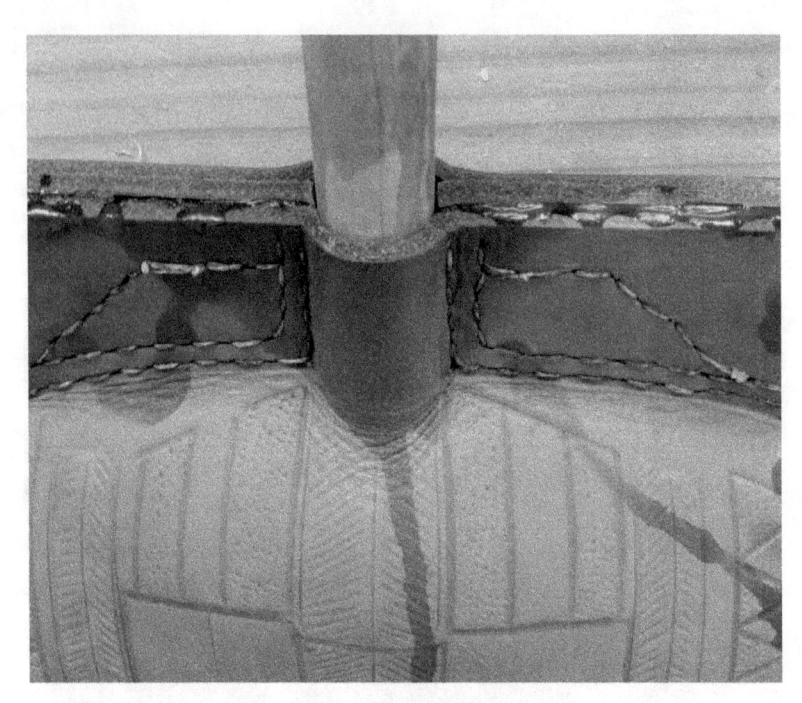

Photo 125. Re-shaping the neck.

Photo 126. Shoulders have been cut and holes being made with chisels.

Dye.

You've been using water to mould your costrel. It's going to be severely watermarked at this stage. You can choose to dye it to hide the stains, or soak it in water one last time and leave it upside down in a cool and shady place to dry and even out the watermarks. For a jolly jape, when the costrel is soaked, empty it, lift it to your mouth and try blowing into it. This way you can be in a position of some authority when mocking academics who have claimed that blow-moulding like a balloon or whoopie-cushion isn't only possible, but a likely manufacturing method.[56]

---

[56] Gardiner et al, (2005) *Before the mast*, p 454.

If the leather ends up with black marks from the iron in your tools or metal filings in your workshop, they can be cleaned off by wiping with lemon juice on a cloth.

Blacks are documented, browns known from manuscript illuminations, other colours may be possible, or you can just leave it undyed. If you intend to use one of the bitumen-based water tank sealers, do yourself a favour and dye the costrel black. The pigment from the sealer will seep through the leather and leave it spotty black whether you want it to be black or not.

Seal.

I could write a dissertation on the different sealers. As a matter of fact, I already have.[57] I'll leave reading it and picking a suitable sealer as an exercise for the reader. I'm using a 50/50 rosin/beeswax blend.

Tools required: Disposable brush (the local chain hardware has packets of two test-pot brushes for around A$3); disposable funnel (I use a 600 ml (1 pint/16 fl. oz.) soft drink bottle and just cut the top part off); disposable ladle from the Op shop; sharp knife; ventilation; PPE; (optional: heat source like a gas ring; hot air gun; wood chisels - 13mm (½") and 6mm (¼")).

Materials required: Sealer of your choice; beeswax for the outside; leather dye; aluminium foil.

---

[57] Robinson, W. (2011). *When good pitches turn bad…*. Retrieved 9 October 2021, from https://leatherworkingreverend.wordpress.com/2011/04/03/when-good-pitches-turn-bad/

> **Safety tip:** Molten pitch burns deeply, and sticks to the burn. If you do manage to burn yourself, flood the burn with plenty of cold running water for at least 5 minutes to cool both the burn and the pitch. The cooled pitch may peel away from the burn, but if it doesn't, don't pull it. Cover the burn and seek medical assistance.

Depending on your sealer, you may need to heat it up or melt it. If you're using a liquid brushable sealer or food safe epoxy, follow the instructions on the tin and re-join us in the next paragraph. Apply just enough heat to melt the sealer, but not so much that it expands with the heat or boils or starts smoking. With brewer's pitch or pitch blended with wax, I look for a viscosity similar to a good summer weight motor oil. Flames coming from the sealer is God's way of telling you're doing something seriously wrong.

Wrap the entire costrel in the aluminium foil, and poke a hole into the costrel's mouth. This keeps the sealer from going all over the outside.

Prepare your Sealer of Choice™ as before and jam the funnel in the costrel's mouth. Ladle a good amount of sealer into the costrel (I use about a cup of sealer for each litre of the costrel's volume) and then try to roll it around so you cover all the leather on the inside with sealer, taking care to not also give yourself a molten pitch beauty treatment. Briefly put the costrel on the work surface with one end facing down – 15 seconds should be enough. Pour the sealer back into the pot and then hold the costrel upright. Wait a couple of minutes for the pot to return to heat and the costrel to soak up the sealer. Repeat the sideways exercise with the other end. Repeat twice more, and then leave it to set for a couple of hours. If you're using a liquid sealer, leave it for at least the length of time indicated on the container.

Photo 127. Propped up on spare wood so it doesn't roll.

Photo 128. Foil cover to keep the sealer away from the outside of the leather.

Testing.

You can test the sealing at this point. Fill the costrel with water, and leave it standing overnight in a container with a larger volume than the costrel. If it leaks, let it dry and do another coat or two with the sealer. Using multiple thin coats is better than one thick coat.

Neck gasket.

The neck gasket's purpose is to cover the raw edges on the side of the neck and create a smoother surface for the stopper, and to provide a better seal. It's present on almost all extant stoppers.

1. Take a piece of 1.2-1.6 mm (3-4 oz.) leather, skive (shave a bevel of thickness away so the leather will sit flatter on seams) the upper edge and one side and press it into position in the neck.
2. This is one of those situations where stitching with boar bristles is easier than with needles, as the thread has to be saddle or running stitched into a really tight space. If you are using needles, slope the awl so the point nearly comes out the top of the costrel neck. Aim for 5-6 mm per stitch (4-6 stitches per inch). A piece of 6 mm (¼") dowel can help hold the leather in place while you push with the awl.
3. Saddle stitch in place.
4. Trim the top edge flush with the neck of the bottle. I get best results by starting from the inside and pulling the knife back towards the bottle neck.

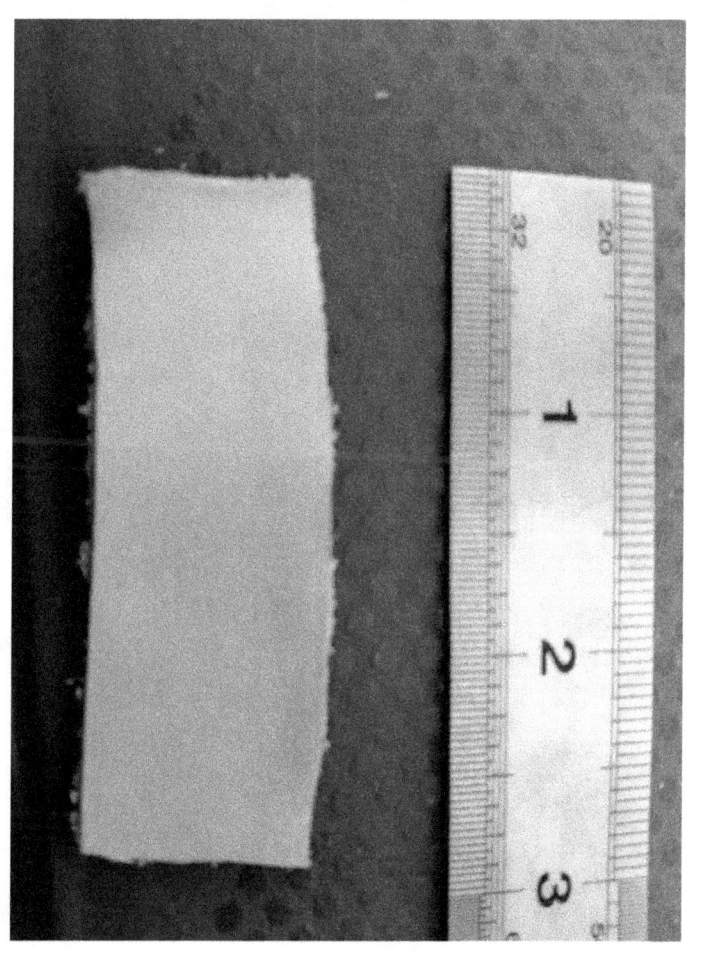

Photo 129. Gasket piece with one long edge and one short skived.

Photo 130. Neck gasket starting, the overlap is on the back.

Photo 131. Neck gasket stitching in progress.

Photo 132. Completed and trimmed neck gasket.

Finishing.

Gently melt some beeswax and with a disposable brush, baste the outside of the costrel. You're looking for it all to soak into the leather, without leaving a layer of wax on top. Gentle use of a heat gun or hair dryer and a wipe with a rag can help. To finish, use a beeswax furniture polish to get a good soft shine.

To get rid of the taste of the pitch, leave the costrel filled overnight with the cheapest, nastiest wine you can find. Next morning, depending on your ethics, pour it down the drain or rebottle it and give it to your friends as home-made retsina. You may need to repeat a couple of times, I'd just make sure you give the second lot of retsina to different friends.

Photo 133. Painting molten wax on the ends. Keep adding wax to the seams until they won't take up any more.

Photo 134. The heat gun treatment. Gently apply heat while the leather absorbs the wax. Take care not to burn the leather or melt the lining.

Make a Stopper.

Using corks in leather bottles isn't really the way to go. It seems cork stoppers weren't imported into England in large enough numbers to leave a record until the end of the first quarter of the seventeenth century and then were still prohibitively expensive until nearly the end of that century. (Rogers, 1866. pp. 608-9). All the extant stoppers are tapered wood, some of the Mary Rose stoppers have an additional layer of leather to assist with sealing.

Material required: Stick, dowel or wood offcut, at least 20mm (¾") wide and 50-75mm (2-3") long; 1.5-2mm (2-3 oz.) leather 30mm (1 ¼") wide and at least 65mm (2 ¾") long; thread; wax; cut nail or tack; hanging cord (optional: cut tack).

Tools required: pencil; knife; chisels; awl; saddle needles; drill to match the cord (optional: files; bone folder).

I'm using a bit of field maple branch from one of my trees in the backyard in the photos below. This is the same timber as a London example published in Egan (1998), and is used for its ultra-fine grain and corresponding dimensional stability when it gets wet. The shape is taken from one of the Mary Rose examples.

1. Take a branch, stick or offcut of an appropriate timber and remove the bits that don't look like a stopper with any of cutting, filing, grinding, whittling or other application of brute force until it fits the neck of the costrel. If you aren't going to fit the leather sleeve, congratulations, you have finished.
2. Bore the top of the stopper to take a cord.

3. If you are fitting the sleeve, you need to further reduce the diameter of the stopper by the thickness of the leather. How you do it depends on the style you're doing. Some, like the one I'm doing, have a shoulder to help stop the leather slipping up when it's being jammed in the bottle. Others have the leather sitting proud of the wood. I usually reduce the diameter of the wood with files and finish the shoulder with a knife.
4. Wrap the leather tightly around the wooden core and then slice through both layers with a single knife cut. This leaves a piece of leather that is an exact fit for the core. You may find you need to stretch the upper side of the rectangle of leather to get it to fit the taper, the extant originals are fairly rough fitting at the top and bottom.
5. Sew using edge – flesh stitches and tie off with overhand knots in each hole. Once finished, dampen the seam and rub it flat with your preferred slicker.
6. Pin with a cut tack near the top of the leather.
7. Thread the cord through the hole and tie to the suspension slot on the costrel.

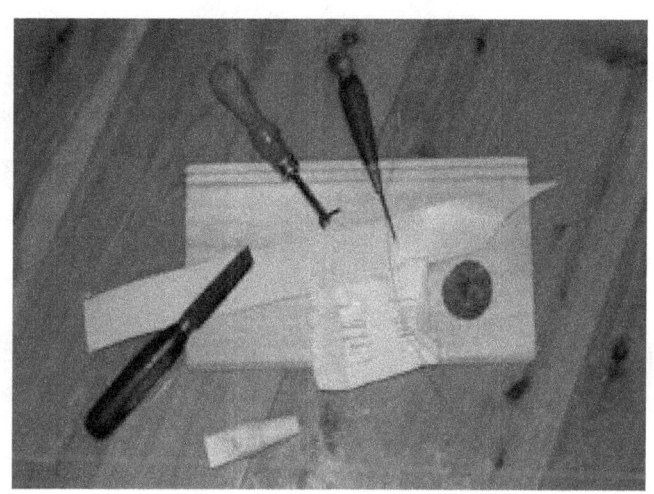

Photo 135. All the tools you need to do this job.

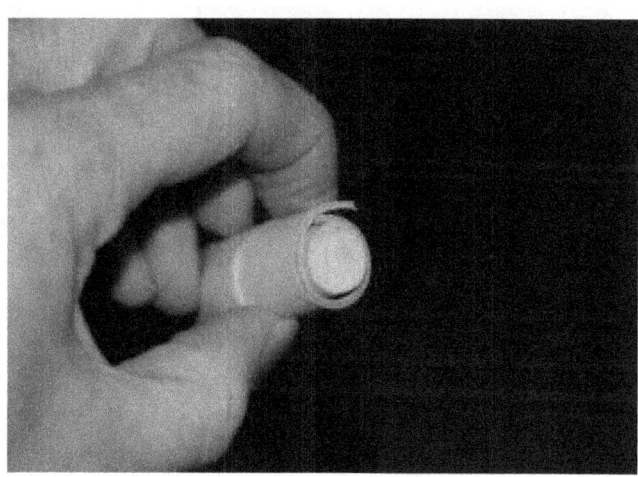

Photo 136. Fit the leather tightly to the stopper and cut the ends flush.

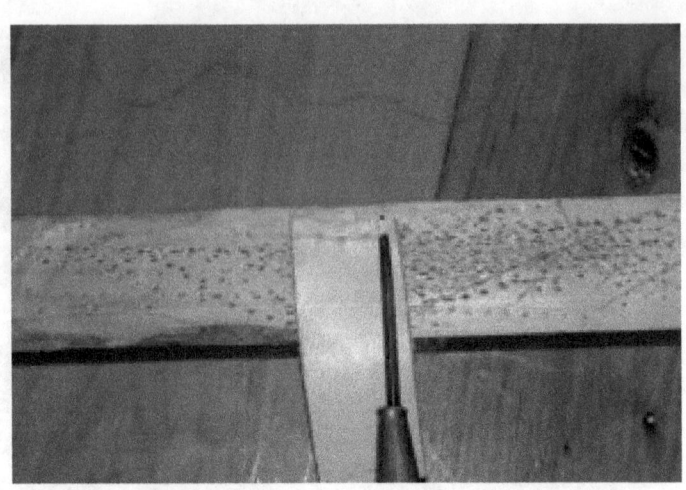

Photo 137. Use an edge-flesh seam.

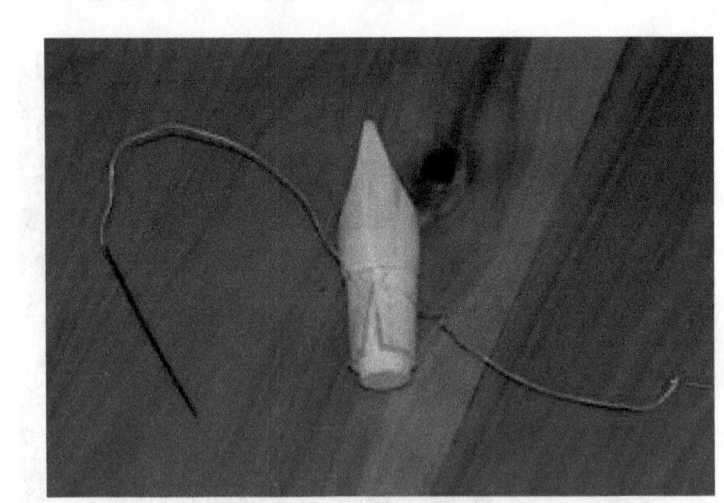

Photo 138. Stitch the seam and tie off.

I've found that often the first time you fit a stopper to your bottle, one or other of the lower corners of the seam turns back on itself – as can be seen in the photo above. I don't worry too much as it can also be seen on some of the extant originals. If it is a problem for you, use a little food-safe glue to hold the leather down before stitching.

Total time for making the stopper: 40 minutes.

Postscript.

A yet to be published leather costrel was found in 2018 at a dig in India Buildings, Cowgate, Edinburgh. The context was two metres (six feet) deep in a small, crudely made stone lined well. The decoration consists of two shields between three wide bands, with outlining and a comb-stamped background. I'm beginning to suspect that this is the medieval equivalent of us having a Nike tick or Coke dynamic ribbon on our drink bottles. A thin leather strip appears to be evidence of a wooden stopper with a gasket. I'm rather smugly pleased that the ends are extant and rounded triangles in shape. Holes for the carrying strap are flat, which makes a contemporary date likely with the MoL example.

Photos are on the AOC Archaeology website (2019, May 17), *News from Current Work at India Buildings, Edinburgh : Exploring Medieval Burgage Plots.*
 https://www.aocarchaeology.com/news/article/india-buildings

The Heater (Shield).

By Andrew Fraser and Stephen Wyley.

The Heater Shield.	**When:** 14th century CE
Material: Wood, canvas, leather and wool (padding)	

Introduction.

A shield was used by infantry and cavalry as a protective device in combat and they ranged in size from the large rectangular *'scutum'* of the Romans to the small round *'targe'* of the late 16th Highland Scots. A shield known as a *'heater'* was a type of shield with a flat top and sides that curve down to a point at the bottom and was in use mainly from the 12th to the 14th centuries CE.

Shields changed shape and reduced in size over time in response to changes in combat style and improvements and prevalence of leg armour. The improvements of leg armour meant that the shield did not have to be so long and heavy. Examples of the developmental timeline include:
- the kite shields of the Bayeux tapestry (1066 CE), reaching from shoulder to thigh resembling a teardrop shape;
- to the shield of Goliath in the Maciejowski Bible (1250 CE) which shows a straight top and the curved sides reaching from neck down to his thigh.
- to shields of the knights in the Queste del Saint Graal (1380 CE) showing the curved shape of the body of the shield, straight top, curved sides down to point at bottom, reaching from shoulder to hip.

Photo 139. Heater shield of the Black Prince, 1330-1376. Canterbury Cathedral, England. Catalogue of the Heraldic Exhibition, Burlington House, 1894 (published 1896). The Princes' shield measures 73 cm (28¾") tall, about 60.5 cm (24") wide, 8 cm ($3\frac{5}{32}$") deep curve, and the shield body is made from 15 mm ($\frac{19}{32}$") thick poplar.[58]

Heaters were usually held on the left side of the body, leaving the weapon side free. The nobility used the heater to display their heraldic devices so the wielder could be identified when their helmet visor covered their face.

---

[58] Steane, John (1999). *The archaeology of the medieval English monarchy*, supplemental information from the Canterbury Cathedral Archives and Library for the measurement of the depth of the curve of the shield.

The origin of name *'heater'* can be described as a neologism, or a new word, supposedly created by Victorian antiquarians due to its resemblance to a *'flat iron'*, a triangular shaped piece of metal with a handle, used to iron cloth, and heated on the wood stove. [59]

There are a number of extant heater shields and they can be found across Europe, see Table 22.

Table 22. Heater – Examples of extant standard heaters.	
Date	*Store and collection*
1220 CE	Swiss National Museum, Zurich, Switzerland - Seedorf-Shield-Swiss.
1376 CE	Funeral attire of the Black Prince (d. 1376) in Canterbury Cathedral, UK.
14th century CE.	Marburg Uni Museum, Inv 3183 – 40 x 36.5 x 4.5 cm (15¾" x $14\frac{3}{8}$" x $1\frac{25}{32}$")

Illuminated manuscripts and other documents like the Fenwick Roles also provide a colourful representation of heaters, see Table 23.

---

[59] Tarassuk & Blair (1979). And I felt the need to explain what a flat iron was to an audience in the 22nd century…

Table 23. Heater – Comparison of Heaters from manuscripts.

Date	Collection details and Stored	Comment
Late 12th or early 13th centuries CE	'Camilla and Turnus besiege Montalbanus' from the Eneide of Heinrich von Veldeke manuscript, German (MS. germ. fol. 282, f.46v, Staatsbibliothek zu Berlin	Straight top, curved top corners curving down to point at bottom, covering just from chin to hip.
1250 CE	Maciejowski Bible / Morgan Crusader Bible, c. 1250 (M.638, f.23r, Goliath, The Piermont Morgan Library, New York	Wide straight topped, sides curving down to point, reaching from neck to thigh.
1250 CE	Histoire de Merlin by Robert de Boron. Ms. français 95, fol. 24r, Paris, Bibliothèque Nationale	Straight top, curve sides down to point at bottom, from shoulder to hip.
1270 CE	Psautier de St. Lois, BNF, _folio 43v	Straight topped, triangular shape, with slight curve to point at bottom, reaching from shoulder to hip.
1316 CE	BL - 10293 Lancelot du Lac c. 1316 fol. 197v.	Straight top, curve sides down to point at bottom, from shoulder to hip. Crossed enarmes at

Table 23. Heater – Comparison of Heaters from manuscripts.

Date	Collection details and Stored	Comment
		top of shield.
1380 CE	BnF Fr. 343 Queste del Saint Graal c. 1380, fol. 47v	Straight top, curve sides down to point at bottom, from shoulder to hip.
Dates to the reign of Henry V (1413-1422) CE	Fenwick's Roll of Arms, Temp HV and HVI, College of Arms reference: Arundel MS 8 f.64v	Flat topped with curved sides to a point at the bottom.

Ply versus Plank.

Most medieval shields, be they round, kite or heater in shape, were made from planks of light timber like linden or poplar, glued together and covered in leather or fabric. The most convenient modern way is to glue planks together on a form and cover them with fabric and/or leather. See Ciana de Carla's project Cennini (2020), which uses poplar planks (8cm wide by 1.25cm thick) which also goes into the various layers of decoration (using materials like gesso, pastiglia, bole and gilding).

If you don't have suitable planks, the alternative is using thin sheets of plywood glued together over a form work.

The construction phrase consists of:

- Making the form;
- Applying the glue to layers of plywood on the form;
- Gluing canvas to faces and edges of the shield;
- Attaching the enarmes;
- Painting the design on the outer face of the shield.

1) **Making the Form - Used to create the curved shape of the heater.**

Materials. Pine and screws

Table 24 Shield form parts measurements

Shield form pieces	Measurements
3 x Frame supports	1m x 7cm x 1cm (40" x 2¾" x $\frac{3}{8}$")
6 x Curved forms	40 x 10 x 2cm (16" x 4" x ¾")
5 x Form bracings	18cm x 7cm x 4cm (7" x 2¾"x 1½")

Tools.

Pencil and ruler, jigsaw (electrical) or coping saw, hand saw, drill and screwdriver bit.

Construction Instructions.

1. Mark out and cut frame supports to length.
2. Mark out and cut curved forms to length and the cut curved shape with jigsaw.
3. Mark out and cut from braces to length.
4. Pre-drill holes and then screw through the frame supports into the base of the curved forms, attach curved forms at either end of the form.

5. Use a form bracing as a spacer, screw the curved form in place, then screw the form base at the top between the two forms.
6. Continue repeating step 5. Offsetting each form bracing so as to be able to screw the form bracing in place un-hindered by the previous bracing. See Photos 141 to 143.

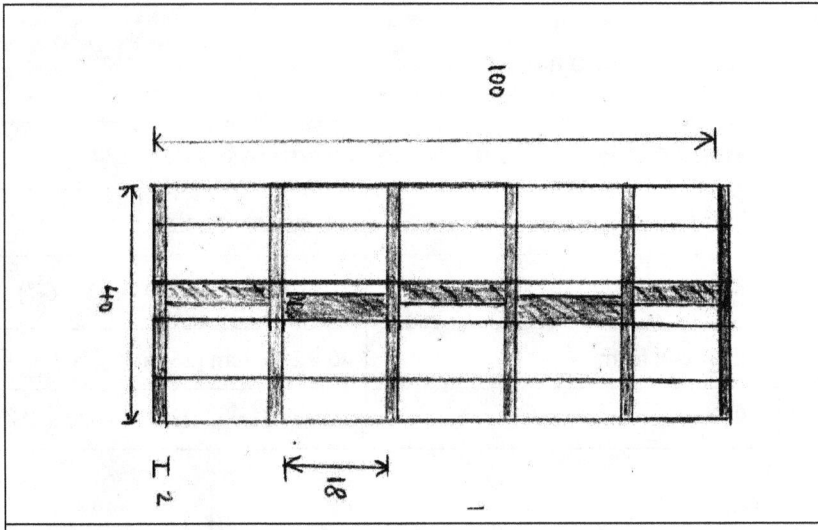

Drawing 51. Shield Form Plans, curved form and bracing. Dimensions in cm.

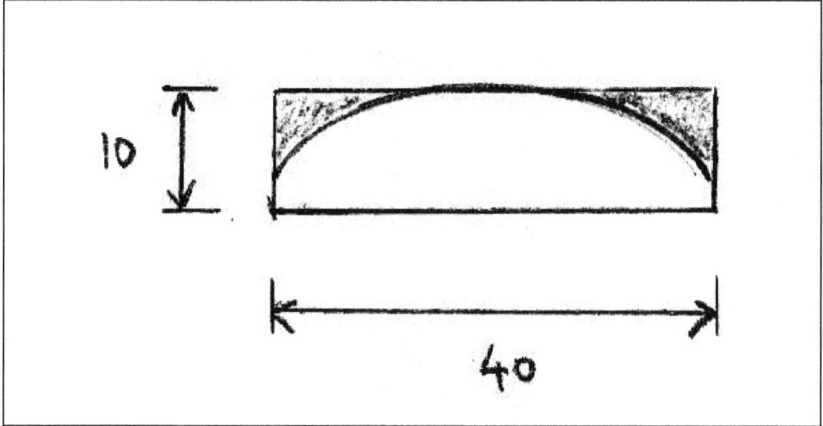

Drawing 52. Form Plans - curved form. Dimensions in cm.

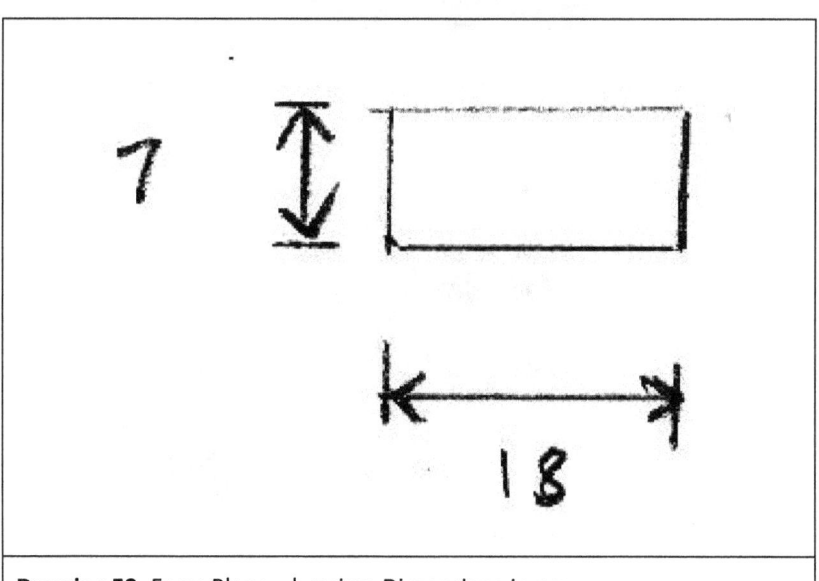

Drawing 53. Form Plans – bracing. Dimensions in cm.

Photo 140. Parts of the Shield form.

Photo 141. Bottom of the Shield form.

Photo 142. A completed Shield form.

Photo 143. A completed Shield form, end on.

2) Applying the glue to layers of timber or plywood on the form.

Materials.

Timber – poplar or linden boards or plywood (pine) –3mm ($\frac{1}{8}$") thick. Plywood sheets come in a range of sizes, see your local supplier. Note: Curved plywood is used in the manufacture of furniture so check out if there is a supplier near you. It saves a lot of work.

Glue (wood glue/ PVA).

Tools.

String, a nail, a pencil and ruler, hacksaw (electrical) or coping saw, hand saw, rasp or knife, ratchet straps and or clamps.
Construction Instructions.

1) Apply glue to the surface of timber (using a brush or plastic spreader).
2) Lay the timber down on the form glue side facing each other.
3) Wrap the ratchet straps around the form and the timber. Note: 'G' clamps can be used but you will need a lot of them.
4) Tighten the straps until the timber meets the form.
5) Allow to dry (check the glue manufacturer's instructions). Depending on the atmospheric conditions the gluing time may vary, err on the side of

longer is better.[60] Repeat with a second layer of timber if you want a thicker shield.[61]

3. **Marking out and cutting the shield blank.**

The size of the heater should follow the proportion in drawing 55. The heater should provide protection for the user's hand, elbow and forearm, so for width I recommend the distance from your elbow to your knuckles when made into a fist plus 10cm (4"). Divide this distance into three units to get the proportions for the shape of the shield, as shown in the diagram below. I.e. 40cm + 10 = 50 cm, so 1 unit = 16.6 cm (16" + 4" = 20", so 1 unit = 6.67"), you will have to determine your specific unit to suit your arm.

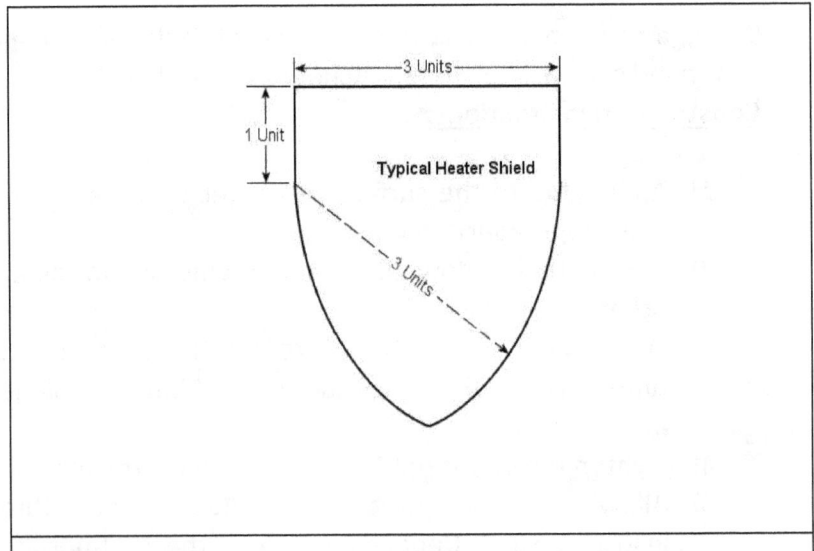

Drawing 54. The size of a typical heater can be determined by this drawing.

---

[60] '*Cuppla days, Beautiful*' – Con the Fruiterer.
[61] Shields were cheap and disposable, better a shield gets hit than you.

1) Attach a string or stick to the nail at the base of the straight edge of one side. Attach the pencil and scribe a line that joins the base of the straight edge of one side down to the centre of the bottom.

2) Swap the nail to the other side and repeat. The two lines should intercept to make a point. Note: A stick is fine for a flat shield but a string is better for a curved shape.

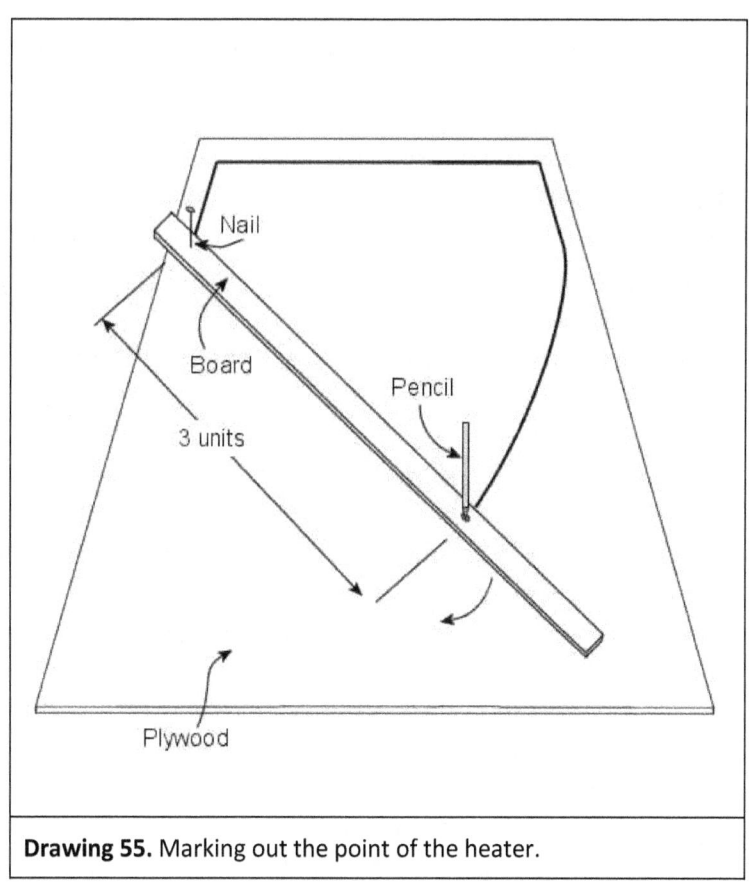

Drawing 55. Marking out the point of the heater.

3) Remove blank from form, mark out shape of heater using information from start of part 2 and drawing 55 and 56. I recommend using a string rather than a stick with holes in it.
4) Cut shield blank out of sheet ensuring that only the shield is cut and not the workbench. Wear the PPE.
5) Round off edges with rasp, file or sandpaper.

4) Shield covering.

Materials.

Glue (wood glue/ PVA), covering (canvas, linen or leather).

Tools.

Brush or plastic glue spreader (a 5 x 10cm (2 x 4") piece of plastic ice cream container), scissors (but not the good ones, and definitely not your partner's clothes making scissors!).

It appears the strength of a shield was increased by adding covering material which could also be decorated. See part 7.

Construction Instructions.

1) Spread a uniform coverage of glue over the surface of the shield, leaving no gaps.
2) Drape the cloth/leather over the shield, allowing for coverage of the edges and some of the back.
3) Spread the cloth/leather over the surface and smooth any wrinkles or bubbles towards the edges using your hands.
4) Cut cloth/leather parallel to the edges of the shield. Allow enough material to overlap the top of the rear surface of the shield.

5) Allow glue to dry before putting on another layer or adding the enarmes.

Note: When using cloth on the front of the shield I like to give the back of the shield a layer of cloth too, adding to the strength of the shield without adding too much extra weight.

5) **Wool padding.**

It is recommended that the wool padding is added before the enarmes because they get in the way of attaching the padding.

Materials. Wool (felt) or cloth

10mm ($\frac{3}{8}$") wool felt or multiple layers of folded wool cloth making up to 10mm ($\frac{3}{8}$").

Tacks: Length? Less than the thickness of the shield. (i.e. Cobblers' tacks). If the tacks are too long and poke out the front, cleat the points over back into the shield.

Tools. Scissors /knife, tack hammer.

Construction Instructions.

1) Cut wool to size.
2) Tack to the inside of the heater where the forearm, wrist and back of hand comes into contact with the heater.

6) The Shield Enarmes (straps).

Enarmes (etymology from old French, to provide straps to a shield, from the Latin *'armus'* = shoulder) are the straps on the back of shields which are used to hold, move and carry a shield.

The guige strap was used to strap the shield to your back when the hands were busy, running around the neck and over the shoulder. For right handers the top part is riveted to the top left hand corner, and bottom part is riveted to the bottom right hand corner, with the joining buckle near the left hip. Measurements have not been provided because we are all different shapes and sizes, and wear different amounts of armour.

On a heater there were usually two straps, one to be held in the hand and the second around the forearm. This could be adjustable but there are many other variations.

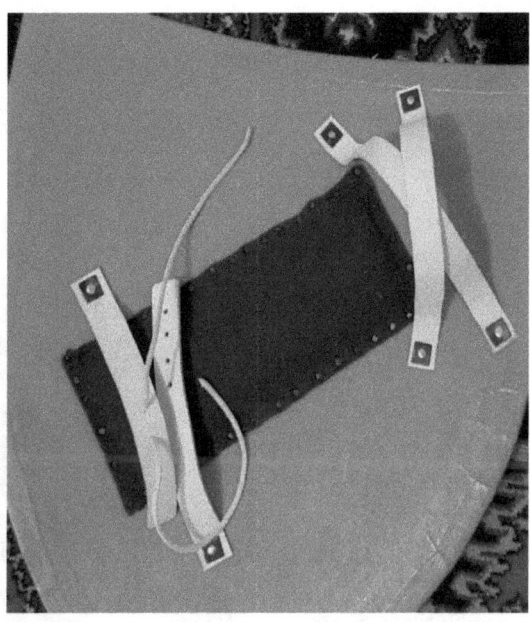

Photo 144. The Enarmes of the Shield. Cross straps at the bottom to grip with. The two straps at the top are adjustable to fit over the top of the forearm, The same effect could be obtained with a belt buckle and a corresponding strap with holes in it.

The upper arm strap could be adjusted. The tight fit enabled the user to wield the shield in defence and attack. If the shield flapped around it was a danger to the user.

The straps needed to be positioned to provide sufficient protection to the user's arm and hand, and were placed so the centre of gravity and ergonomics ensured the shield was easy to use.

The straps were usually attached to the shield by rivets and washers.

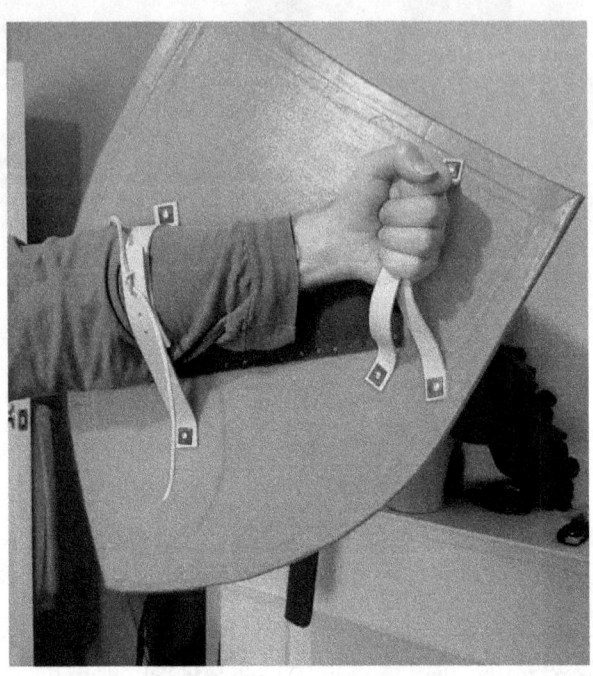

Photo 145. Arm gripping the handles and forearms straps in place. Rivets and square washers are used to hold the straps to the shield.

Materials.

Leather (veggie tanned) straps, thickness = 3mm x 20mm (8oz x ¾"). The length of strap depends on the size of the arm and the additional thickness of the armour worn on the arm.

Square washers made up from 1mm (18ga) mild steel at 15mm ($\frac{5}{8}$") square with a 6mm (¼") hole in the centre. See Appendix 12 for making square washers.

Rivets: mild steel (round head) 30 x 6mm (1¼" x ¼"). Long enough to go through the wood, covering and leather and have enough to rivet over.

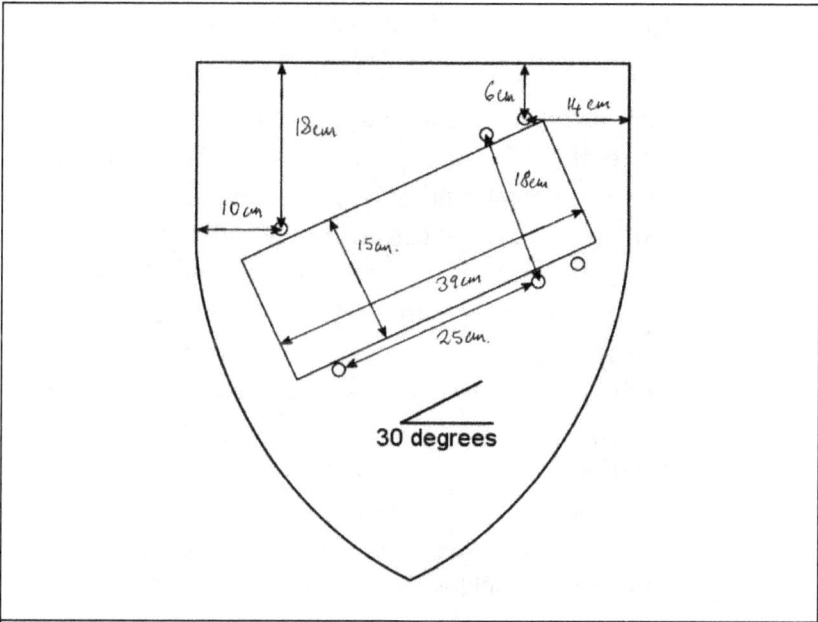

Drawing 56. An example of the position of enarmes and padding, this may vary depending on the size of the person, and the amount and type of armour worn on the shield arm and hand.

Tools.

Strap cutter or knife, awl or hole punch, hammer and anvil, drill and drill bit, bolt cutters, rivet set.

Construction Instructions.
1) Cut straps to width from sheet of hide.
2) Cut to length. Note: Straps need to be long enough to fit the person using the shield.

Is the user going to wear a gauntlet/glove/ armour or just padding on their forearm?
3) Mark and drill holes in the shield. Ensure the rivet is a snug fit, you may need to use a hammer to persuade the rivet through the hole.
4) Cut hole in ends of straps at least 10 mm ($\frac{3}{8}$") from the end of the strap and in the middle of the end.
5) Place the hole of the strap over the rivet, then the washer. You should only need about 5 mm (¼") of rivet exposed, cut off excess with bolt cutter.
6) Place head of rivet on rivet on anvil (I recommend using a *'rivet set'* to preserve the shape of the rivet head), washer is over rivet, and leather strap is lined up in the right direction (especially for the first of the strap rivets).[62]
7) Continue until all straps are riveted in place.
8) Cut holes in each end of the forearm straps, threading thong through the holes. The more expensive option is to use belt buckles.
9) Test straps and thonging for best fit.

---

[62] The idea of riveting is to peen the end over the washer in an even manner without damaging the material around the rivet or bend the rivet. So lots of small taps around the edge of the end of the rivet are used to produce a 'mushroom' effect.

7) Painting the Shield.

The choice of decoration is up to you. Consider the proportionality to the shield size and replicating the colours. As previously stated in the piece on painting the Treaty of Calais chest (see Table 2), many medieval paints contained toxic substances which could be harmful to your health and that of the user. Some ingredients are hard to obtain and prepare.

I recommend you practice painting the design on another surface before starting on the shield itself.

Material.
Paints in the required colours.

Tools.
Pencil, eraser, ruler, stencils, palette, paint brushes and paints.

Photo 146. Shield with gesso primer and white fish painted on it. Note The fish have no personal heraldic significance, Andrew just likes fish.

Photo 147. Shield with red background for fish.

Construction instructions.

1) Ensure the surface is clean of dust and grease.
2) Mark out the design in pencil with a ruler or template.
3) Paint light colours first, add the darker colour last. See photos 144 and 145.
4) Touch up painting if required.
5) Coating of clear lacquer to provide some surface protection.

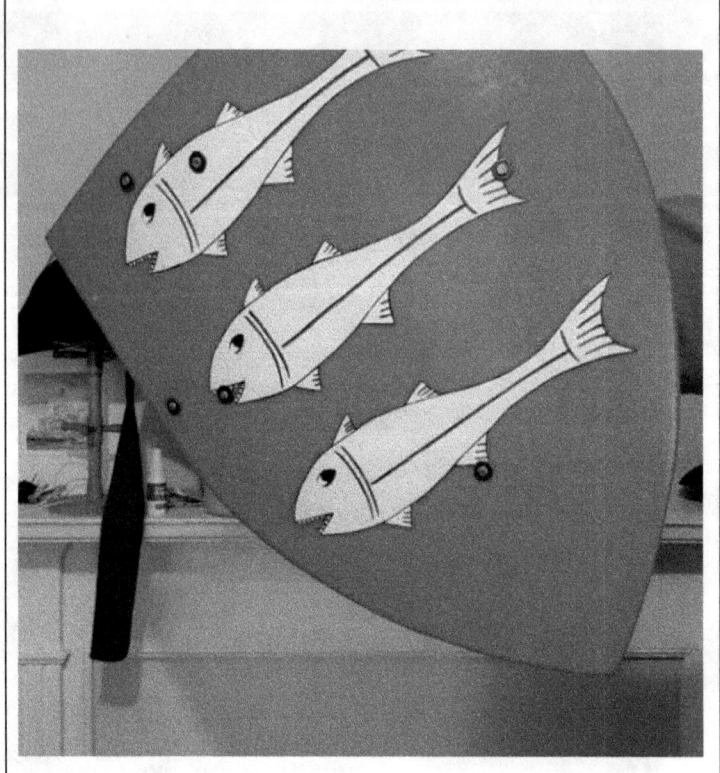

Photo 148. A completed shield with rivets showing where the straps are.

Appendix 1 – Nail making.

Nails were used in all types of timber construction and furniture making as a fastener and even in the 14th century were made in the thousands. As an example, there was a purchase of 18,000 nails for the construction of part of King's Hall College in Cambridge in 1378 CE (Goodall, 2011, pages 163 - 164). Nails came in various shapes and sizes. Depending on the job the heads were square, round, rounded or rectangular and had flat, raised, faceted or headless profiles. The shank of a nail could be round, square or rectangular.

Materials.
Mild steel round bar, 6mm diameter, 50mm (¼" x 2") per nail.

Tools.
Forge (coke, charcoal or gas), anvil, tongs (or vice grips), hammer, cut off, nail header.

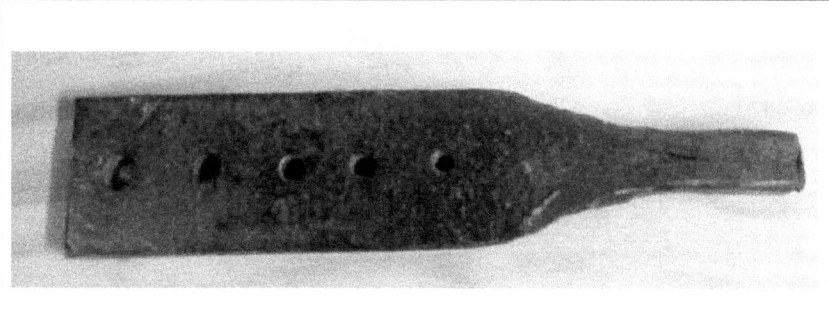

Photo 149. Nail header with a range of sized holes, based on the Mastermyr find (Arwidsson & Berg, 1983), made by S.Wyley.

Photo 150. Metal cut-off edge on, normally affixed in the hardy hole of an anvil.

Photo 151. Metal cut-off, side on showing the shape of the blade.

PPE – Leather apron, gloves, safety glasses, hearing protection (plugs or muffs).

Construction process.

1) Cut 1 metre of stock (you can hold this in your off gloved hand). Small lengths can be held in the tongs.
2) Heat up 100 mm (4") of stock in forge to cherry red.
3) Hammer end of stock to a tapered shape (square cross section is simplest, round cross section is fiddlier).
4) Reheat if necessary.
5) Use *'cut-off'* to cut through most of the nail at about 50 mm (2") from the end of the stock, place it in the nail header and break off the nail.
6) Reheat the thick end if necessary.
7) Strike the top of the nail in the four quarters to produce a *'pyramidal'* shape.
8) Turn nail header over, hang off side of anvil and knock nail out of nail header by knocking nail header against anvil. Note: You may place the nail header with the nail in water then knock out the nail.[63]

Notes: You can heat up some store-bought nails and modify the heads with a hammer while in a vice. After heating the nails a second time, dunk them in some oil to blacken them.

Safety Tip. Beware of heating up galvanised nails because it is a health risk from the fumes.[64]

---

[63] See Schwarz (2011).
[64] Thanks to Bjorn the Blacksmith for reminding me.

Cut nails look the same once in position as forged nails and cost so much less (costs for cut nails is 50c each versus $2 - $4 (AUD)).[65] per forged nail

Appendix 2 - Wider boards and how to make them.

Access to timber used in period European furniture can be difficult in some countries and the only recourse is locally grown timbers like Pinus Radiata. To compound the problems, access to wide boards (over 30cm (12")) is not as easy as it was in the medieval period, so an immediate solution is to butt join two or more boards together. Boards can be glued and clamped together overnight if they are <u>not</u> going to be placed under stress (e.g. the front or back of a chest, where the pieces are supported on three sides). However, if the board is the lid of a chest (without battens) you will need to dowel and glue the boards together to provide mechanical strength to the joint.

---

[65] Prices are based on 2020 prices in Australia.

Photo 152. Two board table top.

Photo 153. Two board table top, underside with cross beams or battens.

"We plant trees not for ourselves, but for the future generations." (Caecilius Statius, 220-168 BCE).

Materials.

Timber boards (longer than required, just in case), dowels (I find that old arrow shafts make a great 8mm ($\frac{5}{16}$") dowel.) Store bought dowels are grooved to provide a greater surface area for adhesion, some compression and air channels to prevent *"hydraulicing"* so it's an idea to groove your shaft before you insert it), glue, damp cloth rag (to clean up water soluble glue such as PVA).

Tools.

Drill (hand or electrical), wooden mallet, saw, pencil, ruler, set square, bench vice, sash clamps, G-clamps, file and sandpaper.

Construction process.

1) Using a pencil mark a centre line along the edges of the timber to be joined using a *'finger gauge'*.
2) Using a pencil mark where each dowel will be placed (for a 90cm (36") chest lid about 20 mm (¾") thick place a make every 10cm (4"), starting 10cm (4") in from the edge, thus ending up with 6 dowels.
3) Punch each mark with a punch or a nail, so the drill does not wander when drilling.
4) Drill holes for dowels, 3cm (1¼") deep, using a depth gauge on the drill bit or some masking tape around the bit, even a texta mark on the drill bit. I use an 8 mm ($\frac{5}{16}$") drill bit because that is the diameter of the arrow shafts I use.

5) Cut dowels 55 mm ($2\frac{1}{16}$") long and round both ends with a file or sandpaper.
6) Place the first board in a bench vice in a horizontal position.
7) Dry fit test, modify where necessary to get a good fit.
8) Squirt a small amount of glue into the dowel holes (about 5 ml (1 tsp)).
9) Run a bead of glue along the edge of the first board on the first board.
10) Tap dowels with a wooden mallet into the holes on the first board.
11) Squirt a small amount of glue into the dowel holes (about 5 ml (1 tsp)) of the next board.
12) Line up holes in the next board with dowels, tap top of the second board with wooden mallet so that both boards meet.
13) Wipe off excess glue with a damp cloth rag.
14) Lay flat on bench top, clamp with sash clamps, remember to protect the edges from damage of pressure of sash clamps using waste timber. If you don't have any sash clamps you can use timbers nailed to the bench top and fox wedges to hold the work.
15) Clamp end of timbers with 'G' clamps.
16) Depending on sizes of boards, you may need to weigh down the centre of the boards (e.g. a table top or a door), I used a small anvil.
17) Allow to cure for at least 12 hours (depending on glue), remove clamps and clean up. You may need to take a plane to the centre rib to take off excess glue or a raised edge if the boards have cupped.
18) Cut off ends if there has been any slippage of the boards, and shave off any raised timber at joins.

Notes:

'Finger gauge' – hold a pencil between your pointer finger and your thumb, with the tip of the pencil on the mark and the tip of your pointer finger on the opposite face, draw a line with the pencil. If the timber is over 30 mm (1¼") thick use 50 mm (2") deep holes and 95 mm (3¾") long dowels.

Photo 154. Finger gauge.

You can also use what is called a *'Marking Gauge,'* consisting of a sharp metal prong sticking out of the end of a stick surrounded by a movable block. The block slides to the desired length and is held in place by an adjustable thumb screw.

Appendix 3 – Hutch chest – Large.

How do you make a larger chest from a plan for a small one?
Ratios and proportionality are based on the timber available. See 'Resizing plans to fit the length or width of the plank available' on page 36.
Change in fabrication of the front:
- The one board used for the front and back becomes three, held together with dowels;
- The centre board has a horizontal grain and the front legs have their grain running vertically.

The fittings for the large chest can be the same as in the smaller chest. The hinges are in Drawing 7, the hasp in drawings 59 and 60 and the hasp plate and loop in drawings 61 and 62.

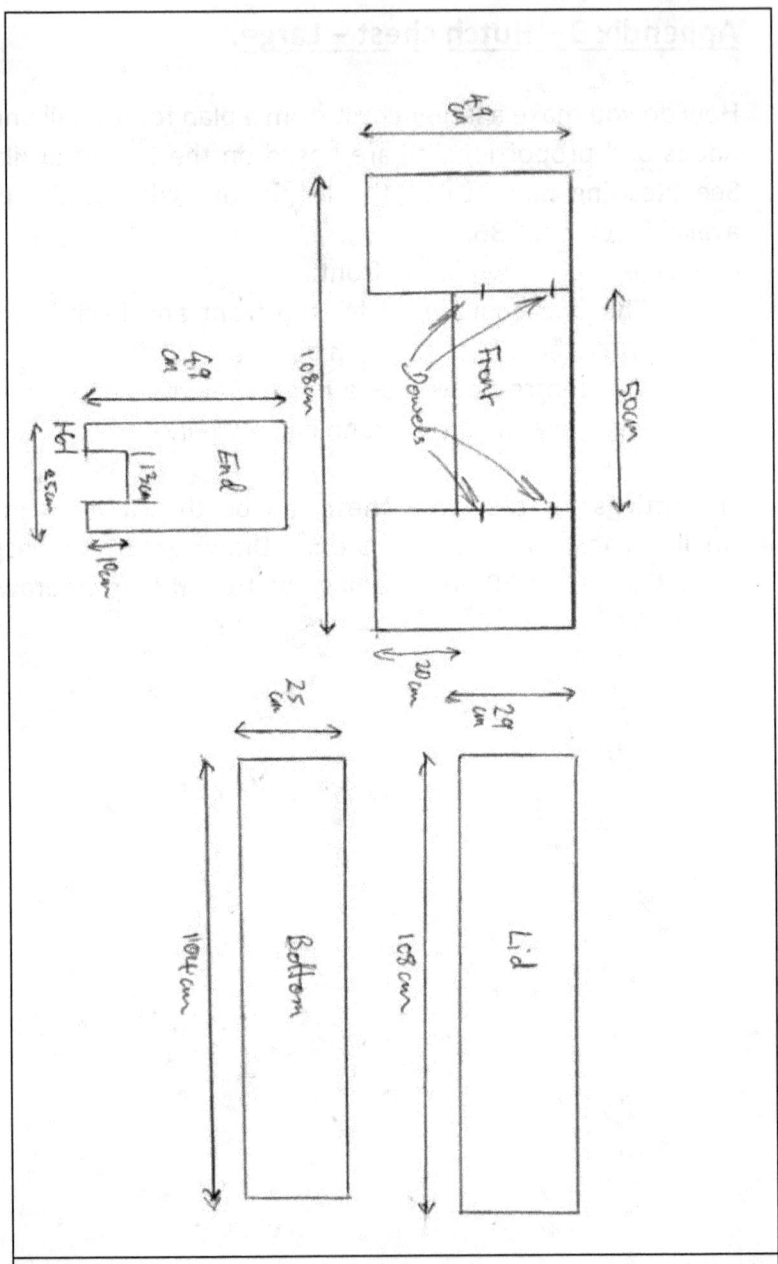

Drawing 57. Plans for a large hutch chest. Dimensions in cm.

Appendix 4 – Hutch chest – Small.

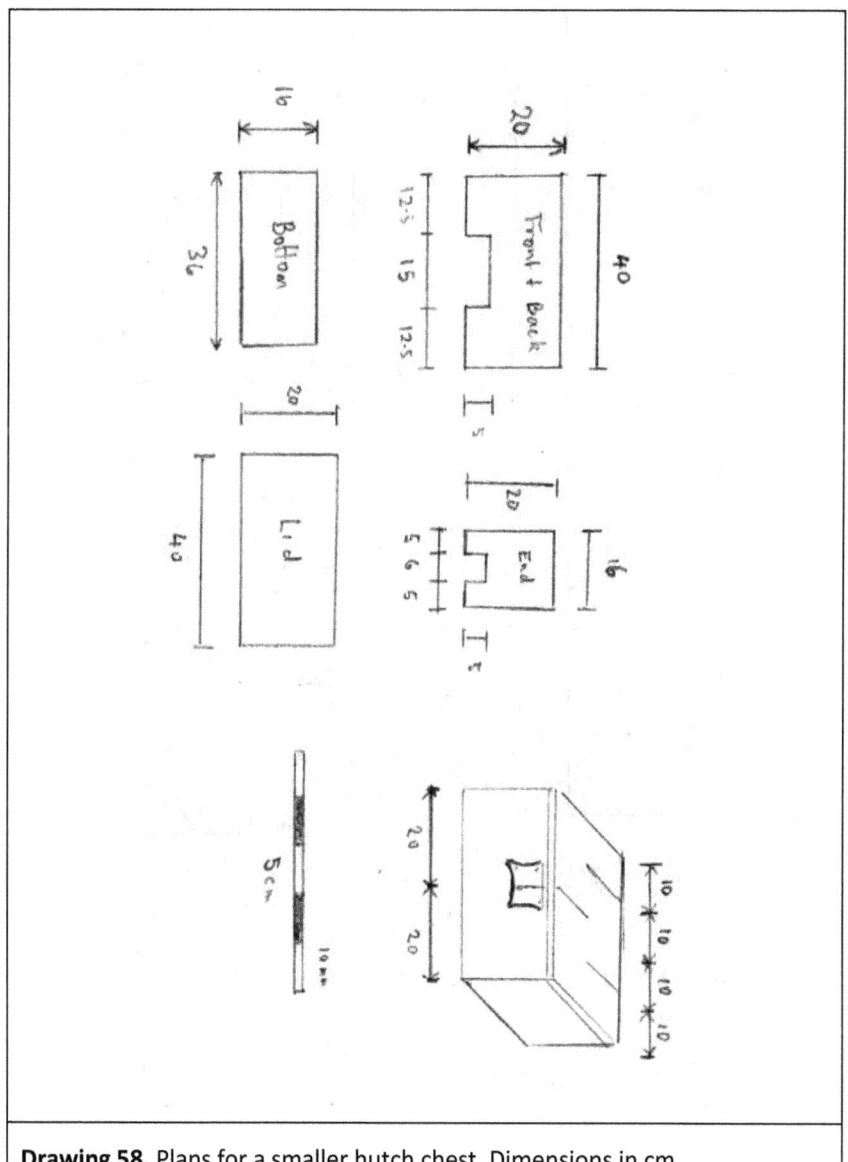

Drawing 58. Plans for a smaller hutch chest. Dimensions in cm.

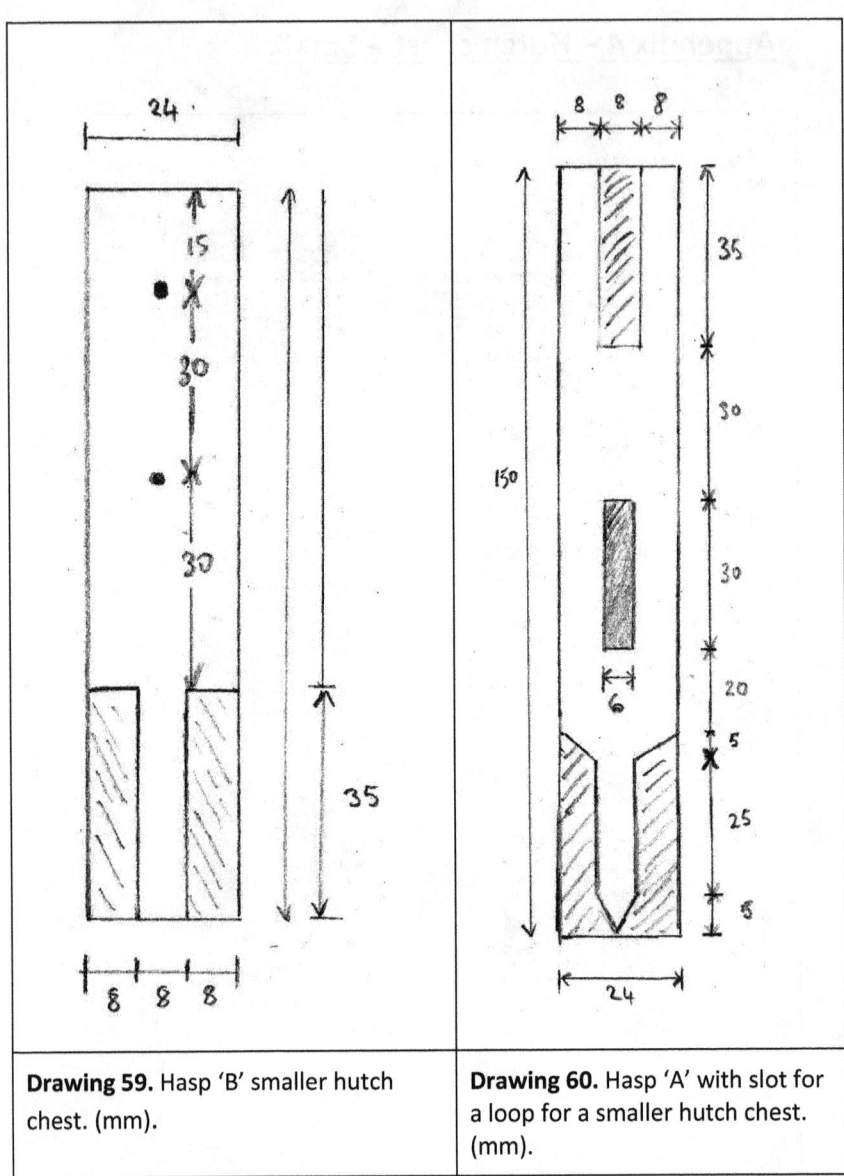

Drawing 59. Hasp 'B' smaller hutch chest. (mm).

Drawing 60. Hasp 'A' with slot for a loop for a smaller hutch chest. (mm).

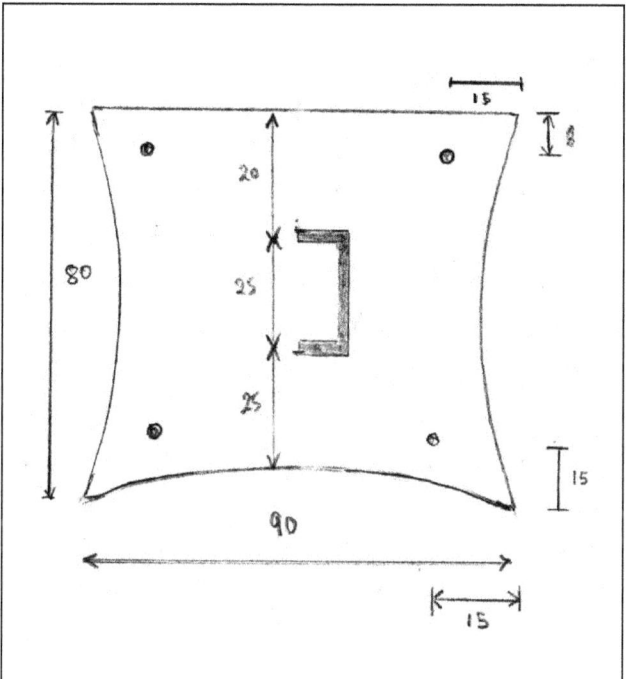

Drawing 61. Hasp plate for a smaller hutch chest. For the hasp loop use drawing 60. Dimensions in mm.

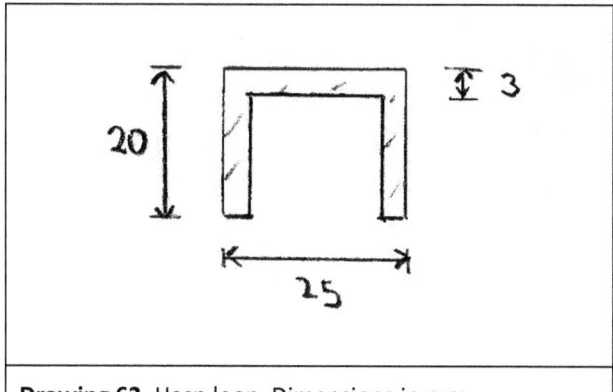

Drawing 62. Hasp loop. Dimensions in mm.

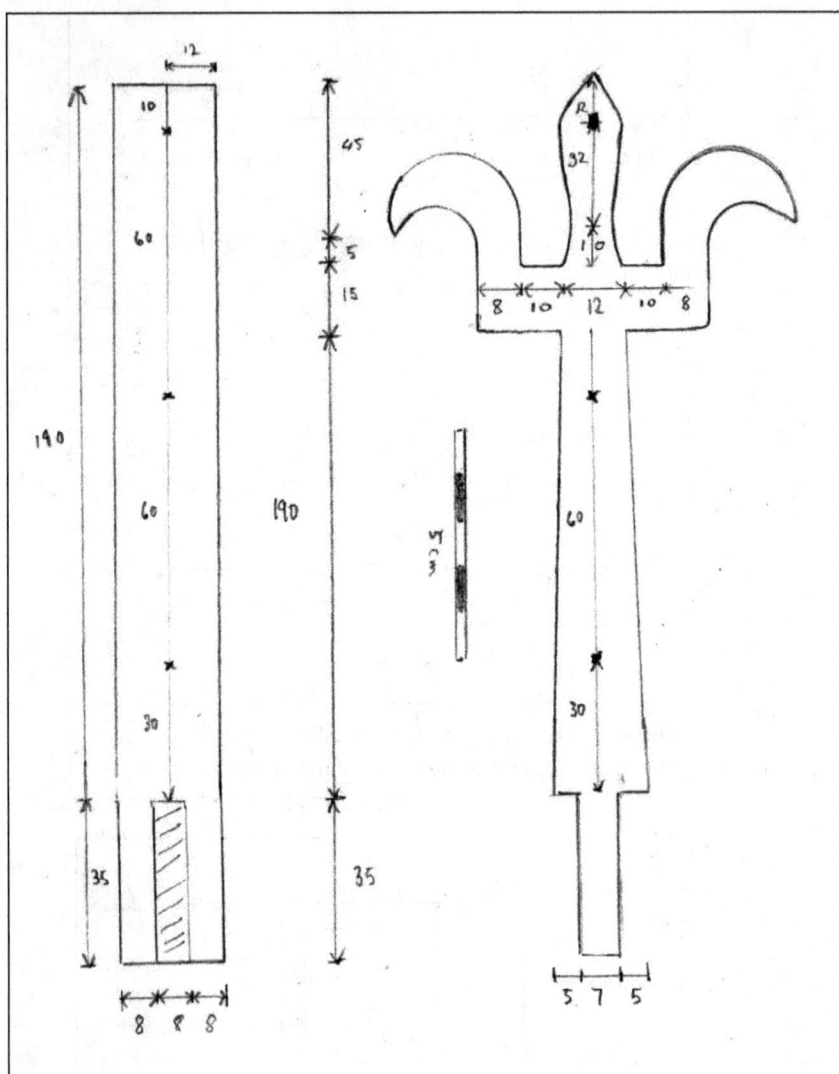

Drawing 63. Hinges for a smaller hutch chest. Dimensions in mm.

Appendix 5 – Treaty of Calais chest.

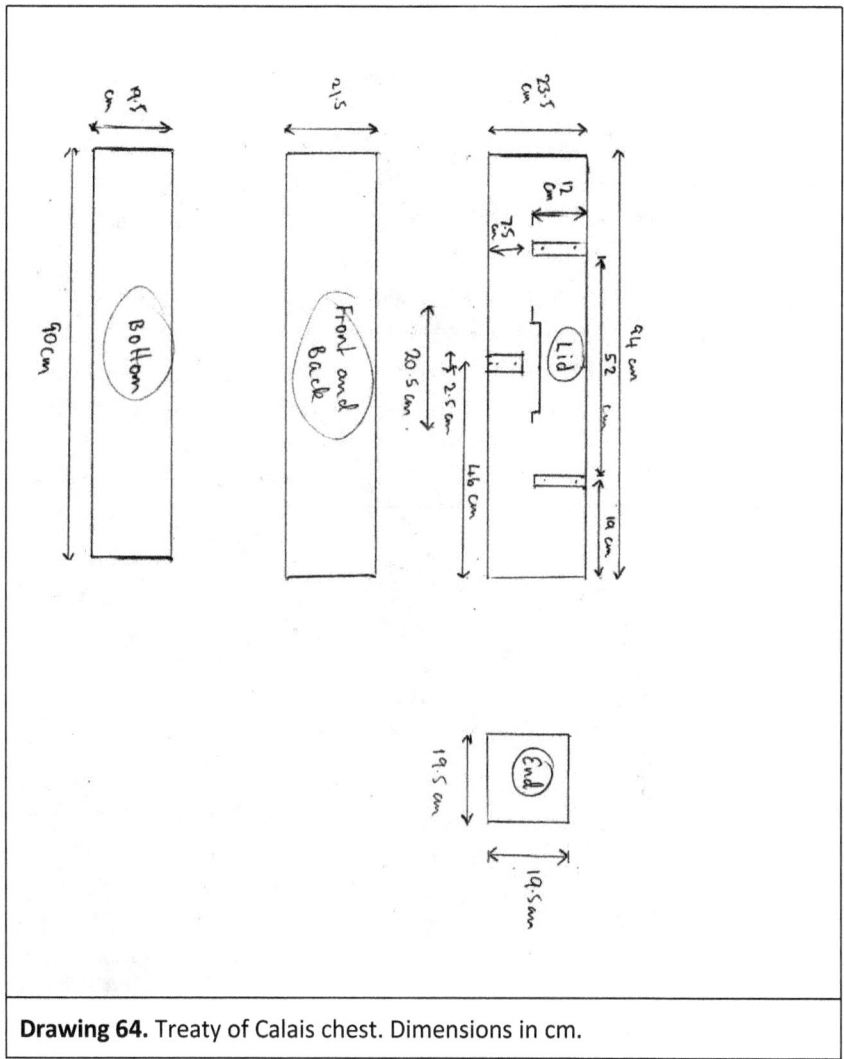

Drawing 64. Treaty of Calais chest. Dimensions in cm.

Note: A full *'how to'* article is planned for the next 14th century volume including a suitable lock. Stay tuned…

Appendix 6 – Bede's Chair – Flat pack.

Making a flat pack version.

1. Add two rails on either side of the sides so the back boards can slide down into to form the back.
2. Attach wooden pegs to either end of the top railing to fit into the holes in the top of the sides so you can take it on and off.
3. Attach the beam (using nails or dowels and glue) under the leading edge of the seat to permanently attach it to the seat, and help hold the seat together. The beam's front edge needs to be shaped to match the rounded shape of the seat.

Photo 155. Close up off block supporting back of seat, mortise hole and bar across bottom edge of chair.

Photo 156. Inside one of the sides of the flat pack chair, including the two runners for the back boards, the block supporting back of seat, mortise hole for the seat tenon and bar across bottom edge of chair.

4. Make up the sides and seat using glue and dowels to make wider boards if boards of the full width are not available.

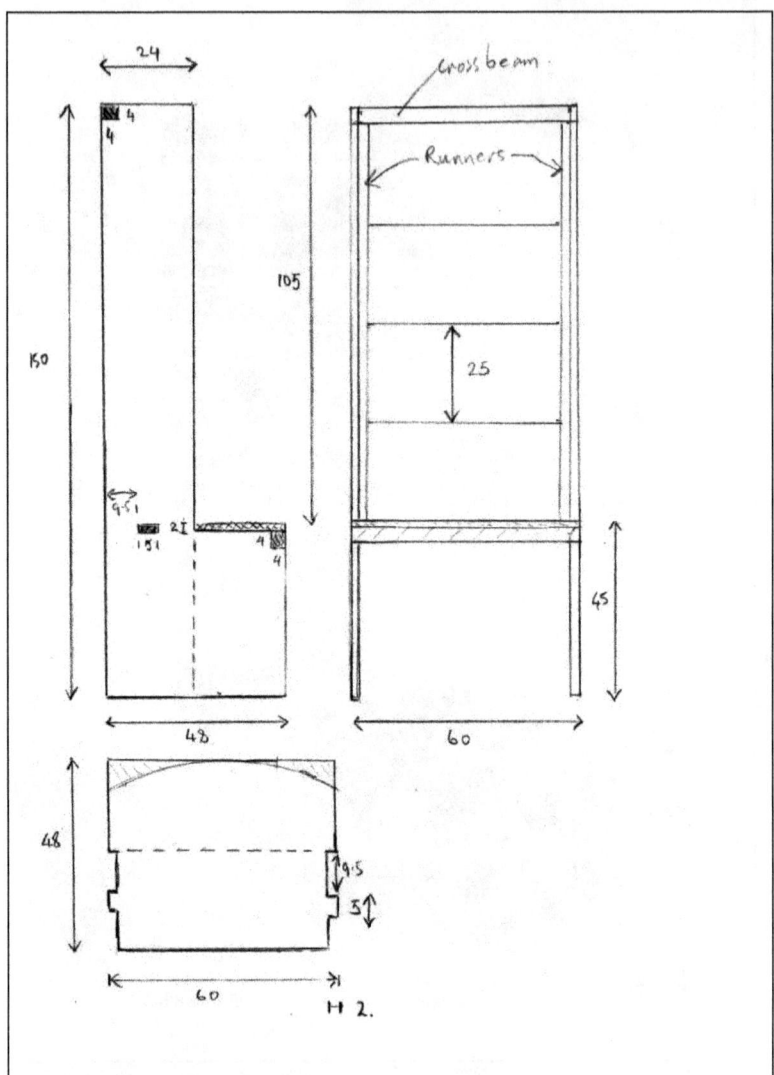

Drawing 65. Plans for a version of Bede's Chair made with smaller planks dowelled together. Dimensions in cm.

Appendix 7 – Bed, longer version based on the bed I made for myself.

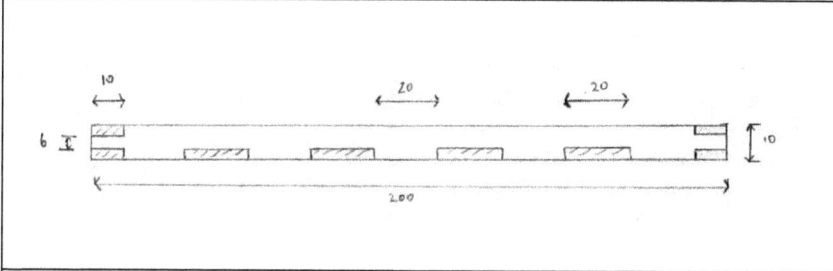

Drawing 66. Side rail. Blocks attached inside of the rail are provided for supporting plywood sheets. Long strips along the inside lower edge can also be used to support planking. See drawing 23. Dimensions in cm.

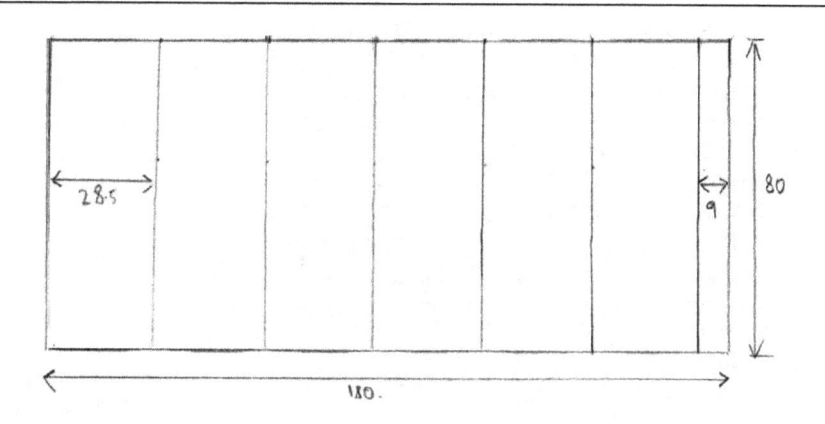

Drawing 67. Planks can be used to support a tick or mattress on the bed. Note that you may need to notch the corners to fit corner posts. Dimensions in cm.

Appendix 8 – Useful conversions.

Table 25. Metric to customary and imperial conversions.	
1 metre = 100 cm	39.3701 inches / 3.28 feet / 1.09 yard
1 centimetre = 10 mm	0.3937 inch
1 millimetre	0.03937 inch
1 yard = 3 feet	91.44 cm
1 foot = 12 inches	30.48 cm
1 inch	2.54 cm
Volume	
1 litre	4 metric cups / 1000 ml
1 litre	1.06 US quarts / 33.8 US fl oz.
1 litre	0.88 Imperial quart / 35.2 Imp fl. oz.
1 US quart	4 US cups / 32 US fl oz. / 946 ml
1 Imperial quart	4 Imp cups / 40 Imp fl.oz. / 1136 ml
1 US cup	240 ml
1 metric cup	250 ml
1 Imperial cup	284 ml
1 US teaspoon	4.9 ml
1 metric teaspoon	5 ml
1 Imperial teaspoon	5.9 ml
Weight	

1kg = 1000 g	2.2 lb
1lb	0.454 kg
1oz	28.35 g
Leather thickness	
0.8 – 1.2 mm	2 – 3 oz.
1.2 – 1.6 mm	3 – 4 oz.
2.8 – 3.2 mm	7 – 8 oz.
5.5 – 6.4 mm	14 – 15 oz.

Closest customary fraction to metric size:

Metric	*Closest gauge number*	*Closest inch*
0.8mm	20ga	1/32"
1.2 mm	18ga	
1.6 mm	16ga	$\frac{1}{16}"$
3 mm	10-11ga	$\frac{1}{8}"$
6 mm	4ga	¼"
1 cm/10 mm		$\frac{3}{8}"$
19mm		¾"
25 mm		1"

Solvents.

Australia and New Zealand mineral turpentine is the same as the USA's mineral spirit and the UK's white spirit. Do not use Australian white spirit (drycleaning solvent) or Australian white oil (pesticide).

Gum Turpentine/ Spirit of Turpentine is a useful if more expensive vegetable-based alternative.

Residents of the state of California will need to formulate their own oil-based timber treatment with an approved solvent or obtain something acceptable from commercial sources.

Linseed oil may be sold as flaxseed oil in some jurisdictions.

Appendix 9 – Chest lock Survey – Chests with turnkey locks from 10th to 16th century.

Aim: To determine if there is significant information available about chest turnkey locks to identify changes in locks over time.
Method: By accumulating information based on origin, dating, and design to support the aim of the survey.

Table 26. Chest turn locks (where the key rotates about a central point) survey.

Date – CE	Description	Hasp position	Key hole	Lock plate shape	Lock Typology
948	St. Severin Shrine, Germany	Left	Centre	Rectangle	5AB
1000	The Body of John Chrysostom arrives in Constantinople Monologian of Basal VI, ms Vat gr. 1613 Fol. 353	Left	Right	Rectangle	5AC
Late 11th	York Minster, Burial, 105 (1080/92)	Left	Centre	Rectangle	5AB
Late 11th	York Minster, Burial, 94 (1080/92)	Left	Centre	Rectangle	5AB

Table 26. Chest turn locks (where the key rotates about a central point) survey.

Date – CE	Description	Hasp position	Key hole	Lock plate shape	Lock Typology
12th	Bunratty Castle, Ireland, Crusader, AccNo. 328, Item no. 8	Left	Right	Rectangle	5AC
12th	Bunratty Castle, Ireland, Crusader, AccNo. 292, Item no. 3	Right	Centre	Rectangle	5CB
Early 12th	Winchester, Hampshire, Cat. No. 1146	Left	Centre	Rectangle, dished	5DA
Late 12th	Hindringham Church, Norfolk, England	Left	Rightish	Rectangle, 4 concave edges	5AB
1244-1254	Maciejowski Bible Coffers (MS M 638, Folio 6 verso, 46)	Left	Right	Square	5BC
1244-1254	Maciejowski Bible Coffers (MS M 638, Folio 6 verso, 47)	Left	Right	Square	5BC

Table 26. Chest turn locks (where the key rotates about a central point) survey.

Date – CE	Description	Hasp position	Key hole	Lock plate shape	Lock Typology
1252-1284	Cantigas de Santaa Maria MS T.I. 1 - Códice Rico. Page 2 - panel XXV La Virgen Entre El Cristiano Y El Judio CSM: 025 F39r	Left	Centre	Rectangle 3 concave edges, not top edge.	5AB
1270-1350	Billings Gate Park, Excavations City of London 1983, Cat. No 276	Left	Centre	Rectangle, 4 concave edges	5AB
1290	Casket of the Blessed Juliana of Collalto (Byzantine) (1st lock)	Left	Centre	Circular – Starburst	5AB
1290	Casket of the Blessed Juliana of Collalto (Medieval) (2nd lock)	Right	Centre	Rectangle	5CB
13th	Newport Church, Essex, England	Centre	Right	Rectangle	5BC
13th	Stoke D'Abernon Church, Surrey, England	Left	Centre	3 rectangular locks	5AB

Table 26. Chest turn locks (where the key rotates about a central point) survey.

Date – CE	Description	Hasp position	Key hole	Lock plate shape	Lock Typology
13th	Chobham Church, Surrey, England	Left	Right	3 rectangular locks	5AC
13th	Winchester, Hampshire, Cat. No. 1142	Left	Centre	Rectangle	5DA
Around 1300	Oxford Chest – Merton College, Oxford University	Left	Centre	Rectangle	5AB, three locks.
1350-1400	Billings Gate Park, Excavations City of London 1983, Cat. No 279	Left	Centre	Rectangle, concave edge on left side	5DA
1375	Kloster Isenhague – Chest TR-NR-409 / ISN Ba 83	Left	Right	Rectangle, 4 concave edges	5AC
1381-1399	the *'Pillagers'* in the Chroniques de France ou de St Denis (Chronicles of France and St. Denis) – British Library – MS Royal 20 C VII 41v	Right	Centre	Rectangle, 3 concave edges, not top edge.	5CB

Table 26. Chest turn locks (where the key rotates about a central point) survey.

Date – CE	Description	Hasp position	Key hole	Lock plate shape	Lock Typology
1390-1400	Marhamchurch Antiques, Stock No. MARH0129	Left	Centre	Rectangle, 4 deep concave edges	5AC
1400-1450	Trig Lane, Upper Thames Street, Excavations City of London 1944, Cat. No 283	Right	Centre	Rectangle, concave edges	5DA
14th	Vestment Chest, Collection of Haddon Hall, Bakewell, England	Left	Centre	Rectangle with Fleur di lis on corners	5AB, Two locks.
14th – 15th	Museum des Kunsthandwerks, Neg NR. FD 161 019– Leipzig, Germany	Left	Centre	Square, with pointed corners, and raised body.	5AB
15th	Hewn timber chest, Collection Hereford Catherdral, UK	Centre	Right	Rectangle, 4 concave edges	5BC

Table 26. Chest turn locks (where the key rotates about a central point) survey.

Date – CE	Description	Hasp position	Key hole	Lock plate shape	Lock Typology
Late 15th	Lady Margaret Beafort's Travel Chest (E27/case 6), British National Archive, UK	Left	Centre	Rectangle	5AB, two locks
Late 15th	Newbury, Berkshire, Cat. No. 1145	Left	Centre	Rectangle	5DA
1480	Marhamchurch Antiques, Stock No. MARH0184	Left	Centre	Square	5AB
First half 16th	Cheshunt Church, Hertfordshire, England	Left	Right, under latch	Rectangle, 3 concave edges, right hand side is straight	5AC
1530	Period Oak Antiques, Stock No. 1048	Left	Centre	Rectangle	5AB

Table 27. The numbers of different types of lock in this (short) survey.

5AB	5AC	5BC	5CB	5DA
14	6	4	3	5

Table 28. The number of locks per century from the survey.

Lock type 5	10th	11th	12th	13th	14th	15th	16th
AB	1	2	1	4	1	3	1
AC	0	1	1	1	2	0	1
BC	0	0	0	3	0	1	0
CB	0	0	0	1	0	0	0
DA	0	0	0	1	0	2	0
Totals	1	3	2	10	3	6	2

Notes:

Photo 157. A rectangular dug out chest with iron strapping was put up on the '*Medieval Boxes*' Facebook group (posted 15th September 2021) from St James church, Kington, Worcestershire (date unknown). I would hazard a guess at a production date in the 15th century. The interesting thing is that the chest has two locks of two types, the left lock has a hasp on the left (type 5AB) and the other lock has a hasp on the right (type 5BC). Photo by Mark Griffin.

Ottaway (Anglo-Scandinavian Ironwork from 16-22 Coppergate) states that 12 slides which could have been used for double hasped locks were found (i.e. Cat. No. 3594, 3595, 3956, which were all straight, whereas Cat. No. 3598 had a hook at one end).

Appendix 10 – Typologies of locks.

I have found two lock typologies (Goodall's and Linlaud's) which classifies a variety of locks but not all, hence I have developed my own chest lock typology, see Table 29 and 30.

Wyley's lock typology.

Table 29. Lock typology for slide locks (as you are looking at the outside of the lock).			
Number of hasps	*Hasp position(s)*	*Typology code*	*Example*
1	Left A	1A	Kaagenden - Denmark
	Centre B	1B	Lejre – Grave 321
	Right C	1C	None found
	Right with snib	1D	Fyrkat - Denmark
2	Left and right A	2A	Mastermyr - Sweden
3	Left, centre and right A	3A	Oseberg 149
Other types of locks.			
Spring displacement at right angles to lock plate		4A	Oseberg 178
Spring displacement is parallel to lock plate		4B	Mastermyr lock no. 4

Table 30. Lock typology for turnkey locks (5) (as you are looking at the outside of the lock).

Hasp	Key hole	Typology code	Example
Left A	Left A	5AA	None found
	Centre B	5AB	Cantigas de Santaa Maria.
	Right C	5AC	Bunratty Castle - Ireland
Centre B	Left A	5BA	None found
	Centre B	5BB	None found
	Right C	5AC	Maciejowski Bible coffers
Right C	Left A	5CA	None found
	Centre B	5CB	Casket of the Blessed Juliana of Collalto (Medieval)
	Right C	5CC	None found
2 Hasps, left and right	Centre A	5DA	City of London

Note: *'None found'* so far as part of this *'short'* survey.

Goodall's Lock typology.

1a. operated by a key with a projection on their bit and a spring held sliding bolt with horizontal enlarged and perforated centres set on a flat lock plate.
1b. a flat lock plate with the lock mechanism attached to the rear face with a hole for the staple of a hasp, held closed by the end(s) of a slide bolt. The bolt slides on 'U' shaped staples, held in place by a spring, and variates two hasps with one hooked.
1c. lock attached to the inner face of dished or embossed cases which could be attached to a door or furniture (without having to chisel out a space for the lock mechanism in the timber).
1. Has a bolt which engages in a staple or other keeper outside the lock case.

Linlaud's Lock typology. [66]

Most of the lock can only be opened from one side of the lock. or for a limited number of locks in Line 2 are opening of the system from two sides.

Table 31. Line 1 (Systems using gravity).	
Pegs	Aligning pegs.
Sliders	Simple sliders, Nipple sliders.
Line 2 (Spring Systems)	

---

[66] I admit up front my French translations skills are poor and I am relying on google translate and my understanding of locks and keys.

Welded bolts	Padlock subtype A; Padlock sub type B; Lock subtype C; Lock subtype D Not solid with bolt; T shaped key; L shaped key.
Bolt with notches	Wooden bolt, full shank key, subtype A; Hollow barrel key without rake, subtype B; Metal bolt, hollow cannon key and rake, subtype C; Metal solid shank key, subtype D; Proto benardes[67] with full shank key, subtype E.
Grooved Spring and bearded bolt	Metal bolt with 1 beard, subtype A; Solid shank key with wooden bolt, subtype B; Metal bolt with rolled up key, subtype C; Solid shank wrench, subtype D; Benardes.

---

[67]"Clef benarde," a key that is not piped (foree) (Hamilton and Legros) or furnished with grooves, and which can be opened from both sides, is from "Bernard," which in old French signifies a fool, hence a "clef bernarde " or "benarde" is an inferior kind of key (Littre)." ' Pitt-Rivers (1883) pp. 3-5.'

Appendix 11 - Trenails (Wooden pegged Construction).

By Wayne Robinson.

Photo 158. Pegged hanging salt box of Buda, Hungary. W. Robinson. Pegs are 3 mm (⅛").

Photo 159. Original trenailed building frame, Plas Mawr, Conwy, North Wales. Trenails are 45 mm (1¾"). Photo by W Robinson.

Wooden pegs can be used as a cheap and attractive alternative to nails, with many extant examples, ranging from small boxes and clamp-front hutch chests to massive building frames. While differing in scale, the techniques are broadly similar in both cases.

Materials.

- Wood for pegs. It needs to be well seasoned and straight grained; oak barrel offcuts or fruitwood pieces sold for use in food smokers work well. In the example below, I'm using an offcut of oak from the hanging salt box project in chapter 6,
- Glue. I like liquid hide glue, but it does take a long time to set. It doesn't really matter what type you use. PVA works well.

Tools.

- Heavy chisel. We need momentum here so a bit of mass helps,
- Bench hook[68], or some sacrificial surface to cut against that can also support the blanks vertically,
- Mallet for striking the chisel,
- Metal hammer for driving the pegs.
- Drill and drill bit in the desired size or gimlet/s[69]. I'm using a gimlet in the photos below.

Construction process.

Making the pegs.

Most furniture sized pegs vary between about 3 mm (⅛") and 10 mm (⅜"). These are easily made from waste timber. The size of your pegs will depend on the thickness of the timber and the type of joints you are using. For the salt box below I'm doing simple butt joints in 12 mm (½") oak wainscot. I like to keep the

---

[68] A board with a lip for hooking over the front of a workbench, and a back fence for working against. https://en.wikipedia.org/wiki/Bench_hook
[69] https://en.wikipedia.org/wiki/Gimlet_(tool)

width of the pegs below one third of the thickness of the boards, so I'm using 3 mm (⅛").

1. Stand the block of oak on one end, leaning against the vertical support of the bench hook.
2. Place the edge of the chisel on the upper end grain, parallel to the short axis and 3 mm (⅛") or so in from one end. Face the bevel towards the smaller end.
3. Grasp the chisel in one hand, and strike the chisel with the mallet. A rectangular piece of timber should split off, possibly shooting across the room and disappearing under the beer fridge. Repeat.
4. Pick up a smaller piece, we now want to do a split at right angles to the first so that we end up with an approximately square section. Splitting wood for pegs ensures there is no cross-grain to create weaknesses. Simply press the edge of the chisel into the end grain. The wood will stick to the chisel. Lift the wood and chisel and drop from a low height onto the bench. Keep your hands above the edge of the chisel and try to stop the chisel from hitting the bench.
5. Using the chisel or a knife, round a third of the length of the peg. Just shaving the corners off the square so you have eight similarly sized faces is usually enough for small pegs. This square part of the peg should engage and distort the round hole for maximum strength.
6. Taper them a little so they'll fit easily in the hole and bevel the nose of the peg.

Photo 160. Offcut of oak and a 32 mm (1¼") chisel. Mass is more important than size, it will work as long as the edge is wider than the offcut.

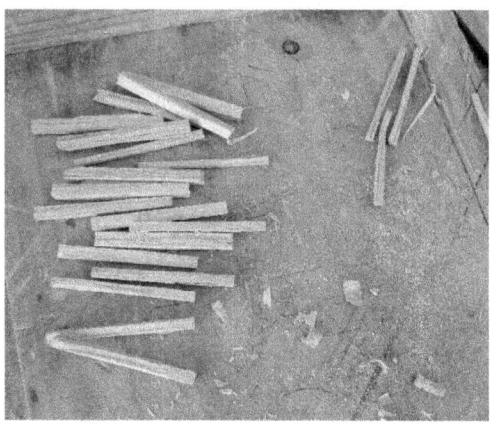

Photo 161. Oak split into pegs, the ones on the right are rejected as too small, but may be useful for other projects.

Photo 162. Rounding the nose of the peg.

Photo 163. Tapering the pegs.

Fitting the Pegs.

1. Bore the holes for the pegs. If your construction is small with simple rebate joints, like the salt box, you can glue the rebates and assemble the item first, then support it and drill the holes. For mid-sized items, you can drill the long grain face, do the gluing next, then finish drilling the end grain using the other board as a template. Large mortise and tenon construction is out of the scope of this appendix. Schwarz (2013), Schwarz (2020) or Follansbee and Alexander (2012), are in the bibliography with examples of *'drawboring'*.[70]
2. Glue the rounded end of the pin. I drop some glue onto a take-away container lid and just roll the end of the pin in that.
3. Push the pins into place with hand pressure, then knock them in with a metal hammer. Listen to the noise, the sound will increase in pitch as the peg goes in and you'll get a hollow thump when the pin hits the bottom of the hole. If you break one, add a little glue and press the broken piece into the end grain of the peg to avoid having a hole. Give it a very light tap to consolidate the parts.
4. Leave it to set overnight, I don't care what the glue label promises. You can clean up any glue that's squeezed out while it's still wet with a toothbrush or rag and warm water.
5. Cut the pegs off just proud of the surface with a saw. Use a fine saw, and protect the flat surface with masking tape if there's any risk of marking the surface with the saw teeth.
6. Pare the remaining part with a chisel, working from the outside towards the middle so the grain is supported. If the chisel is

---

[70] A drawbored mortise and tenon has the peg hole in the tenon offset toward the shoulder of the tenon. The peg follows a curved path and pulls the joint tight as it is driven in.

really sharp, you'll be left with a burnished surface on the end grain of the peg.

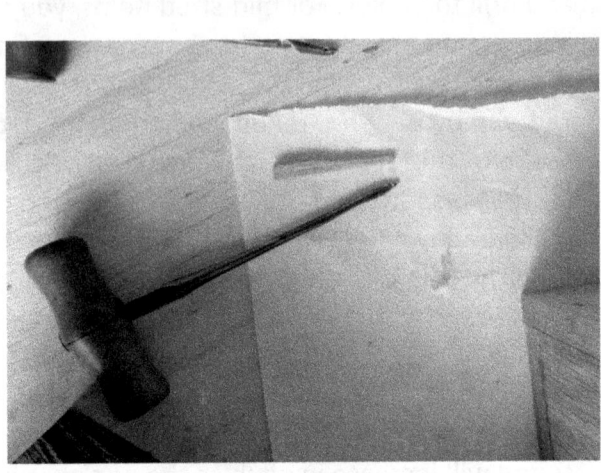

Photo 164. Gimlets are great for this sort of task because they leave a tapered hole.

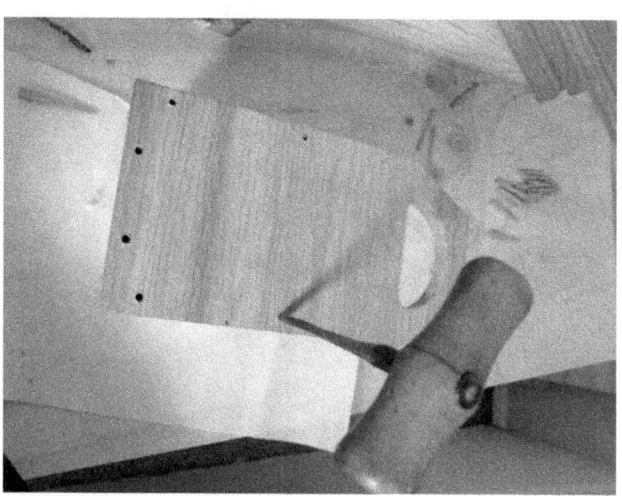

Photo 165. Bore the holes for the pegs, don't go too close to the edge.

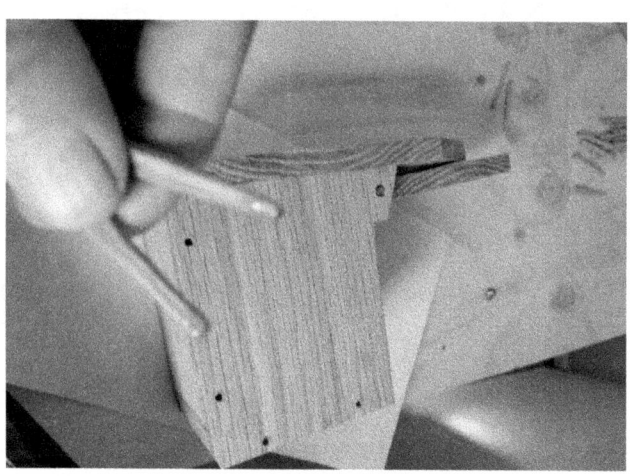

Photo 166. Spread glue of your choice on the end of the peg.

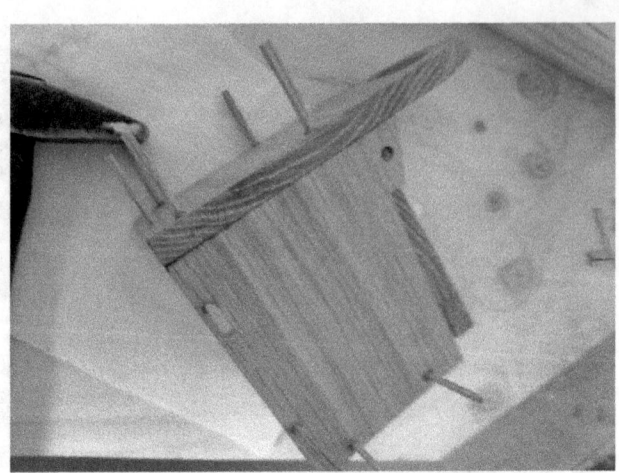

Photo 167. Knock the pegs in with a metal hammer. Listen for the sound to get higher as the peg goes in.

Photo 168. I broke one. You're in luck, you can see how I fix broken pegs.

Photo 169. Glue the broken off bit in place, so there isn't a hollow when you trim it later.

Photo 170. When the glue is dry, trim close to flush. The saw has no offset on the teeth, you can also protect the timber with masking tape before cutting the pegs.

Photo 171. Near enough is good enough with the initial cut. You will trim the end grain with a sharp chisel after this.

Photo 172. Pare the end flush with a sharp chisel, this helps seal and polish the end of the peg.

Photo 173. The finished pegged joint.

Some other examples of peg use.

Photo 174. 6 mm (¼") square oak pegs in oak 17th century table box by the author. Distortion of the hole by the peg corners can be clearly seen.

Photo 175. 9 mm (⅜") round Victorian Ash pegs holding the legs on my workbench. The pegs are 200 mm (8") long with the hole on the leg tenon offset by 6 mm (¼") towards the shoulder.

Photo 176. 22 mm (⅞") tapered trenails cut by axe from a reclaimed French oak barrel stave.

Photo 177. The trenails are left long and have the corners bevelled like on the roof frame at the start of the appendix. The holes securing the leg to the carving stump are deliberately angled for extra strength.

Appendix 12 – Making square washers.

Materials. Mild steel sheet, 1mm thick.

Tools.

Ruler and pencil, hack saw, angle grinder with cutting disc or a pair of straight WISS cutters, punch, anvil, drill and drill bit.

Construction process (Cold).

1) Mark out multiple squares on a flat sheet or strip.
2) Mark out squares and punch mark the holes.
3) Drill 6 mm (¼") holes in the sheet. It's much easier to hold a large sheet than individual washers.
4) Cut the washers from the sheet. This saves time and drilling multiple washers.
5) Clean up edges with a file (or tumble with grit). Ensure the rivets fit into the hole in the washer.

Photo 178. The tools for the job.

Photo 179. Marked and punched.

Photo 180. Drilling using a pedestal drill press.

Photo 181. Cut to length with a pair of tin snips.

About the authors.

Stephen Francis (Sven) Wyley.

Born in 1962 in the town of Colac (Victoria, Australia) and now lives in Melbourne (Victoria), son of a nurse and a fibrous plaster, worked in analytical and research science (from EPA to CSIRO) for 25 years, then moved in occupational health and safety because safety paid more and he had desire to make the world a safer place one workplace at a time, and after another

20 years in safety (13 years as a state government safety inspector) is now a self-employed author and craftsperson.

Sports and martial arts figured predominantly in his life which included Freestyle wrestling (represented Australia), Archery (Longbow, Victorian State champion and competed at the nationals), Fencing (foil, epee and sabre at intervarsity competitions), and attaining a blue belt in Shudokan Aikido.

A living historian and re-enactor since joining the New Varangian Guard Inc. in 1984, then started Sven the Merchant (a business making and selling medieval goods mainly consisting of furniture, arrows and leatherwork) in 2004[1].

And now it's passing on the legacy in the form of workshops and the 'How to" books.

[1] Stephen Francis Wyley, not to be confused with his cousin or an actor in Ireland of the same name.
https://www.imdb.com/name/nm3184249/

Youtube site of Sven Skildbiter, from Arrows to Wrestling.
https://sites.google.com/site/svenskildbiter/
https://www.youtube.com/channel/UCYaAcfT7OzRoQv2RzNC829A

Andrew Fraser.

Andrew Fraser started re-enacting in: 1999, his interests include; medieval arts and culture, wood and leather working, black smithing and reconstruction of the medieval middle class and their material culture.

Wayne Robinson.

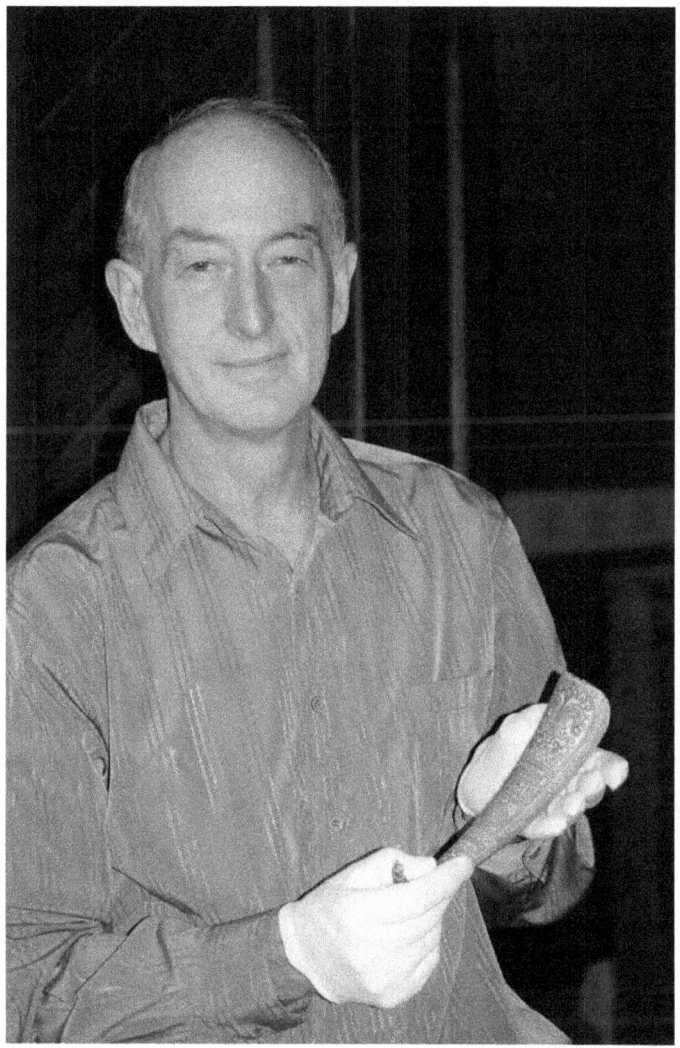

Wayne Robinson and one of Robert Mindum's shoe horns.

Wayne Robinson is the product of an upbringing by three generations of his family. He worked in technical development roles in a variety of industries. Accidentally retired, Wayne is working on the Renaissance Person thing, although the sonnets are proving to be an embuggerance.

A re-enactor of some vintage, having joined 1066 in 1982 and going on to be a member at different times (and occasionally, founder) of more re-enactment groups than can possibly be healthy. He is currently a member of The Pike and Musket Society, concentrating on the middle class London militia of 13 November, 1642, and The Company of the Staple, based on a merchant company in Calais in 1376.

He is sufficiently skilled in ancient, medieval and early modern period leather work, fletching, paint, woodwork and metalwork to bluff convincingly. Much to his own surprise, he finds himself to be a world authority on the carved horn work of Robert Mindum (active 1593-1613).

Publications include: *The Reverend's Big Book of Leather* (2005) and *The Reverend's Big Blogge of Leather* (2009); *A Catalogue of Shoehorns by Robert Mindum* (2014-); *The Opus of Robert Mindum - 1593 to 1613* (2018-); a small part in Wyley, Robinson and Joyce's (2021) *Historic Viking Replicas Vol 1*; with *The Double Armed Man - a New Invention* in perpetual preparation, based on a series of articles written earlier this century about William Neade's 1623 method of arming pikemen with longbows.

Bibliography.

Archaeology.

Holl, I. (1966). *Mittelalter liche Funde aus einem Brunnnen Von Buda*, Budapest.
Arbman, Holger (1940). *Birka 1 Die Graber: Tafeln. [The Graves: Plates] Birka,* Kungliga Vitterhets Historie och Antikvitets Akademien).

Arms and Armour.

Kohlmorgen, J. (2002). The Medieval Equestrian Shield: Historical Development from 975 to 1350 and A Guide to Building a Combat Shield.
Stone, G.C (1961). *A Glossary of the construction, Decoration and use of arms and armour in all countries in all times*, New York.
Tarassuk L. & Blair C. (1979). *The Complete Encyclopaedia of Arms and Weapons*, New York.

Costrel.

Baker, Oliver. (1921) *Black Jacks and Leather Bottells.* Cheltenham: privately printed for W.J. Fieldhouse, Austy Manor, near Stratford on Avon, by Ed. J. Burrow & Co Ltd, Cheltenham Spa and 93 Kingsway, London.

Boccacio, Giovianni (c.1410) | Rafael Schwemmer (Programming and Design) | Douglas Kim (Programming, S. (2021). *Des cas des nobles hommes et femmes.* e-codices – Virtual Manuscript Library of Switzerland. Retrieved 25 September 2021, from http://www.e-codices.unifr.ch/en/list/one/bge/fr0190-2

Buigne, Gace de la (artist) (c.1387-1389). *Gaston Phébus, Livre de la chasse*. Retrieved 25 September 2021, from https://commons.wikimedia.org/wiki/File:Gaston_Ph%C3%A9bus,_Livre_de_la_chasse._67r.jpg

de Ferrières, Henri (c. 1374-1377). *Le songe de Pestilence*. Belgica, digital library of the KBR. Retrieved 25 September 2021, from https://uurl.kbr.be/1065691

De' Grassi, Giovannino (1395-1400). *Historia Plantarum*. Biblioteca Casanatense, Rome. Retrieved 25 September 2021, from http://opac.casanatense.it/Record.htm?Record=19931939124917591119

Egan, Geoff & Bayley, Justine | Museum of London (1998). *The medieval household: daily living c. 1150-c. 1450*. HMSO, London, UK

Gardiner, J., Allen, M.J., Alburger, M.A. and others. (2005). *Before the Mast – Life and Death Aboard the Mary Rose* (Archaeology of the Mary Rose Volume 4). Portsmouth, UK: The Mary Rose Trust.

Limburg Brothers (artists) (c.1412-16). *Très Riches Heures du Duc de Berry*. Retrieved 25 September 2021, from https://commons.wikimedia.org/wiki/File:Les_Tr%C3%A8s_Riches_Heures_du_duc_de_Berry_octobre.jpg

Morgan Library and Museum (2019). *The Crusader Bible online exhibition*. Retrieved 25 September 2021, from https://www.themorgan.org/collection/crusader-bible/54

Museum of London. (2021). *Costrel*. Retrieved 24 September 2021, from https://collections.museumoflondon.org.uk/online/object/309508.html

Robinson, W. (2011). *When good pitches turn bad….* Retrieved 9 October 2021, from https://leatherworkingreverend.wordpress.com/2011/04/03/when-good-pitches-turn-bad/

Rogers, Arthur George Liddon. (1866), *A History of Agriculture and Prices in England: From the Year after the Oxford Parliament (1259) to the Commencement of the Continental War (1793)* (Cambridge Library Collection - British and Irish History, General). Oxford, UK: Clarendon Press

Waterer, J.W. (1981) *Leather and the Warrior: An Account of the Importance of Leather to the Fighting Man from the Time of the Ancient Greeks to the Second World War.* Northampton, UK: Museum of Leathercraft.

Waterer, J.W. (1944) *Leather in Life, Art and Industry.* London, UK: Faber and Faber.

Heraldry.

Fox-Davies, A.C. (1954). *Complete Guide to Heraldry*, Cape Town.
Volborth, C. (1981). *Heraldry, Customs, Rules and Styles*, Dorset.
Woodcock, T. and Robinson, J.M. (1988). *The Oxford Guide to Heraldry*, Oxford.
Walker, G., (1999). *Heraldry and the 12th Century Shield*, Varangian Voice, Issue No 52 August.

Leatherwork.

Baker, Oliver. (1921) *Black Jacks and Leather Bottells.* Cheltenham: privately printed for W.J.
Cowgill, J., M. De Neergaard, N. Griffiths, (2005). *Knives and Scabbards*, Museum of London.
Egan, G. (2010). *The Medieval Household, Daily living c. 1150 - c. 1450*, London.
Gardner, J. (Ed.) (2005). *Before the Mast, Life and death aboard the Mary Rose.* The Mary Rose Trust.
Goubitz, O. (2009). *Purses in Pieces. Archaeological finds of late medieval & 16th century leather purses, pouches, bags and cases in the Netherlands*, Waanders.
Grew, F., M. De Neergaard, N. Griffiths, (2001). *Shoes and Pattens*, Museum of London.
Waterer, J.W. (1981) *Leather and the Warrior: An Account of the Importance of Leather to the Fighting Man from the Time of the Ancient Greeks to the Second World War.* Northampton, UK: Museum of Leathercraft.
Waterer, J.W. (1944) *Leather in Life, Art and Industry.* London, UK:

Metalwork.

Eras, V. (1974). *Locks & Keys throughout the Ages*, Great Britain.
Goodall, Ian H. (2012). *Ironwork in Medieval Britain (Society for Medieval Archaeology Monographs*, No. 31, UK.

Other.

Adams, R. (2005). *Adhesive Bonding: Science, Technology and Applications*, Elsevier.

Burlington Fine Arts Club (1894) *Illustrated Catalogue of the Heraldic Exhibition*, Burlington House.

Egan, Geoff & Bayley, J. (Justine) | Museum of London (1998). *The medieval household: daily living c. 1150-c. 1450*. HMSO, London, UK.

Gardiner, J., Allen, M.J., Alburger, M.A. and others. (2005). *Before the Mast – Life and Death Aboard the Mary Rose* (Archaeology of the Mary Rose Volume 4). Portsmouth, UK: The Mary Rose Trust.

Hawthorn & Smith, Trans. (1979), *Theophilus, On Divers Arts, The Foremost Medieval Treatise on painting, glassmaking and metalwork*, New York.

Rogers, Arthur George Liddon. (1866), *A History of Agriculture and Prices in England: From the Year after the Oxford Parliament (1259) to the Commencement of the Continental War (1793)* (Cambridge Library Collection - British and Irish History, General). Oxford, UK: Clarendon Press.

Travers, C. (2006). *Beginning Illumination, Learning the Ancient Art step by step*, Schiffer Publishing.

Wyley, S., (2014). *A Few Things Re-enactors can do to make their encampments better – Inspector General of the Encampment Inspectorate*.

Woodwork.

Cynegetica (Cod Z 479), folio 36r, held in the Bibliotheca Marciana Venice Italy.

Diehl, D. (1997). *Constructing Medieval Furniture, Plans and Instructions with Historical Notes*, Stackpole Books, USA.

Diehl, D. & Donnelly, M. (1999). *Medieval Furniture, Plans and Instructions for Historical Reproductions*, Stackpole Books, USA.

Diehl, D. & Donnelly, M. (2012). *Medieval and Renaissance Furniture, Plans and Instructions for Historical Reproductions*, Stackpole Books, USA.

Follansbee, Peter. (2019). *Joiners work.* Lost Art Press, Covington, KY, USA.

Gilbert, V. & Lopez, J. (2002). *Woodworking class Cabinetmaking*, Pavilion Books.

Heelas, Edgar H. (1944). *Craftwork in Wood*, Oxford University Press, Glasgow.

Horwood, R. (2002). *The Woodworker's Handbook*, Caxton Publishing.

Jackson, A. & Day, D. (1993). *Collins Complete Wood Worker's Manual*, London.

Jenning, C. (1974). *Early Chests in Wood and Iron*, HM Stationary Office, London.

Jones, Peter (1987). *Shelves, Closets & Cabinets*, New York.

Mercer, Henry, C. (reprint 2012). *Ancient Carpenters' Tools: Illustrated and Explained, Together with the Implements of the Lumberman, Joiner and Cabinet-Maker in Use in the Eighteenth Century*, New York.

Morris, C. A. (2000). *Archaeology of York: Craft, Industry and Everyday Life: Wood and Woodworking in Anglo-Scandinavian and Medieval York, v. 17*, Fasc. 13.

Roe, F. (reprint 2007). *Ancient Church Chests and Chairs*, London.

Raftos P. & Beatson P. (2004). *A Vento-Byzantine Chest? Casket of the Blessed Juliana of Collalto*, Varangian Voice Issue 68, Australia.

Schleining, L. (2001). *Treasure Chests, The Legacy of Extraordinary Boxes*, The Taunton Press.

Tate, W.E. (1969). *The Parish Chest: a study of the records of parochial administration in England*, London.

Hill. P. (1997). *Whithorn and St.Ninian: The Excavation of a Monastic Town (1984-91).* Stroud, Gloucestershire, United Kingdom: *Alan Sutton Publishing.*

Goodall, I. (2011). *Ironwork in Medieval Britain, An Archaeological Study: Society for Medieval Archaeology (Monograph 31)*. Abingdon, Oxon, United Kingdom: Routledge.

Further Reading.

Abbott, M., (1991). *Green Woodwork: Working with wood the Natural Way*, Wiltshire.
Corkhill, T., (1980). *The Complete Dictionary of Wood*, Marboro Books.
Drijber, T, Wolters, WT, Meishke, IR et al (1980). *Thuis in de late middeleeuwen - Het Nederlands burgerinterieur, 1400-1535* (Exhibition Catalogue) Overijssels Provincial Museum, Zwolle, Netherlands.
Eames P, (1977) *Medieval Furniture in England and France and the Netherlands from the 12th to 15th centuries* (Furniture Hist. Soc. Journal 13).
Foley, D., (1962). *Toys through the Age*, Chilton.
Johnson, H., (1980). *The International Book of Wood*, London.
Kolchin, B.A., (1989). *Wooden Artifacts from Medieval Novgorod*, Oxford.
Lucas, A. (1934). *Wood Working in Ancient Egypt*, Empire Forestry Journal, Vol. 13, No. 2 (DECEMBER).
Werner, A., (1999). *London Bodies The Changing Shape of Londoners from Prehistoric Times to the Present Day*, Museum of London.
Wright, L., (2004). *Warm & Snug: The History of the Bed*, Sutton Publishing.

Links.

Archeology.

Holl, I. (1966). *Mittelalter liche Funde aus einem Brunnnen Von Buda*, Budapest. http://real-eod.mtak.hu/3198/1/MTA_StudiaArcheologica_04.pdf downloaded 25/09/2021.

Ottaway, Patrick (1989) *Anglo-Scandinavian ironwork from 16-22 Coppergate, York : c.850-1100 A.D.* PhD thesis, University of York.
https://etheses.whiterose.ac.uk/10826/ Download 8/7/2023.

Ottaway, Patrick (1992) Anglo-Scandinavian Ironwork from 16-22 Coppergate (The Archaeology of York) Fascicule 17/6. York: York Archaeological Trust.
https://www.collections.yorkarchaeologicaltrust.co.uk/s/publications/item/74495#lg=1&slide=0
Downloaded 5/08/2023.

Photo of remains of chest from Birka Grave 639.
http://www.vikingage.org/wiki/index.php?title=File:Box_-_Sweden,_Birka_Grave_639_(Arbman_1940_Taf.259).JPG
Downloaded 8/7/2023.

Arms and Armour.

Heraldry – Fenwicks Rolls
https://www.theheraldrysociety.com/wp-content/uploads/2021/09/Fenwicks-Roll-paper.pdf downloaded 1/6/2022
How to make Heraldic Parade Shield - 3th Century Swiss Seedorf Shield, bearing the arms of Sir Arnold von Bienz by Ciana di Carla, 2020.

https://projectcennini.com/heraldic-parade-shield/ Downloaded 8/12/2021
http://www.schlachtschule.org/instruction/SwordandShield.pdf download 2/6/2022
Wyley, S. (2002), Enarmes, The Straps of a kite shield. https://www.angelfire.com/wy/svenskildbiter/armsandarmour/enarmes.html Downloaded 8/12/2021
The Heraldic Exhibition of 1894: preserving Britain's national heritage.
http://journal.sciencemuseum.ac.uk/browse/issue-10/the-panstereomachia/the-heraldic-exhibition-of-1894-preserving-britain-s-national-heritage/ Downloaded 10/12/2022.

Shield Construction, The shield of the Black Prince. https://willscommonplacebook.blogspot.com/2009/07/shield-construction.html Downloaded 10/12/2022.

Bede's Chair.

https://www.flickr.com/photos/leatherworkingreverend/albums/72157644631514085
https://www.periodoakantiques.co.uk/antique-sales-archive/a-very-rare-example-of-a-late-15th-century-box-seated-table-chair-english-circa-1490-27-stockno-1053/ downloaded 29/11/2020.
https://hoveloghage.wordpress.com/2015/03/13/korstolen-i-hol-kirke/ downloaded 16/07/2021

Bellows.

Digital Collections of the Württemberg State Library / Manuscripts / Württemberg State Library; *Cod.bibl.fol.23* (first half of the 9th century). [Digitised manuscript] Retrieved 30 April 2023, from http://digital.wlb-stuttgart.de/purl/bsz307047059

Herr Jakob von Warte, Manesse Codex (UBH Cod. Pal. germ. 848, fol. 46v), Universitätsbibliothek Heidelberg, Cod. Pal. germ.

Chairs.

https://thomasguild.blogspot.com/2015/10/norwegian-medieval-furniture-chairs-and.html downloaded 2/11/2020.
Bronze throne of Dagobert the 1st.
https://merovingianworld.com/2019/03/01/merovingian-things-2-the-throne-of-dagobert/ downloaded 9/6/2021.

Chaucer's Works (ed. Skeat) Vol. III Clarendon Press (1900)- Wikisource, the free online library. (2021). Retrieved 13 June 2021, from https://en.wikisource.org/wiki/Chaucer_%27s_Works_(ed._Skeat)_Vol._II

Chests.

Catalogue of extant chests and caskets by S.Wyley. http://www.geocities.ws/chestsandcaskets/catalogueofextantchestsandcaskets.html Downloaded 8/7/2023.

The David Bruce's Ransom chest (E39/36Case) - National Archives (Kew - United Kingdom. https://discovery.nationalarchives.gov.uk/details/r/C2352296 downloaded 31/08/2021.

Fitzsimmons, Paul. | Marhamchurch Antiques. (2021). *14th century oak clamp front chest*. Retrieved 25 June 2021, from https://www.marhamchurchantiques.com/antique/14th-century-oak-clamp-front-chest/

The medieval chest at St Mary's church, Horsham: an important unrecorded pin-hinged, clamped chest, Sussex Archaeological Collections, 155, 2017, 203-7
https://www.researchgate.net/publication/321490083_The_medieval_chest_at_St_Mary's_church_Horsham_an_important_unrecorded_pin-hinged_clamped_chest_Sussex_Archaeological_Collections_155_2017_203-7 downloaded 2/1/2021.

Chest with two different types of locks on the *'Medieval Boxes'* Facebook group
https://www.facebook.com/groups/2243848865688255/user/100009493898796 Downloaded 9/10/2021.

The Pillager's Chest.
https://www.bl.uk/catalogues/illuminatedmanuscripts/record.asp?MSID=8466&CollID=16&NStart=200307 downloaded 29/11/2020.

St Thomas Guild. (2012, December 17) *Medieval chests from Kloster Isenhagen*. Retrieved 29 April 2023, from https://thomasguild.blogspot.com/2012/12/medieval-chests-from-kloster-isenhagen.html

Frame saws.

https://thomasguild.blogspot.com/2014/03/the-medieval-toolchest-frame-saw.html downloaded 16/9/2021.
Furniture.

Berry, Nicholas. |Early Oak Reproductions (2021). *Oak Furniture Construction* | Mortise and Tenon Joint. Retrieved 24 June 2021, from https://www.earlyoakreproductions.co.uk/news-blog/oak-furniture-construction/news-blog-5256-mortise-and-tenon.php

Treaty of Calais Chest.

https://www.nationalarchives.gov.uk/museum/item.asp?item_id=7 downloaded 29/11/2020.
http://www.webexhibits.org/pigments/intro/medieval.html downloaded 22/11/2020.

Hutch chest – 1200-1300.
https://collections.vam.ac.uk/item/O93911/chest-unknown/ downloaded 1/1/2021.

Hanging Salt Box.

Speculum humanae salvationis (1485-1509) British Library Harley Ms2838 [Digitised manuscript]. Retrieved 30 April 2023, from https://www.bl.uk/manuscripts/FullDisplay.aspx?ref=Harley_MS_2838

Murner, T., (1512). *Die Narrenbeschwörung*.

Heraldry.

A procedural heraldry generator and editor by Azgaar
https://github.com/Azgaar/Armoria Down loaded 21/9/2023

Coat of arms throughout Europe, Anatolia, the Holy Land & the New World, from about 1100 and onwards.
https://wappenwiki.org/index.php/Main_Page Downloaded 21/9/2023

Leatherwork.

https://leatherworkingreverend.wordpress.com/author/leatherworkingreverend/ downloaded 21/7/2021.

Costrel from the MoL collection webpage. https://collections.museumoflondon.org.uk/online/object/309508.html Downloaded 5/4/2023.

Locks and keys.

'On the Development and Distribution of Primitive Locks and Keys by Lieut.-General Pitt-Rivers, F.R.S. Illustrated by specimens in the Pitt-Rivers Collection' London: Chatto and Windus, 1883 pp. 3-5 https://web.prm.ox.ac.uk/rpr/index.php/article-index/12-articles/208-primitive-locks-and-keys.html Downloaded 26/12/2021

Sven Skildbiter (2021, February 17). *14th Century Hutch chest lock and how it works* [Video]. Youtube. https://www.youtube.com/watch?v=cC90-fqXthk&ab_channel=SvenSkildbiter

Metalwork.

Nail making https://eaiainfo.org/2021/11/11/nailmaking-in-the-eighteenth-century/ downloaded 12/11/2021.
Roman.
https://www.mortiseandtenonmag.com/blogs/blog/tagged/roman-workbench downloaded 6/9/2021.

Tables.

15th Century Table from Bruges
https://thomasguild.blogspot.com/2012/07/a-15th-century-trestle-table-from-bruges.html downloaded 20/9/2021

Thomas Guild – Tables.
https://thomasguild.blogspot.com/search/label/trestle%20table downloaded 20/9/2021

Larsdatter - Tables
http://www.larsdatter.com/tables.htm downloaded 20/9/2021

Guiron learns of Asue's misdeeds, *Guiron le Courtois* (BNF NAL 5243, fol. 75r), c. 1370-1380
https://gallica.bnf.fr/ark:/12148/btv1b550063539/f155.item
Downloaded 1/10/2021.

Feast of Job, *Bible historiale* (BNF Fr. 164), fourth quarter of the 14th century
http://visualiseur.bnf.fr/ConsulterElementNum?O=IFN-8100218&E=JPEG&Deb=25&Fin=25&Param=C downloaded 20/9/2021

Castration of the Hebrews, *Bible historiale* (BNF Fr. 159, fol. 232v), 14th-15th century
http://visualiseur.bnf.fr/ConsulterElementNum?O=IFN-8100222&E=JPEG&Deb=57&Fin=57&Param=C
Downloaded 1/10/2021

Other.

The Mendelian and Landauer house books – depictions of various crafts and workshops.

https://hausbuecher.nuernberg.de/ downloaded 2/11/2020.

Follansbee, Peter & Alexander, Jennie, (2012). *Drawboarding Demystified* | Popular Woodworking Magazine, Retrieved 27 August 2021, from https://popularwoodworking.com/wp-content/uploads/Drawboring.pdf

Schwarz, C. (2013). *Drawboring Resurrected* | Popular Woodworking Magazine. Retrieved 24 June 2021, from https://www.popularwoodworking.com/techniques/drawboring-resurrected/

Workbenches.

https://thomasguild.blogspot.com/search/label/workbench downloaded 6/9/2021.

Wood work.

Berry, Nicholas. | Early Oak Reproductions (2021). *Oak Furniture Construction* | Mortise and Tenon Joint. Retrieved 24 June 2021, from https://www.earlyoakreproductions.co.uk/news-blog/oak-furniture-construction/news-blog-5256-mortise-and-tenon.php

Egan, Geoff & Bayley, J. (Justine) | Museum of London (1998). *The medieval household: daily living c. 1150-c. 1450.* HMSO, London, UK.

Fitzsimmons, Paul. | Marhamchurch Antiques. (2021). *14th century oak clamp front chest.* Retrieved 25 June 2021, from https://www.marhamchurchantiques.com/antique/14th-century-oak-clamp-front-chest/

Follansbee, Peter. (2019). *Joiners work*. Lost Art Press, Covington, KY, USA.

Follansbee, Peter & Alexander, Jennie, (2012). Drawboarding Demystified | *Popular Woodworking* Magazine, Retrieved 27 August 2021, from https://popularwoodworking.com/wp-content/uploads/Drawboring.pdf

Schwarz, Chris. (2013). Drawboring Resurrected | *Popular Woodworking Magazine*. Retrieved 24 June 2021, from https://www.popularwoodworking.com/techniques/drawboring-resurrected/

Schwarz, C. (2020). *The anarchist's workbench*. Lost Art Press, Covington, KY, USA. This work is available as a free download via https://lostartpress.com/collections/books/products/the-anarchists-workbench.Retrieved 18 July 2020.

Index

Bayeux tapestry, 261
Baynard Castle Dock Costrel, 182
Bede's chair, 46
Bede's Chair, 300
beeswax, 254
Bellows, 158
below the salt, 148
Box bellows, 161
Carbon 14, 48
Chest lock Survey, 307
chest lock typology, 41
Cleating nails, 16
cooking, 159
costrels, 182
egg tempera, 31
fleur di lis, 62
frame saw, 170
Galenic, 102
Goodall's Lock typology, 317
hanging salt box, 319
Hanging Salt Box, 146
heater, 261
Heater Shield, 261
holding devices, 14
Hutch chest – Large, 293
Hutch chest – Small, 295
Hutch' chests, 62
Leatherwork, 42
Linlaud's Lock typology, 317
lock typologies, 315
Luttrell Psalter, 130
Luttrell Psalter Dining Table, 127
Maciejowski Bible, 261
Metal cut-off, 286
Nail making, 285
Painting furniture, 31
Perdix, 12
Pillager's chest, 20
Pillager's Hutch chest, 60
plans, 25
Pot bellows, 161
Queste del Saint Graal, 261
safety, 36
Santa Croce Frame Saw, 170
Santa Croce Sitting Bed., 100
scutum, 261
Smithfield Decretals, 158
square washers, 335
Taciunum Sanitatis, 113
targe, 261
tick, 102
Tool protection, 43
Treaty of Calais, 32
Trenails, 319
trestle table, 128
turnkey, 40
wards, 89
warping, 45
Wider boards, 288
Work tables, 114
Wyley's lock typology, 315

Photographs.

Table 32. Photographs.			
Number	*Description*	*Credit*	*Page no.*
1	One of the 14th C hutch chests Stephen Wyley made from recycled shelving, with a turnkey lock.	Morgan Wyley	Cover photo
2	Fresco of Perdix cutting mortises with a chisel and hammer from the House of Vettii, Pompeii.	Alamy, Reference No. OY58528143 Getty Images, order number 2074452449	12
3 – 6	Cleating nails on inside of chest	Morgan Wyley	16-18
7	Small Hutch chest in pine with hasp closure.	Stephen Wyley	27
8	Large Hutch chest in pine with hasp closure.	Stephen Wyley	28
9	Treaty of Calais Chest (British National Archive - E 30/153 case)	British National Archive	31
10	The heraldry on the Treaty of Calais chest. (British National Archive)	British National Archive	34

11	Replica of Treaty of Calais chest with painting in progress.	Morgan Wyley	35
12	Wooden axe sheath from Haithabu No. 4, HbH.432.003 on an axe based on the axe found near the Mastermyr chest find.	Stephen Wyley	44
13	Bede's Chair – front left	Wayne Robinson	46
14	Bede's Chair – Replica	Stephen Wyley	47
15	Bede's Chair – Top rail from side	Wayne Robinson	49
16	Bede's Chair – Side of seat	Wayne Robinson	50
17	Bede's Chair – Side of seat - detail	Wayne Robinson	51
18	The Pillager's Hutch chest - Replica	Morgan Wyley	61
19	The Hutch chest – Replica, cut out at the end.	Stephen Wyley	70
20	The Hutch chest – Replica, Bottom in place.	Stephen Wyley	70
21	The Hutch chest – Replica, cut out in front and back.	Stephen Wyley	71
22	The Hutch chest – Replica, hinges attached to top of the chest.	Stephen Wyley	75
23	The Hutch chest – Replica, Hinges attached to back of the chest.	Stephen Wyley	75

24	The Hutch chest – Replica, hinges attached to back of the chest.	Stephen Wyley	76
25	The Hutch chest – Replica, the lock plate can be cut out with a cold chisel	Stephen Wyley	82
26	The turned up tip of a hasp	Morgan Wyley	86
27	The Hutch chest – Replica, the key's swivel point is fitted to the top of the key hole.	Stephen Wyley	92
28	The Hutch chest – Replica, the hole in the ward plate lines up with the top of the key hole.	Stephen Wyley	94
29	The Hutch chest – Replica, the slide lugs support the slide, the slide slides into the lug of the hasp.	Stephen Wyley	94
30	The Hutch chest – Replica, front of the lock.	Stephen Wyley	95
31	The Hutch chest – Replica, the back of the lock.	Stephen Wyley	96
32	The Hutch chest – Replica, The chest is complete.	Stephen Wyley	98
33	The Santa Croce Fresco by Agnolo Gaddi – Original – Part - Bed	Scala Archives – PQ000868. 15/9/2021.	99
34	The Santa Croce bed – Replica.	Stephen Wyley	100

35	The Santa Croce bed - The headboard with beading around the outer edge	Morgan Wyley	106
36	The Santae Croce bed - The detail on the corner of the beading on the outer edge of the head board.	Morgan Wyley	106
37, 38 & 39	The Santa Croce bed - mattress support – rope,	Stephen Wyley	110-111
40	The Table - Making Spaghetti – The Replica, end on.	Stephen Wyley	114
41	The Table - Making Spaghetti - Cutting out on of the stretchers with a jigsaw	Stephen Wyley	119
42	The Table - Making Spaghetti - The tenon at the top of one of the legs.	Stephen Wyley	121
43	The Table - Making Spaghetti - The legs and stretcher	Stephen Wyley	122
44	The Trestle Table – Luttrell Psalter - Replica	Morgan Wyley	128
45	The Trestle Table – Luttrell Psalter – close up on legs.	Morgan Wyley	128
46	The Trestle Table – Luttrell Psalter - Brace cardboard template (not to scale).	Stephen Wyley	135
47	The Trestle Table – Luttrell Psalter – Trestle disassembled, the cross beam, the rear leg and the	Morgan Wyley	143

	'A' frame.		
48	The Trestle Table – Luttrell Psalter – The trestle from the back	Morgan Wyley	144
49	The Hanging Salt box of Buda – The Replica	Morgan Wyley	146
50	The Hanging Salt box of Buda – Bottom and front glued, dowelled and clamped.	Stephen Wyley	154
51	The Hanging Salt box of Buda – 4 mm holes predrilled in sides.	Stephen Wyley	155
52	The Hanging Salt box of Buda – Back of box.	Stephen Wyley	156
53	The Hanging Salt box of Buda – Side of box.	Stephen Wyley	156
54	The bellows – The Replica	Morgan Wyley	158
55	The bellows – The Replica – Bottom view of cord cross over	Morgan Wyley	165
56	The bellows – The Replica - Top view of cord cross over	Morgan Wyley	166
57	The bellows – The Replica - Side view of cord cross over	Morgan Wyley	167
58	Frame saw – The Replica	Morgan Wyley	170
59	Frame saw – The Replica – blade attachment	Morgan Wyley	178
60	Frame saw – The Replica –	Morgan Wyley	179

	top of one of the sides with a grove for the tourniquet.		
61	Frame saw – The Replica – Toggle stick.	Morgan Wyley	180
62	The Costrel – The Original	Museum of London. Order number 5476, 23/09/2021.	182
63	The Costrel – The Replica	Wayne Robinson	183
64	The Costrel – The Tools	Wayne Robinson	193
65	The Costrel – cutting out the end jig	Glenda Robinson	196
66	The Costrel – The Replica - Mark the oval with two nails and a loop of string	Glenda Robinson	196
67	The Costrel – Mark the outside piece.	Wayne Robinson	197
68	The Costrel – Saw close to the line.	Wayne Robinson	197
69	The Costrel – Shoulder jig, The tools required.	Wayne Robinson	198
70	The Costrel – The neck jig.	Wayne Robinson	200
71	The Costrel – The neck jig, another view	Wayne Robinson	200
72	The Costrel – The Costrel – Rib jig, The tools.	Wayne Robinson	201
73	The Costrel – Jig for moulding ribs	Wayne Robinson	202

74	The Costrel – Defining the edges of the grooves with a broad chisel	Glenda Robinson	202
75	The Costrel – Trenching the grooves.	Wayne Robinson	203
76	The Costrel – A small router plane can help get it smooth	Wayne Robinson	203
77	The Costrel – Easing the corners of the middle band	Wayne Robinson	204
78	The Costrel – Finished rib moulding jig with push stick.	Wayne Robinson	204
79	The Costrel – Making the shoulder seam templates.	Wayne Robinson	206
80	The Costrel – Shoulder seam template cut to shape.	Wayne Robinson	207
81	The Costrel – Shield template in card	Wayne Robinson	207
82	The Costrel – Triangle template in card.	Wayne Robinson	208
83	The Costrel – Tools used for making the embossing comb.	Wayne Robinson	208
84	The Costrel – Finished comb and test impressions.	Wayne Robinson	209
85	The Costrel – Soaking the cut piece of leather.	Wayne Robinson	211
86	The Costrel – Wet piece of	Wayne Robinson	211

	leather between the outer and inner end mould.		
87	The Costrel – Clamping the end.	Glenda Robinson	212
88	The Costrel – The moulded end with clamps removed	Wayne Robinson	212
89	The Costrel – Two moulded ends showing inside and outside.	Wayne Robinson	213
90	The Costrel – Cutting the end to the correct thickness.	Wayne Robinson	213
91	The Costrel – Soaking the cut piece of leather.	Wayne Robinson	215
92	The Costrel – Working the leather down into the grooves.	Glenda Robinson	216
93	The Costrel – Pressing down a mark left from a chip in the rib jig.	Glenda Robinson	217
94	The Costrel – The leather and I both needed to rest before moving on to the embossing.	Wayne Robinson	217
95	The Costrel – Embossing the shields with the point of the bone folder around the template.	Glenda Robinson	220
96	The Costrel – Both shields done and starting the vertical lines.	Wayne Robinson	220

97	The Costrel – Embossing the triangles in the same way as the shields using the triangle template.	Wayne Robinson	221
98	The Costrel – The leather was starting to dry out	Glenda Robinson	221
99	The Costrel – Backing the ribs with a temporary strip of leather	Glenda Robinson	222
100	The Costrel – Embossing the diagonal hatching/feathering on the ribs	Glenda Robinson	222
101	The Costrel – Embossing the inner triangles and the flat fields	Glenda Robinson	223
102	The Costrel – Embossing complete and the knife cuts made on the shields.	Glenda Robinson	223
103	The Costrel – Wet leather being offered up to the shoulder jig.	Glenda Robinson	225
104	The Costrel – The dowel for shaping the neck is laid on top of the first layer.	Wayne Robinson	226
105	The Costrel – Make sure the top edges of the leather and jig pieces align and tighten.	Wayne Robinson	226
106	The Costrel – Slide the inner part of the jig to shape the shoulders and clamp.	Wayne Robinson	227

107	The Costrel – Back view with all clamps applied.	Wayne Robinson	227
108	The Costrel – Next morning with the jig removed.	Wayne Robinson	228
109	The Costrel – Shoulder gasket pieces.	Wayne Robinson	229
110	The Costrel – Gluing and clamping.	Wayne Robinson	230
111	The Costrel – Start the awl from the side of the neck.	Wayne Robinson	232
112	The Costrel – Using a piece of wood to space the stitches.	Wayne Robinson	233
113	The Costrel – Continue making holes along the seam.	Wayne Robinson	233
114	The Costrel – Start stitching from the neck.	Wayne Robinson	234
115	The Costrel – When you get to the end of the row, leave the ends long.	Wayne Robinson	234
116	The Costrel – Outer seam with a new piece of thread.	Wayne Robinson	235
117	The Costrel – Stitch up to the neck.	Wayne Robinson	235
118	The Costrel – Finished side seam	Wayne Robinson	236
119	The Costrel – The right end and gasket piece pressed into place.	Wayne Robinson	237

120	The Costrel – You have to watch the stitching on both the inside and outside.	Wayne Robinson	238
121	The Costrel – I'm matching the spacing on both rows of stitching.	Wayne Robinson	238
122	The Costrel – Stitching complete.	Wayne Robinson	239
123	The Costrel – It's obvious what needs to be trimmed.	Wayne Robinson	240
124	The Costrel – I had a small gap in the corner from cutting the gasket piece 1 mm too short.	Wayne Robinson	241
125	The Costrel – Re-shaping the neck and ribs.	Wayne Robinson	242
126	The Costrel – Shoulders have been cut and holes being made with chisels.	Wayne Robinson	243
127	The Costrel – Propped up on spare wood so it doesn't roll.	Wayne Robinson	246
128	The Costrel – Foil cover to keep the sealer away from the outside of the leather.	Wayne Robinson	247
129	The Costrel – Gasket piece with one long edge and one short skived.	Wayne Robinson	249
130	The Costrel – Neck gasket starting, the overlap is on the back.	Wayne Robinson	250

131	The Costrel – Neck gasket stitching in progress.	Wayne Robinson	251
132	The Costrel – Completed and trimmed neck gasket.	Wayne Robinson	252
133	The Costrel – Painting molten wax on the ends.	Wayne Robinson	253
134	The Costrel – The heat gun treatment.	Wayne Robinson	254
135	The Costrel – All the tools you need to do this job.	Wayne Robinson	257
136	The Costrel – Fit the leather tightly to the stopper and cut the ends flush.	Wayne Robinson	257
137	The Costrel – Use an edge-flesh seam.	Wayne Robinson	258
138	The Costrel – Use an edge-flesh seam.	Wayne Robinson	258
139	Heater shield of the Black Princes, 1330-1376. Canterbury Cathedral, England.	Burlington House, 1894 (published 1896).	261
140	Parts of the Shield form	Andrew Fraser	268
141	Bottom of the Shield form	Andrew Fraser	268
142	A completed Shield form	Andrew Fraser	269
143	A completed Shield form, end on	Andrew Fraser	269
144	The Enarmes of the Shield.	Andrew Fraser	276
145	Arm gripping the handles and forearms straps in	Andrew Fraser	277

	place		
146	Shield with gesso primer and white fishes painted on it.	Andrew Fraser	281
147	Shield with gesso primer and white fishes painted on it.	Andrew Fraser	282
148	A completed shield with rivets showing where the straps are.	Andrew Fraser	283
149	Nail header	Stephen Wyley	284
150	Metal cut off, edge on	Stephen Wyley	285
151	Metal cut off, side on	Stephen Wyley	285
152	Two board table top	Stephen Wyley	288
153	Two board table top, underside with cross beams or battens.	Stephen Wyley	288
154	Finger gauge.	Stephen Wyley	291
155	Close up off block supporting back of seat, mortise hole and bar across bottom edge of chair	Stephen Wyley	299
156	Inside of one of the sides of the flat pack chair.	Stephen Wyley	300
157	A rectangular dug out chest with iron strapping from St James church, Kington, Worcestershire (date unknown).	Mark Griffin	313

158	Pegged hanging salt box of Buda, Hungary	Wayne Robinson	318
159	Original trenailed building frame, Plas Mawr, Conwy, North Wales	Wayne Robinson	319
160	Offcut of oak and a 32 mm chisel.	Wayne Robinson	322
161	Oak split into pegs	Wayne Robinson	322
162	Rounding the nose of the peg.	Glenda Robinson	323
163	Tapering the pegs.	Glenda Robinson	323
164	Gimlets are great for this sort of task because they leave a tapered hole	Glenda Robinson	325
165	Bore the holes for the pegs.	Glenda Robinson	326
166	Spread glue of your choice on the end of the peg.	Glenda Robinson	326
167	Knock the pegs in with a metal hammer.	Glenda Robinson	327
168	I broke one. You're in luck, you can see how I fix broken pegs	Glenda Robinson	327
169	Glue the broken off bit in place.	Glenda Robinson	328
170	When the glue is dry, trim close to flush.	Glenda Robinson	328
171	Near enough is good enough with the initial cut.	Glenda Robinson	329

172	Pare the end flush with a sharp chisel	Glenda Robinson	329
173	The finished pegged joint.	Wayne Robinson	330
174	6 mm (¼") square oak pegs in oak 17th C table box by the author.	Wayne Robinson	330
175	9 mm (⅜") round Victorian Ash pegs holding the legs on my workbench	Wayne Robinson	331
176	22 mm (⅞") tapered trenails cut by axe from reclaimed French oak barrel stave.	Wayne Robinson	332
177	The trenails are left long and have the corners bevelled like on the roof frame at the start of the chapter	Wayne Robinson	333
178	Square Washers - The tools for the job	Stephen Wyley	334
179	Square Washers - Marked and punched	Stephen Wyley	335
180	Square Washers - Drilling using a pedestal drill press	Stephen Wyley	335
181	Square Washers - Cut to length with a pair of WISS cutters	Stephen Wyley	336
182	Stephen Wyley in his 14th C kit for filming of Troll Bridge at Black Lake, Victoria.	Bronwyn Gregory, Snowgum Films	337
183	Andrew Fraser	Andrew Fraser	339

| 184 | Wayne Robinson | Glenda Robinson | 340 |

Drawings.

Table 33. Drawings.			
Number	Description	Credit	Page no.
1	Conversion to full size chest	Stephen Wyley	24
2	Conversion to available plank size	Stephen Wyley	26
3	Bede's chair – side view plans	Stephen Wyley	57
4	Bede's chair - seat plans	Stephen Wyley	58
5	Bede's chair front on plans	Stephen Wyley	59
6	Hutch chest – Woodworking plans	Stephen Wyley	66
7	Hutch chest – Fleur de lis strap hinges	Stephen Wyley	73
8	Hutch chest – isometric lock internal	Gary Banister	77
9	Hutch chest – isometric lock – the key turns	Gary Banister	78
10	Hutch chest – The parts of a key	Stephen Wyley	79
11	Hutch chest – The measurements of the key	Stephen Wyley	79
12	Hutch chest – Lock,	Stephen Wyley	80

	slide and ward plate.		
13	Hutch chest – Lock, slide and ward plate dimensions	Stephen Wyley	81
14 & 15	Hutch chest – Hasp A & B	Stephen Wyley	84 & 85
16	Hutch chest – Lug	Stephen Wyley	87
17	Hutch chest – Ward plate	Stephen Wyley	88
18	Hutch chest – Basic ward	Stephen Wyley	89
19	Hutch chest – Slide	Stephen Wyley	90
20	Hutch chest – Spring	Stephen Wyley	92
21	Santa Croce Bed – Headboard	Stephen Wyley	106
22	Santa Croce Bed – Footboard	Stephen Wyley	108
23	Santa Croce Bed – Side rails	Stephen Wyley	109
24	Santa Croce Bed – Mattress support - Planks	Stephen Wyley	110
25	T S Stretcher template	Stephen Wyley	119
26	T S Table top End and stretcher	Stephen Wyley	121
27	T S Table legs – over all, top tenon and mortise for stretcher	Stephen Wyley	124

28	Table leg – side elevation of through tenon	Stephen Wyley	125
29	T S - Table top	Stephen Wyley	126
30 & 31	Table top	Stephen Wyley	135
32	Trestle brace	Stephen Wyley	137
33	Trestle Cross beam	Stephen Wyley	138
34	The angle of dangle for the inside leg	Stephen Wyley	139
35	The angle of the top of one piece of the leg	Stephen Wyley	140
36	Front legs, 'A' front view, 'B' outside view of side of leg with dowels through leg into front piece, 'C' inside view of mortise for front piece	Stephen Wyley	141
37	Expanded view of front legs	Stephen Wyley	142
38	Back legs	Stephen Wyley	143
39	Buda Hanging Salt box - Lid	Stephen Wyley	151
40	Buda Hanging Salt box – Side	Stephen Wyley	152
41	Buda Hanging Salt box – Back	Stephen Wyley	153
42	Buda Hanging Salt box - Front	Stephen Wyley	154

43	Buda Hanging Salt box - Bottom	Stephen Wyley	154
44	SM bellows – Bellow Parts	Stephen Wyley	160
45	SM bellows – Plan view	Stephen Wyley	164
46	SM bellows - Side view (throat/pipe)	Stephen Wyley	165
47	Frame saw - The whole thing	Stephen Wyley	175
48	Frame saw - Side and close up of mortise	Stephen Wyley	176
49	Frame saw - Crossbar and close up of tenon	Stephen Wyley	177
50	Frame saw - Toggle	Stephen Wyley	178
51	Heater - Shield Form Plans, curved form and bracing	Stephen Wyley	267
52	Heater - Form Plans - curved form.	Stephen Wyley	268
53	Heater - Form Plans – bracing.	Stephen Wyley	268
54	Heater - size of a typical heater	Andrew Fraser	272
55	Heater - Marking out the point of the heater	Andrew Fraser	273
56	Heater - An example of the position of enarmes and padding	Andrew Fraser and Stephen Wyley	279

57	Large hutch chest plans	Stephen Wyley	294
58	Small hutch chest plans	Stephen Wyley	295
59 & 60	Small hutch chest plans – Hasp A & B.	Stephen Wyley	296
61	Small hutch chest hasp plate plans	Stephen Wyley	297
62	Small hutch chest Hasp loop.	Stephen Wyley	297
63	Hinges for a smaller hutch chest	Stephen Wyley	298
64	Treaty of Calais chest – Woodwork	Stephen Wyley	299
65	Bede's chair – flat pack	Stephen Wyley	302
66	Bed, longer version – side rails	Stephen Wyley	303
67	Bed, longer version – Plank mattress support.	Stephen Wyley	303

Illuminated Manuscripts and Frescos.

Table 34. Illuminated Manuscripts and Frescos.

Number	Description	Collection details	Page no.
1	Mendal 1	Amb. 317.2 Folio 21 recto (Mendel I), Karl Schreyner (carpenter) - City Library in the Nuremberg Education Campus. Historical and scientific city library, Nürnberg	13
2	The Pillager's	MS Royal 20 CVII, f. 41v, British Library	21
3	The Pillager's – close up of the chest	MS Royal 20 CVII, f. 41v, British Library	22 & 60
4	Taciunum Sanitatis - Making Spaghetti	Nouvella acquisition Latine 1673 Folio 50 (Milan or Pavia, Italy) - Bibliothèque nationale de France (BNF), France.	112
5	The Trestle Table – Luttrell Psalter. Sir Geoffrey Luttrell at dinner.	British Library. Add. MS 42130. Folio no 208r.	128
6	The Trestle– Luttrell Psalter. Sir Geoffrey Luttrell at dinner.	British Library. Add. MS 42130. Folio no 208r.	127
7	Smithfield Decretals - Fanning the	British Library, England. Collection no: Royal 10, EIV, Fol. 142R	157

	fire under a three-legged cooking pot.		
8	The Santae Croce Fresco by Agnolo Gaddi – Part - The carpenters using a frame saw on the cross.	Scala Archives. Image number 0078944. 2/10/2021.	169

Forthcoming works.

Viking Volume 2:
- The Gamla Lödöse weaving knife – Stephen Wyley and Shannon Joyce;
- The Oseberg chair – Darren Delany and Stephen Wyley;
- The Hedeby chest – Stephen Wyley;
- The Winchester chest lock – Stephen Wyley;
- The Gokstad bed – Stephen Wyley;
- The Hørning table – Stephen Wyley;
- The Trondheim hnefatafl board – Stephen Wyley;
- The Hedeby arrows – Wayne Robinson;
- The Grytøy smoothing board – Shannon Joyce;
- The Oseberg bucket – Steven Sinclair;
- The Gokstad backpack – Brodie Henry.

13th century;
Byzantine;
Viking Volume 3;
15th century;
Viking volume 4;
16th century.

Dictionary of Military Architecture, Fortifications and Field works from the Iron Age to the 21 Century.

Previous Publications.

Historical replica constructions in Wood and Metal, Viking Volume 1, issue 2, by Wyley, Robinson and Joyce, 2023.